CARLISLE

THE POSTCARD COLLECTION

Alan Spree

AMBERLEY

First published 2026

Amberley Publishing
The Hill, Stroud, Gloucestershire, GL5 4EP
www.amberley-books.com

ISBN 978 1 3981 3244 3 (print)
ISBN 978 1 3981 3245 0 (ebook)

British Library Cataloguing in Publication Data.
A catalogue record for this book is available from the British Library.

Origination by Amberley Publishing.
Printed in Great Britain.

Appointed GPSR EU Representative: Easy Access System Europe Oü, 16879218
Address: Mustamäe tee 50, 10621, Tallinn, Estonia
Contact Details: gpsr.requests@easproject.com, +358 40 500 3575

CONTENTS

A Short History of Carlisle from Roman Times to the 1950s 4

Map of the Area Covered 8

The Postcard Collection 9

Sources 96

About the Author 96

A SHORT HISTORY OF CARLISLE FROM ROMAN TIMES TO THE 1950s

Roman Times

Carlisle's origins lie in the Roman settlement of Luguvalium. A fort was established in AD 72–3 and a civilian settlement or vicus grew up to the east of this, covering much of the area later enclosed by the medieval city wall. The soldiers in the fort provided a market for the townspeople's goods. In Roman Carlisle, there was probably a forum or marketplace with public buildings around it, including public baths. In Roman times people went to the baths not just to get clean but also to socialise.

By the third century Luguvalium was an important military base and also a centre of administration as a principal town of Civitas Carvetiorum, a self-governing territory of the tribal group known as Carvetii. However, in the fourth century, Roman civilization declined. Troops were withdrawn from Hadrian 's Wall in AD 399.

The Fifth Century to the Eleventh Century

Carlisle may not have been abandoned completely. There may have been some farmers living inside the walls and farming the land outside. However, it seems certain that Carlisle ceased to be a town, and all its Roman buildings fell into ruins.

Some sort of organised community existed in 685. When St Cuthbert visited Carlisle and met the Reeve, a 'fountain' was still functioning. Carlisle and a territory of 15 miles radius were granted to St Cuthbert by the king of Northumbria before 685 – it is likely that an Anglo-Saxon monastic community was placed there, probably in the vicinity of a later cathedral.

Carlisle is said to have been destroyed by Danes *c.* 875 and to have lain desolate until after the Norman Conquest. Archaeological evidence, however, points to some continuing occupation throughout the tenth and eleventh centuries.

In 876 the Vikings captured Carlisle and sacked it. The monks moved away but some people probably continued to live within the walls of the old Roman town. The Vikings held Carlisle until the tenth century when the Saxons captured it. Carlisle was rebuilt and revived by King William Rufus in 1092. He built a wooden castle at Carlisle and encouraged people to come and live here.

Middle Ages

Over the centuries, the name Luguvalium faded from common usage. By 1106, it had evolved into Carleol. This change reflects the linguistic shifts of the period, likely influenced by the local populations and the development of early English. The 'Car' part of Carleol is thought to stem from the Welsh word Caer or Cair, meaning 'fort' or 'fortress', reaffirming the defensive importance of the location throughout history. The addition of 'leol' to this likely represents a linguistic evolution and possibly a reference to an important local family or place.

Carlisle was strategically important because of its position near the Scottish border. In the twelfth century, stone walls were erected around the town, and in 1112 Carlisle Castle was reconstructed in stone.

In 1133 Carlisle was made the seat of a bishop. Between 1135 and 1154 Carlisle was in the hands of the Scots. The Scots laid siege to Carlisle for three months in 1173 but they were unable to retake the town.

Carlisle was given its first charter in 1158. In medieval Carlisle, the main industries were wool and leather – wool was woven and dyed in the town and leather was tanned. Wool and leather were then exported to Ireland. Wine (the drink of the upper class) was imported into Carlisle from France.

In 1223 the friars arrived in Carlisle. There were two orders of friars in Carlisle, Dominicans (called Blackfriars because of their black robes) and Franciscans or Greyfriars.

In 1292 Carlisle suffered a disastrous fire. Most of the buildings in Carlisle were of wood with thatched roofs, so a fire was a constant danger.

Carlisle had a weekly market and an annual fair. In the Middle Ages fairs were like markets but they were held only once a year. People would come from all over Cumbria to buy and sell at a Carlisle fair.

In Carlisle, different trades were organised into guilds to safeguard their members' interests. There were eight of them: merchants, butchers, skinners, shoemakers, tanners, tailors, smiths and weavers. In the early fifteenth century a guildhall was built where these guilds could hold meetings.

The Scots returned in 1315 but again they were unable to capture Carlisle.

In 1349 the Black Death devastated the population of Carlisle. It did not recover fully until the sixteenth century.

The Sixteenth Century and Seventeenth Century

In 1541 Henry VIII closed the priory and the two friaries. He also rebuilt and strengthened the castle. Henry replaced the southern gate of Carlisle with a citadel with two towers. Carlisle suffered outbreaks of plague which decimated the population each time. There was a severe outbreak of plague in Carlisle in 1597, but the population grew and by 1600 Carlisle had around 2,500 inhabitants.

In 1642 there was a civil war between the king and parliament. Carlisle was staunchly loyal to the king. However, after the Battle of Marston Moor in July, Scottish soldiers on parliament's side occupied all of northern England except Carlisle. The city was under siege from October 1644 to June 1645. Finally, Carlisle was starved into surrender. The soldiers then ransacked and vandalised the cathedral.

Carlisle was again struck by an outbreak of plague which killed many people. Carlisle Cross was erected in 1682 and Tullie House built in 1689.

Carlisle in the Eighteenth Century

In the mid-eighteenth century, Carlisle was no more than a medium-sized market town with a population of around 4,000.

In 1745, between 13–15 November, the Siege of Carlisle took place during the Jacobite Rising in which their forces led by Charles Edward Stuart, known as Bonnie Prince Charlie, successfully took over Carlisle and besieged Carlisle Castle. Between 21–30 December Government forces led by Prince William recaptured Carlisle. On 30 December 384 Jacobite prisoners were taken after the Siege of Carlisle. Some were executed while others were sentenced to transportation to the West Indies.

In the later eighteenth century roads to and from Carlisle were improved which allowed the merchants of the town to sell their goods elsewhere and in the last years of the eighteenth century, the Industrial Revolution began to transform Carlisle. The wool industry began to boom. Calico printing started in 1761 and gingham, check and bleaching establishments set up shop. St Cuthbert's Church was built in 1778.

In 1782 a dispensary opened where the poor could obtain free medicines. Carlisle gained its first bank in 1787 and its first newspaper in 1798. The novelist Sir Walter Scott married in Carlisle Cathedral in 1797. Cotton-spinning mills were established from the 1790s.

Carlisle in the Nineteenth Century

In 1801 the population of Carlisle was 9,555. By the standards of the time, it was quite a large town. Carlisle grew rapidly and by 1851 it had a population of over 25,000. Scottish and Irish immigrants swelled the population. The textile industry boomed in Carlisle in the early nineteenth century although many of the weavers lived in poverty. However, in the late nineteenth century the textile industry declined. Other industries in Carlisle in the nineteenth century were biscuit-making, engineering, printing and brick-making.

From 1804 the corporation lit and paved the streets. At first, Carlisle was lit by oil lamps, but after 1819 it was lit by gas. Carlisle gained its first theatre in 1813 and between 1811 and 1815 parts of the town walls were demolished. Lowther Street was laid out on the site of the East Wall. In 1823 a canal was dug from Carlisle to Port Carlisle.

There were outbreaks of cholera in 1832 and 1848.

Carr's biscuit factory was established 1834. The infirmary was built in Lancaster Street in 1841.

There were three banks at the time: the Carlisle Old Bank, which was a private bank; the Carlisle City & District Bank, established in 1836 that amalgamated with London & Midland Bank, established in 1896; and the Carlisle & Cumberland Banking Co., established in 1835 – this bank issued their own notes.

The *Carlisle Journal*, established in 1798, was first of a plethora of newspapers, most of which were short-lived. Those which endured were the *Journal* itself; the *Carlisle Patriot*, first issued in 1815; the *Carlisle Examiner* and *Northern Advertiser*, between 1857 and 1870; and the *Carlisle Express*, founded in 1861, which merged with the *Carlisle Examiner* in 1870 to form the *Carlisle Express and Examiner*.

The railway connected Carlisle to Newcastle in 1838, and the city became a hub of the expanding railway network, being served by seven different lines. Maryport railway opened in

1845, and that to Lancaster in 1846. The southern section of the Caledonian Railway opened in 1847, with through services to Glasgow and Edinburgh from 1848. The Glasgow and South Western Railway followed in 1851. Port Carlisle Canal was replaced by railway to Silloth in 1856 and Midland Railway's Settle–Carlisle line opened for freight traffic in 1875. Citadel station, built between 1847 and 1848, became a hub of the railway network.

In 1848 a company began to supply piped water to those who could afford it. In the 1870s sewers were dug under Carlisle and the first telephone exchange in Carlisle opened in 1885.

From 1886 began the manufacture of tin boxes. The number of foundries increased and specialised engineering, such as crane manufacture (from 1858), developed. John Laing set up a small building firm in 1848, which was to become one of country's leading building and civil engineering contractors.

The Covered Market was built in 1889. Carlisle Council obtained Tullie House in 1890 and built extensions to house a museum and library. In 1893 a park was opened called the People's Park. It was later extended and renamed The Bitts. In 1899 electricity was generated in Carlisle for the first time and the town gained electric lighting.

Carlisle in the Twentieth Century to the 1950s

By 1901 the population of Carlisle was over 45,000. In 1900 electric trams began to run in the streets. They were replaced by buses in 1931. In 1904, on 17 May, Carlisle United FC was formed.

Carlisle gained its first cinema in 1906. In 1912 the boundaries of Carlisle were extended to include Stanwix and Botcherby. In the 1920s and 1930s, Raffles Estate was built.

In 1927 a new power station was erected at Willowholme and was connected to the national grid.

In the early twentieth century the textile industry continued to decline but others that continued included biscuits and railway engineering.

In first half of twentieth century, railways, engineering and metal trades remained major industries. The textile industry, which was in a severe recession at beginning of the century, made a limited recovery during the interwar years, but dwindled after 1945, though some specialised activity continued.

MAP OF THE AREA COVERED

WARDS WITHIN CARLISLE CITY COUNCIL AREA

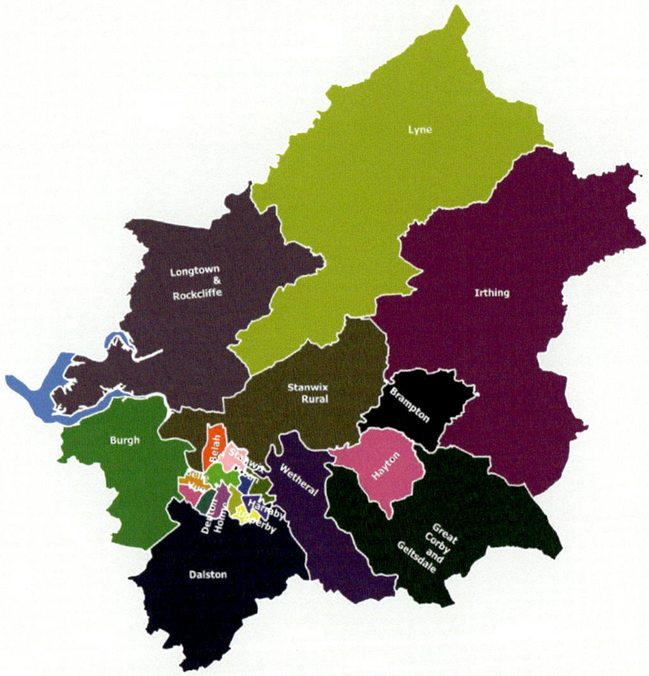

Stanwix Rural	Currock
Stanwix Urban	Dalston
Upperby	Denton Holme
Wetheral	Great Corby and Geltsdale
Yewdale	Harraby
Belah	Hayton
Belle Vue	Irthing
Botcherby	Longtown & Rockcliffe
Brampton	Lyne
Burgh	Morton
Castle	St Aidans

THE POSTCARD COLLECTION

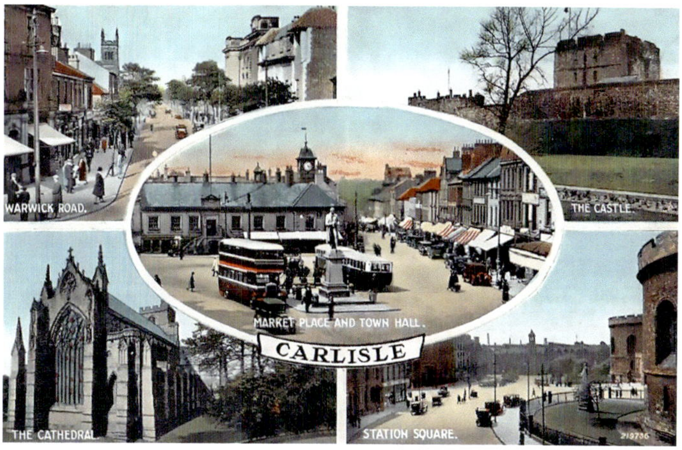

Multi-view Cards

These multi-view postcards show the most visited attractions in the city, and these are all featured in the following pages as well as some of the lesser-known but still significant places in the area. The locations shown are Warwick Road, the castle, the cathedral, Station Square, the law courts, Market Place, English Street and Eden Bridge Gardens.

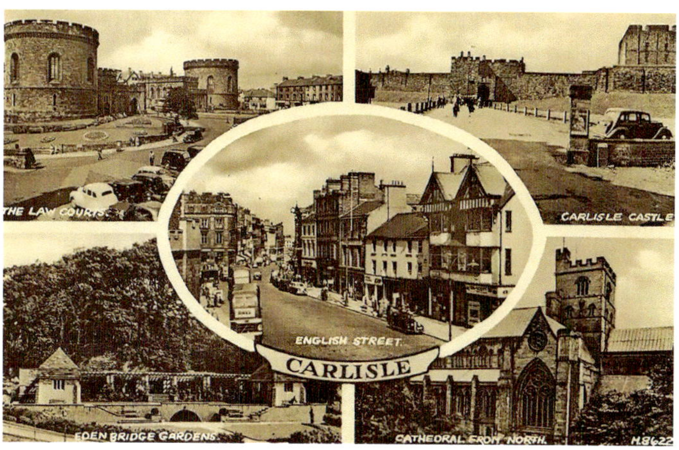

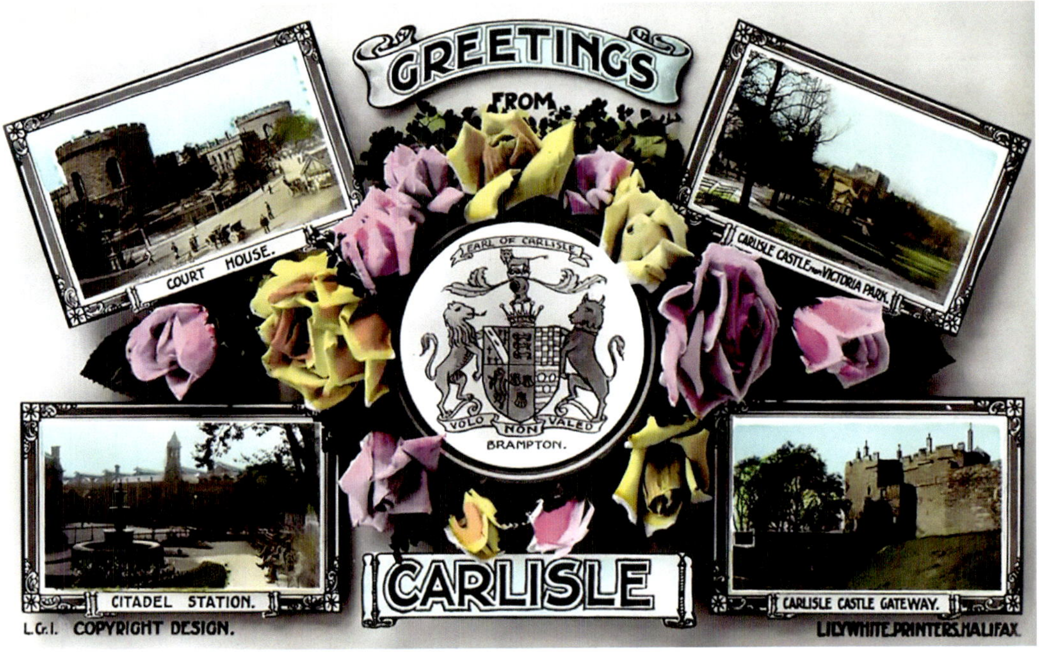

Multi-view Cards

Two impressive designs to catch the eye. The locations shown are the courthouse, the castle, Victoria Park, Citadel railway station and the cathedral.

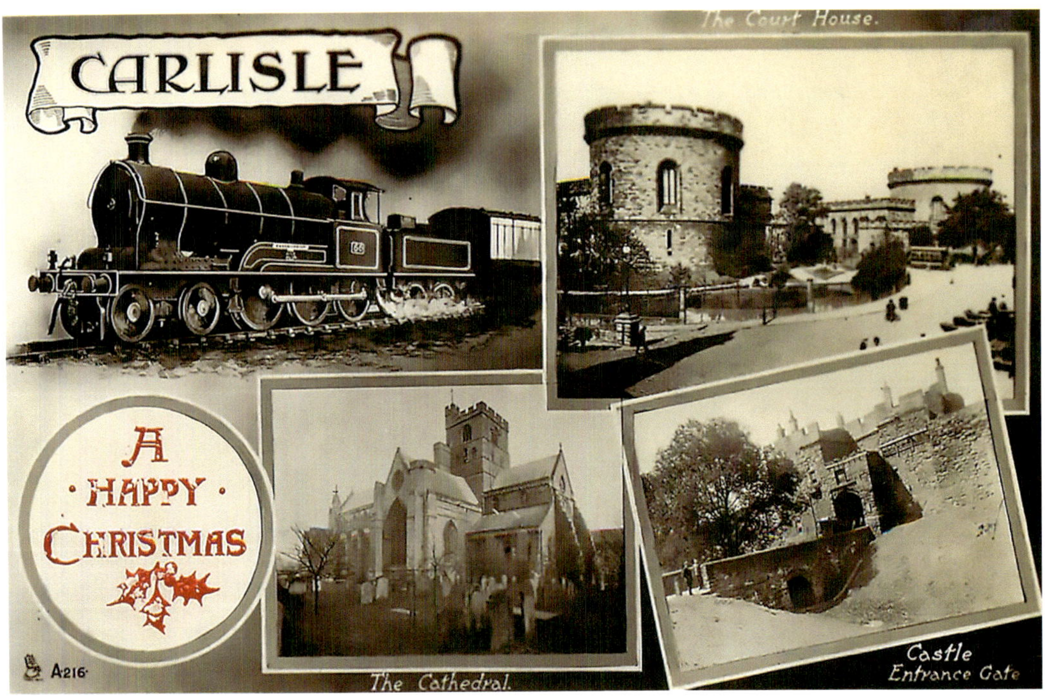

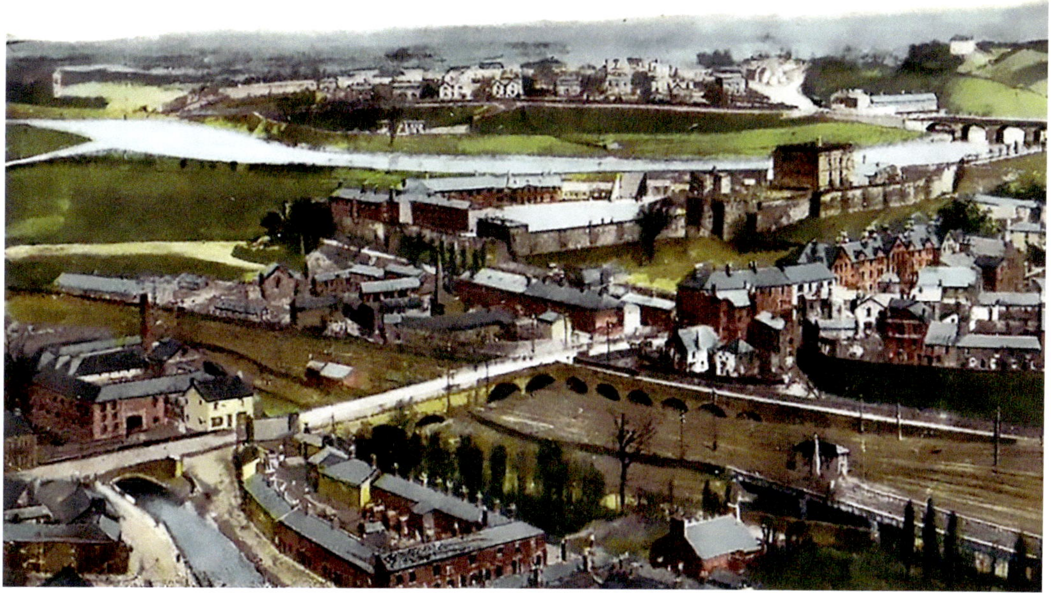

Birds-eye View

These two views span from left to right from the top image to the bottom image. The images show a panoramic view of the city taken from the top of a 300-foot-high chimney. In the image above, the gasworks are to the left and at the bottom. The Victoria Viaduct is clearly seen, as is the Eden bridge in the top right. In the image below is the railway yard. The imposing cathedral and west walls are left centre.

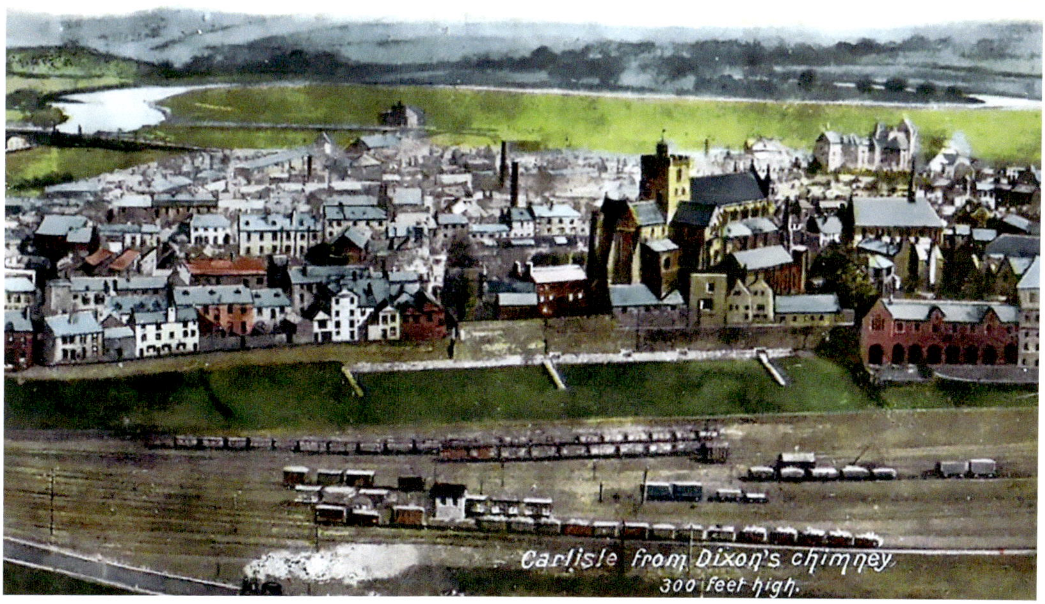

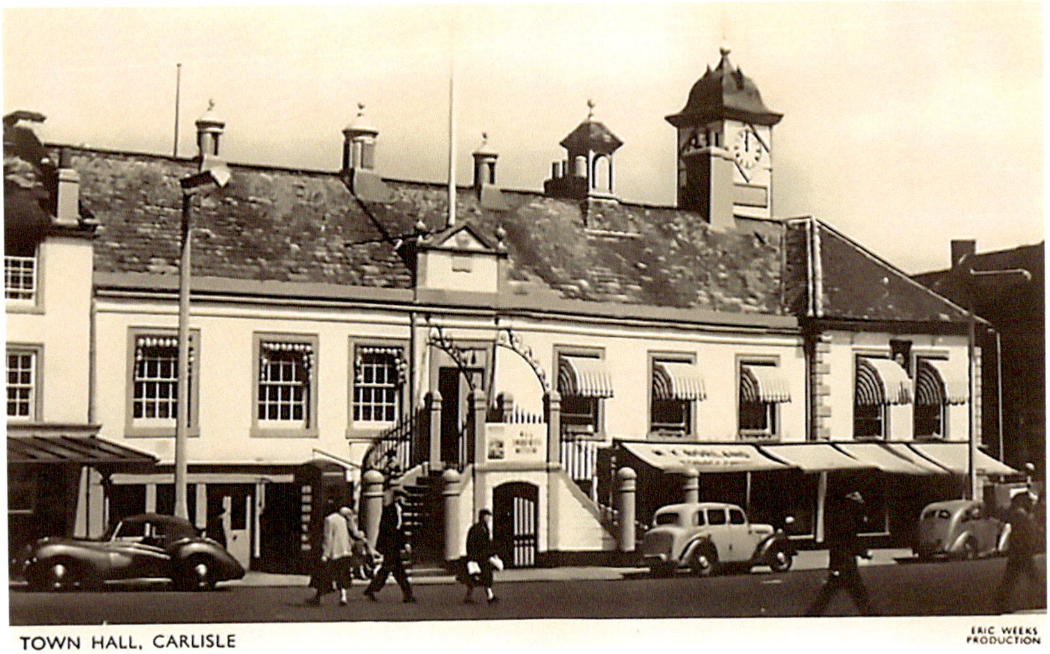

Town Hall

The building was commissioned to replace an earlier 'moot hall' on the site which dated back to 1345. The new building, with commercial facilities on the ground floor and assembly rooms on the first floor, was completed in 1669. It was extended to the east with an extra section incorporating a clock tower in 1717 and to the west with an extra three-storey section in the nineteenth century.

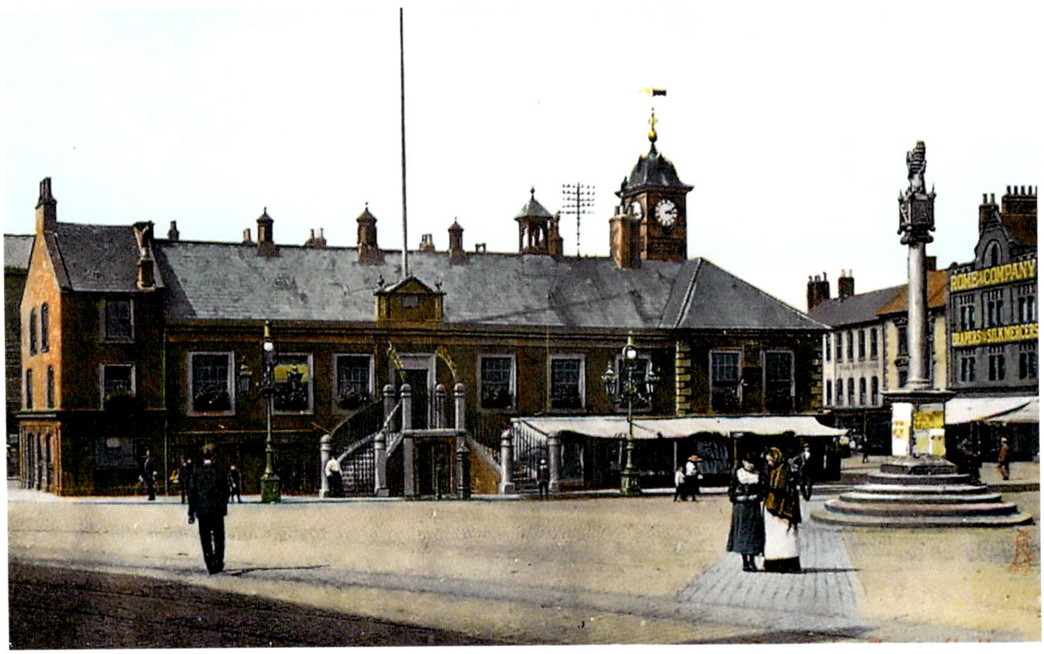

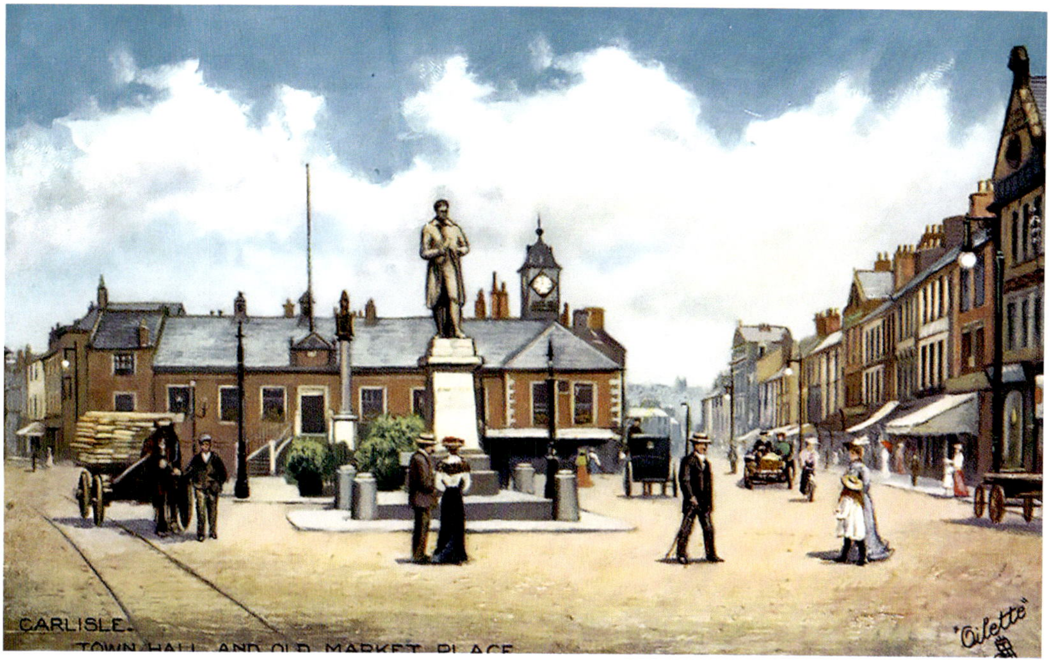

Town Hall

The medieval Market Cross in front of the Town Hall was designed by Thomas Machell and carved from stone by Thomas Addison. It incorporates a sundial and a lion holding a scroll with the city's coat of arms and was erected in 1682.

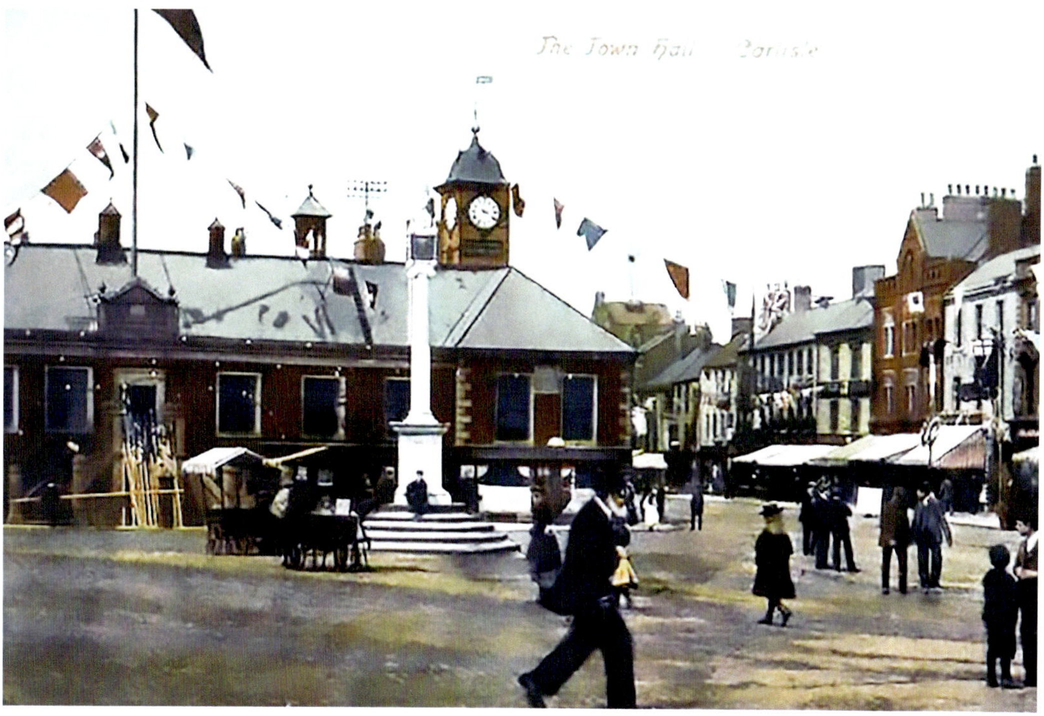

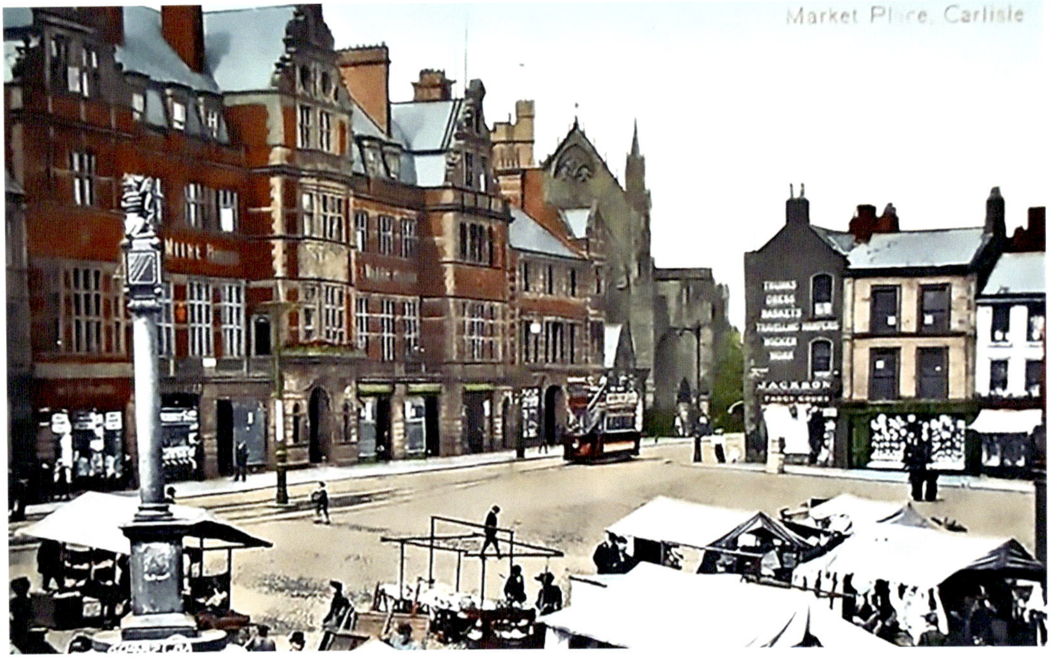

Market Place

The Market Place and adjoining Greenmarket are at the heart of Carlisle city centre. The Market Place is an open space which is formed at the junctions of Castle Street, Fisher Street, Scotch Street and English Street. The image above is looking in a southerly direction with English Street on the left. The image below is looking in a northerly direction with Scotch Street on the right.

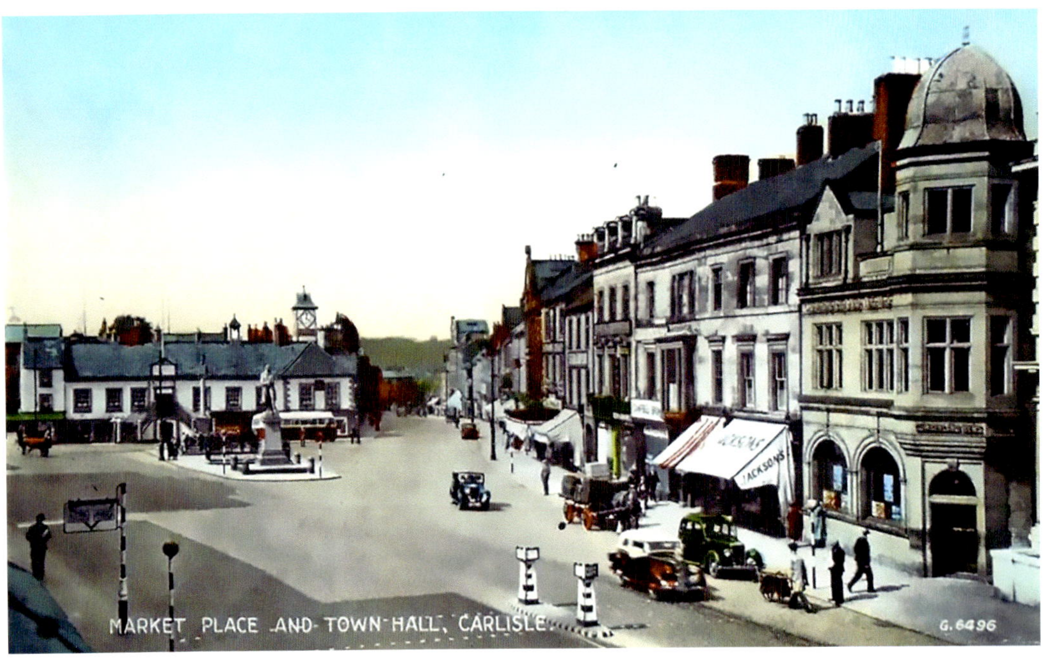

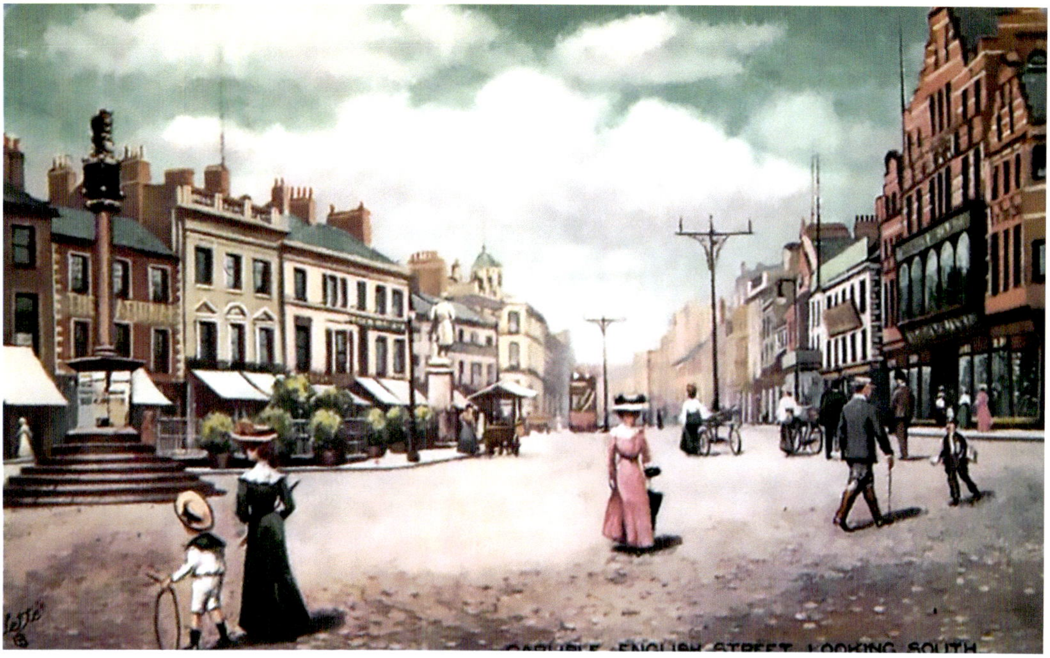

English Street

English Street runs in a south-easterly direction from the junction of Fisher Street in the Market Square to the Assizes, The Crescent, Court Square Brow and Botchergate and is approximately 397 yards long. The image above shows the Market Square monument on the left and the James Steel statue. The images are taken looking in a southerly direction. The image below is from approximately where the tram is situated in the above image.

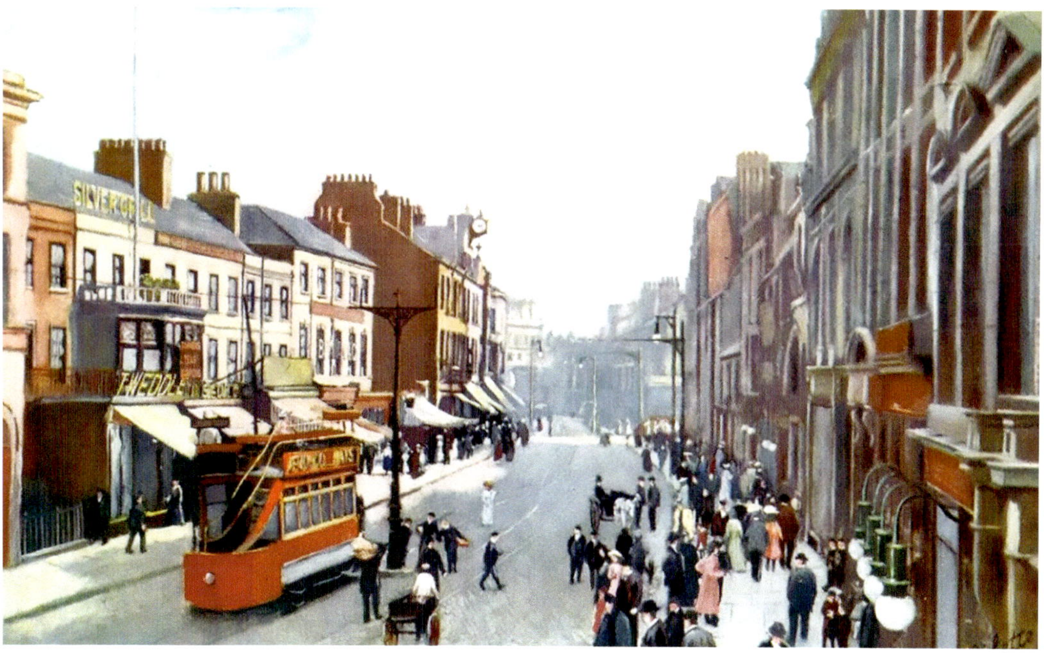

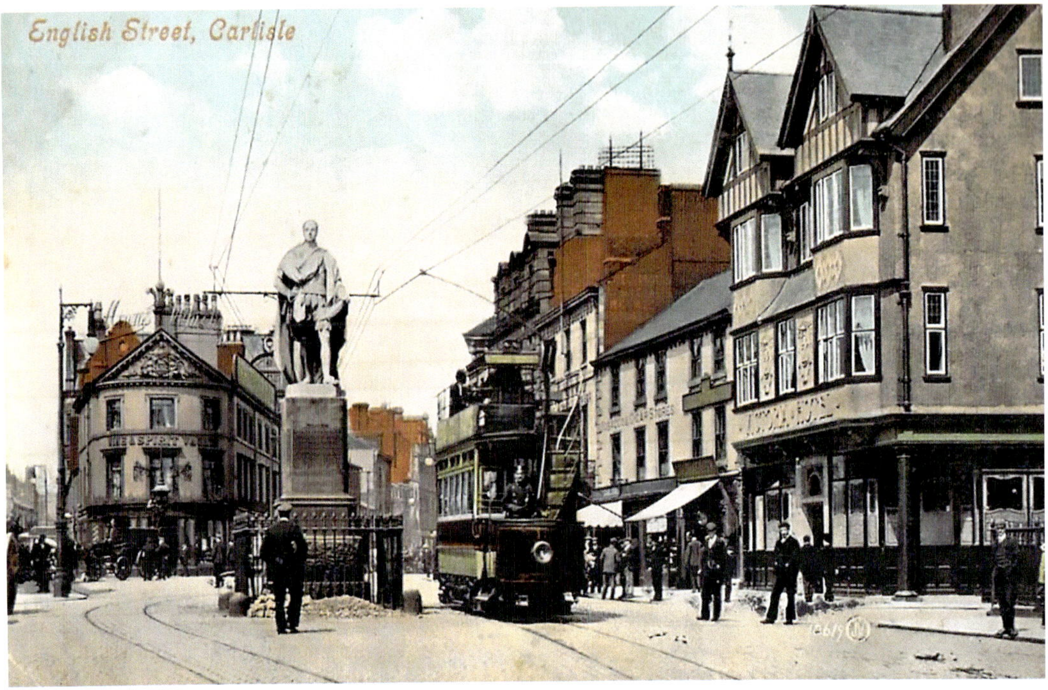

English Street

The statue of Lord Lonsdale is adjacent to the Victoria Hotel on the right. The images are taken looking in a northerly direction from near the Assize Courts. The public house to the left of the statue is the 'Gaol Tap'.

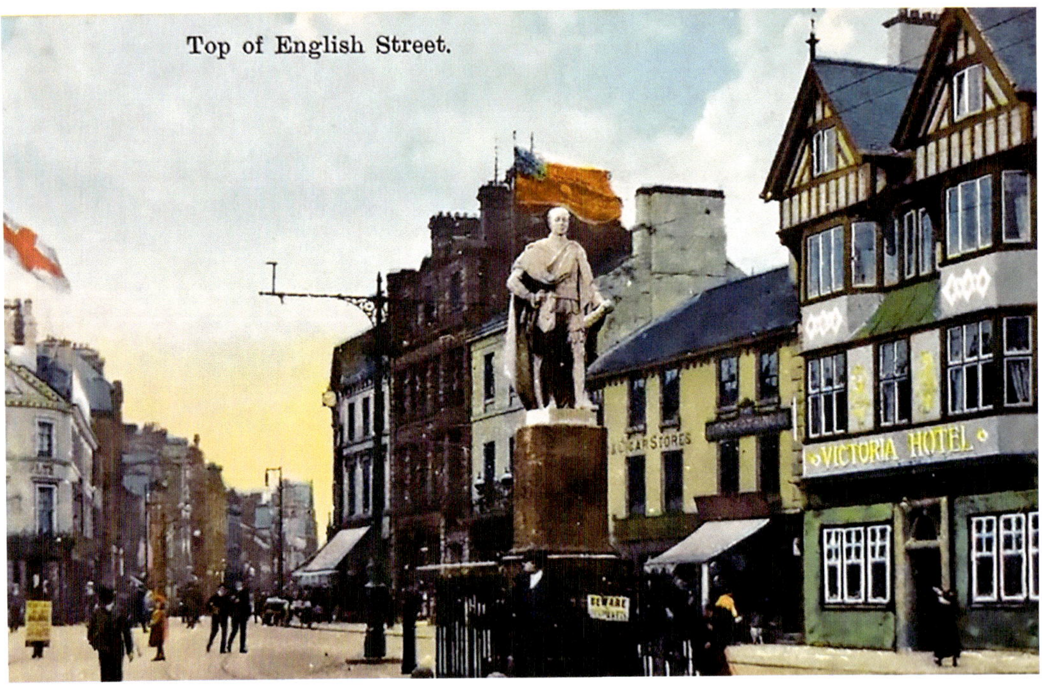

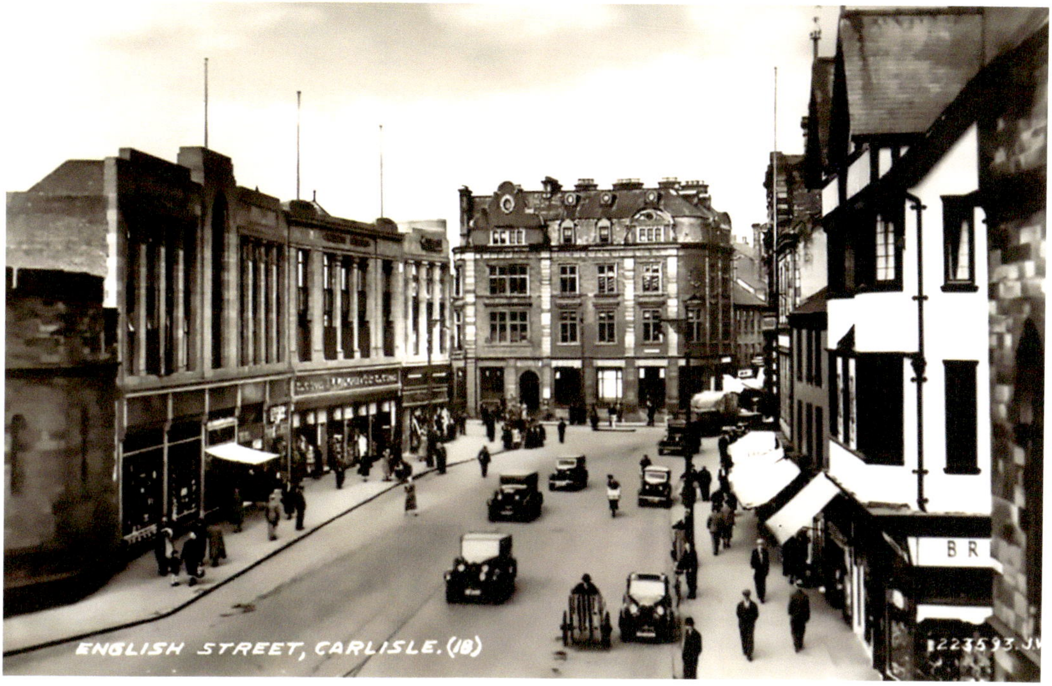

English Street

Both images are taken looking in a northerly direction from the Assize Courts. The road is now for motorised traffic and was the site of the old prison, now built on. Victoria Viaduct is to the left of centre and Devonshire Street to the right of centre.

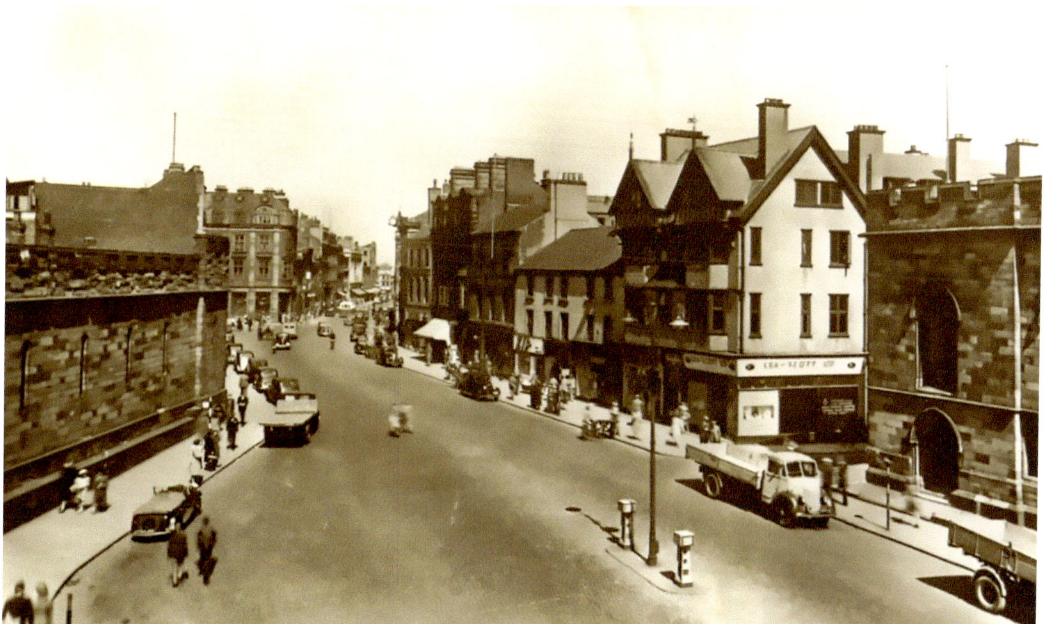

Looking North down English Street, Carlisle

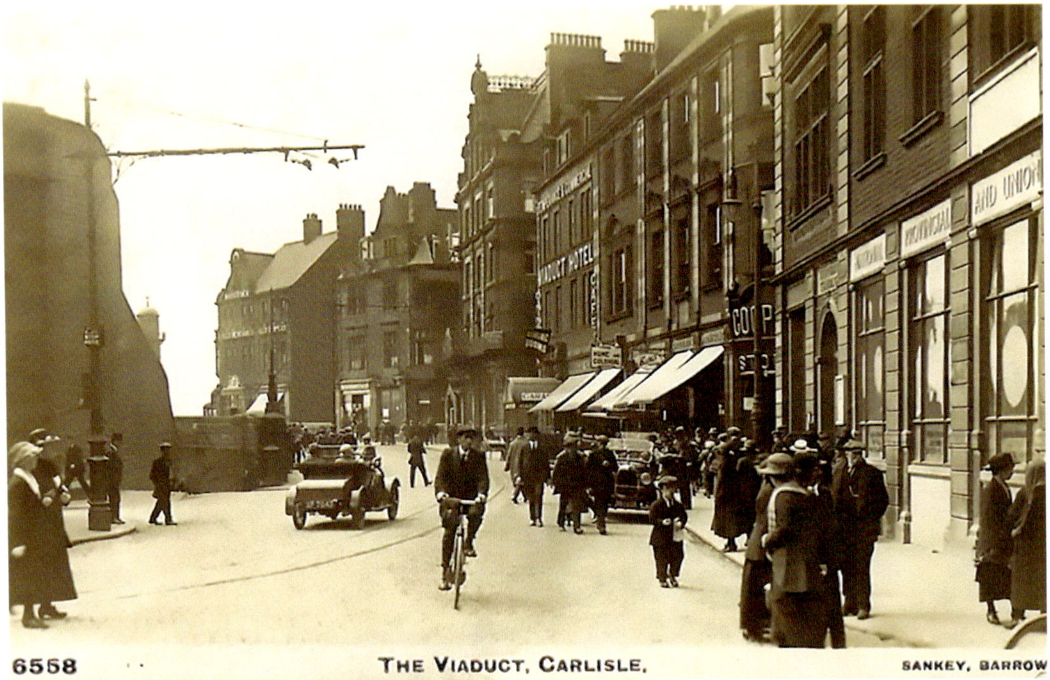

Victoria Viaduct

Victoria Viaduct runs in a south-westerly and then in a southerly direction from English Street to the junction of James Street and Nelson Bridge and is approximately 296 yards long. The two images are looking from near to the junction with English Street.

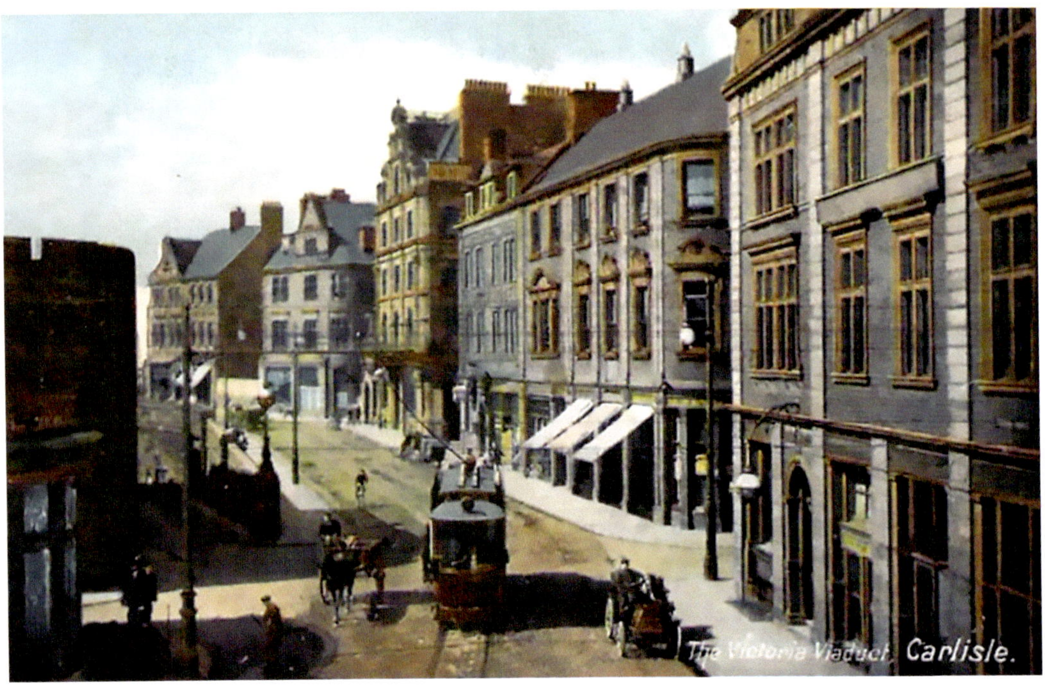

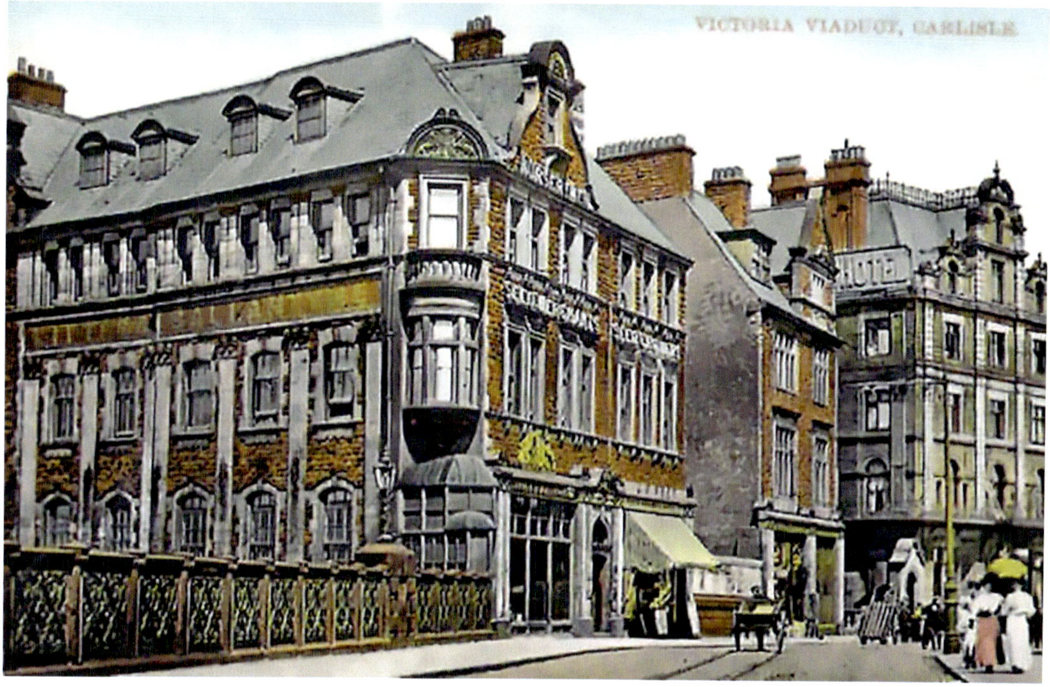

VICTORIA VIADUCT, CARLISLE.

Victoria Viaduct

The image above is taken from where the viaduct crosses the railway and shows the Little and Ballantynes warehouse on the left. The Central Hotel is the building to the right. The image below shows the gasworks at the bottom left and the prison on the right opposite the warehouse.

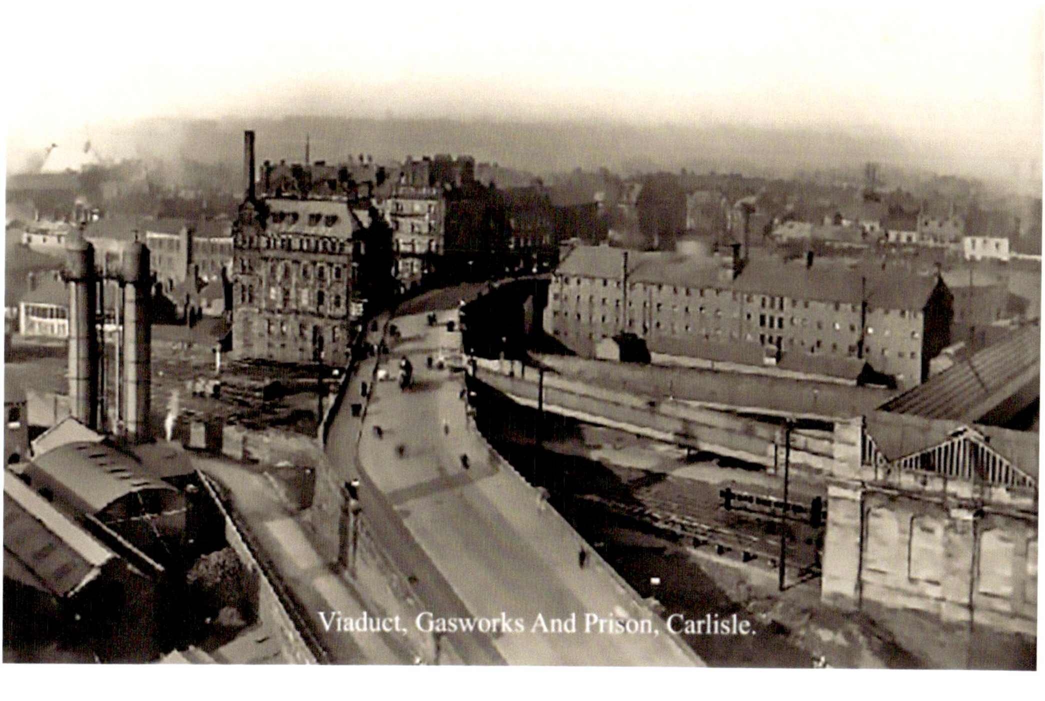

Viaduct, Gasworks And Prison, Carlisle.

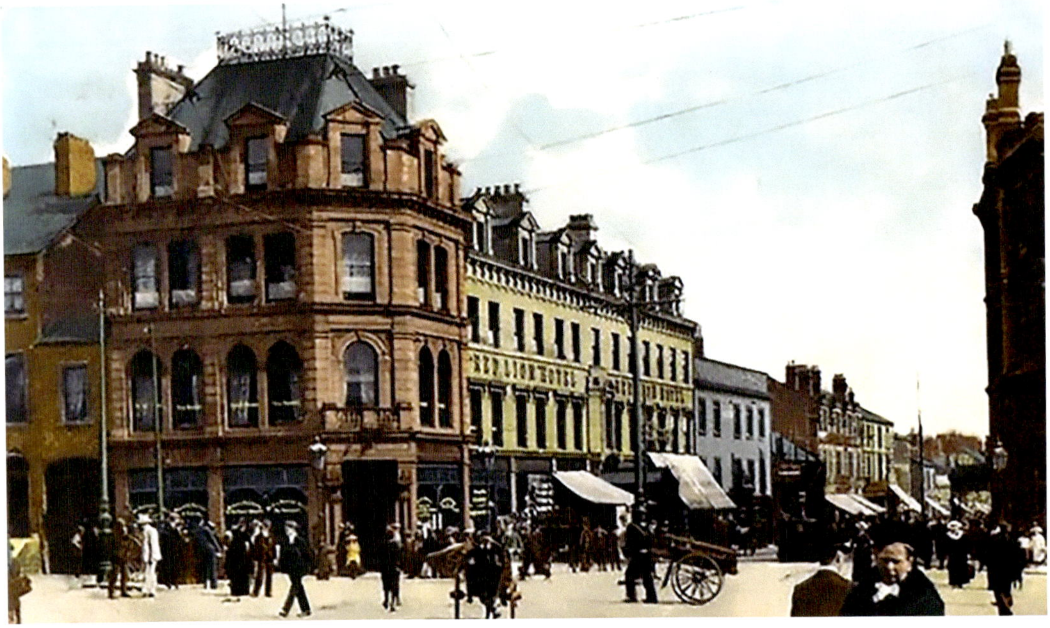

Botchergate

Botchergate runs in a south-easterly direction from the junction of The Crescent, Court Square Brow and English Street to the junction of London Road and St Nicholas Street and is approximately 563 yards long. These images are at the northern end of the street with the York City and County Banking Co. Ltd on the right, which in 1914 became the London Joint Stock Bank Ltd. On the left can be seen the Red Lion Hotel.

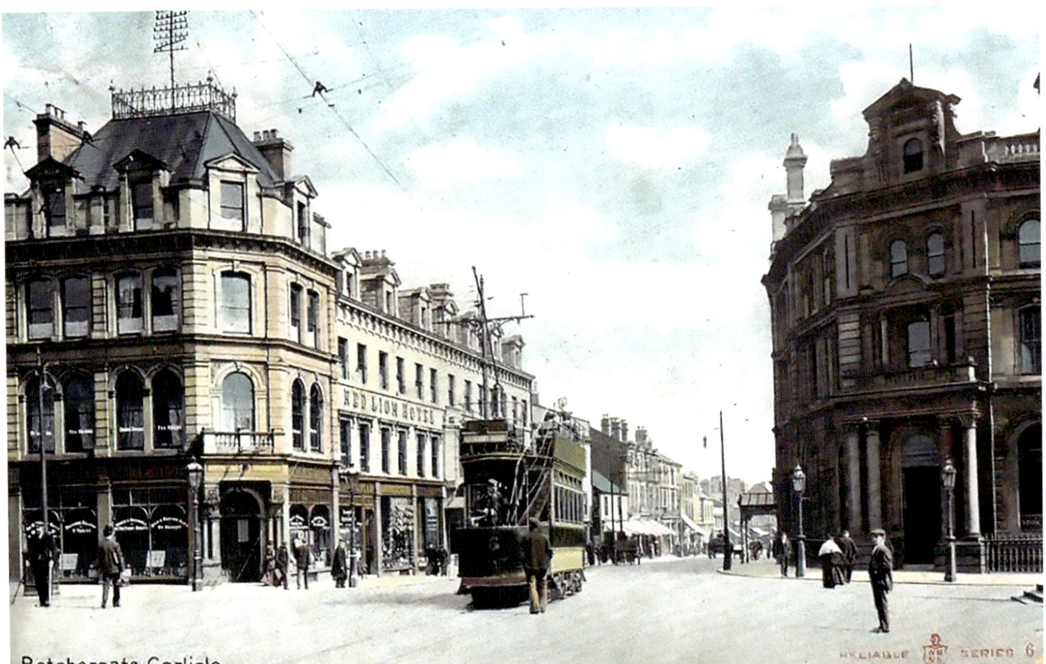

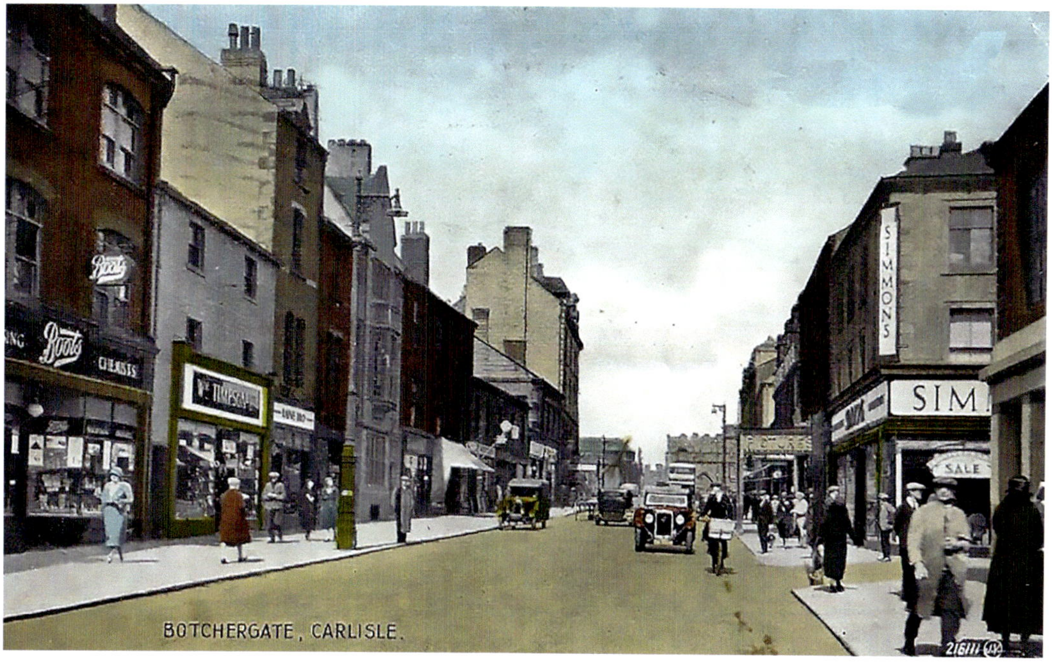

Botchergate

Looking up Botchergate from Portland Place to the northern end. On the above image a Boots store can be seen on the left and Simmons furniture shop on the right. Just past Simmons in the above image and Parker's Ironmongers in the one below is the Carlisle Picture House which opened in 1915.

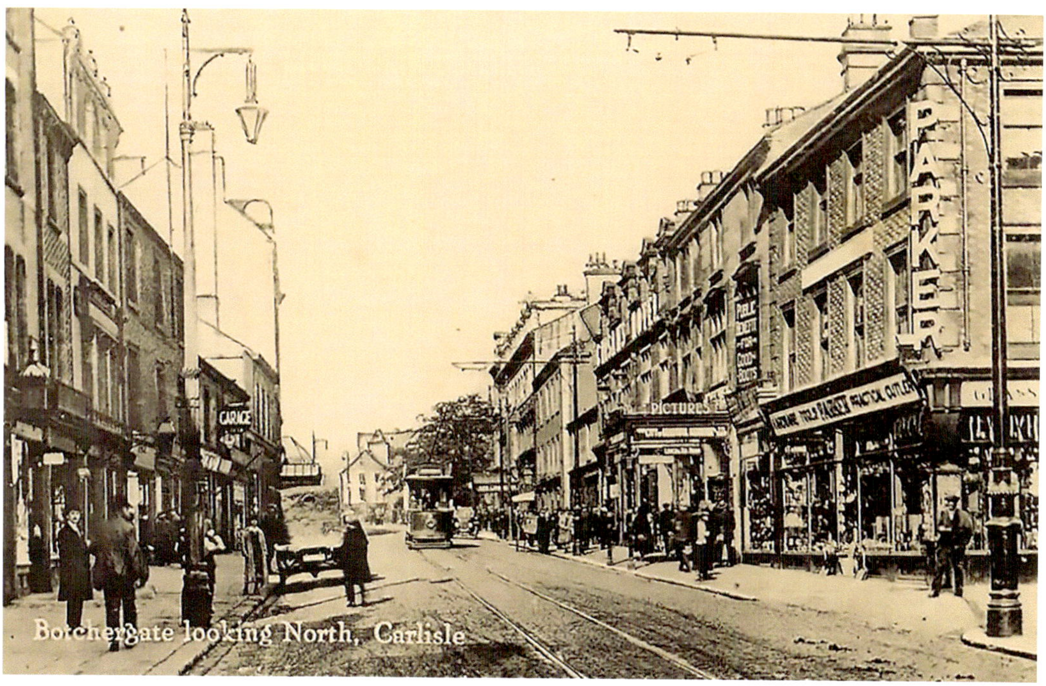

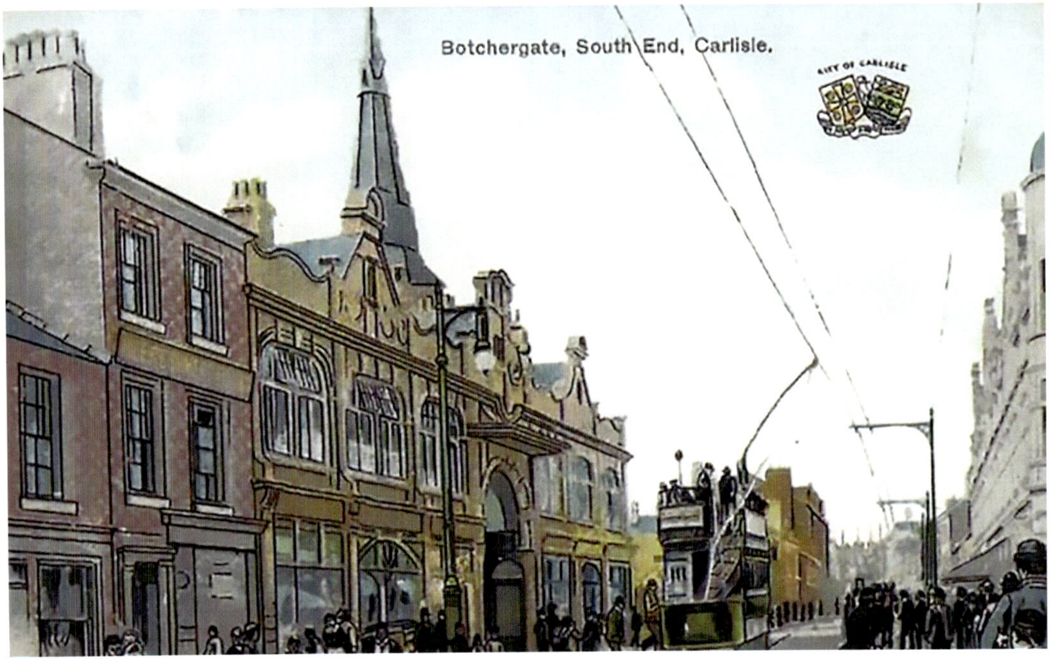

Botchergate

Botchergate, looking towards the southern end. The spire of Christ Church can be seen on the left. The church was built between 1828 and 1830 and closed in 1938; it was demolished in 1953. In the bottom image on the right is the Earl Grey Inn owned by the Carlisle Old Brewery.

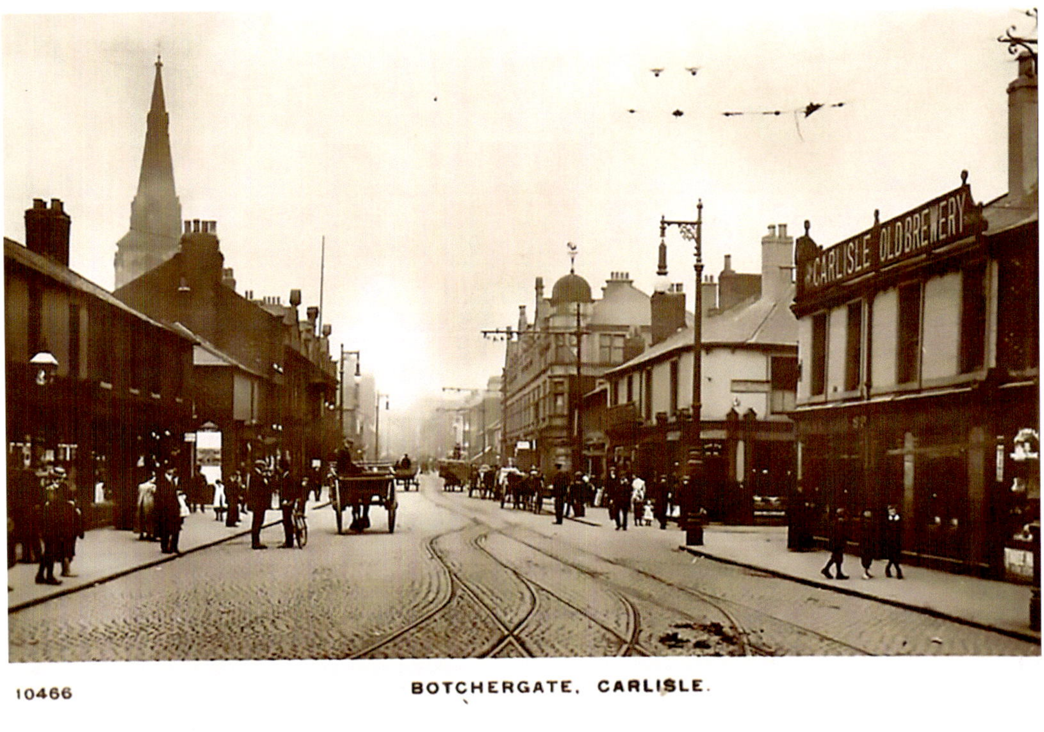

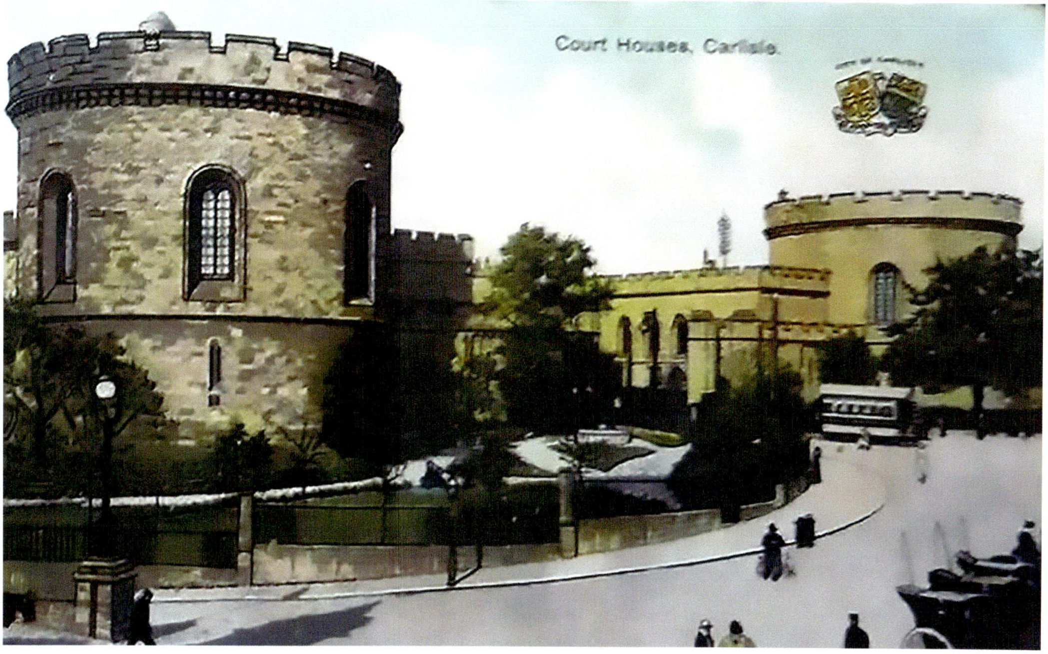

Courthouses (Citadel)

The courthouses are located at the junction of English Street, The Crescent and Court Square Brow. The images are looking north from Court Square Brow. The buildings are known as the Citadel and were commissioned by King Henry VIII to replace the medieval Botcher's gate. The Eastern Tower on the right was modified for use as civil courts in 1812. The Western Tower was completely rebuilt and converted for use as the Crown Court in 1822.

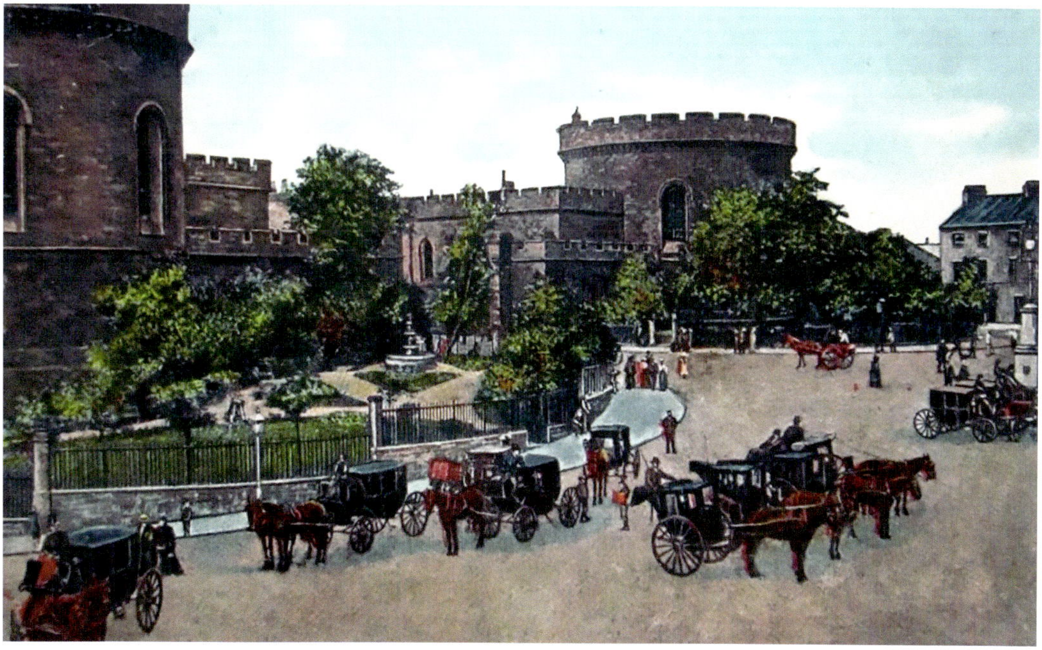

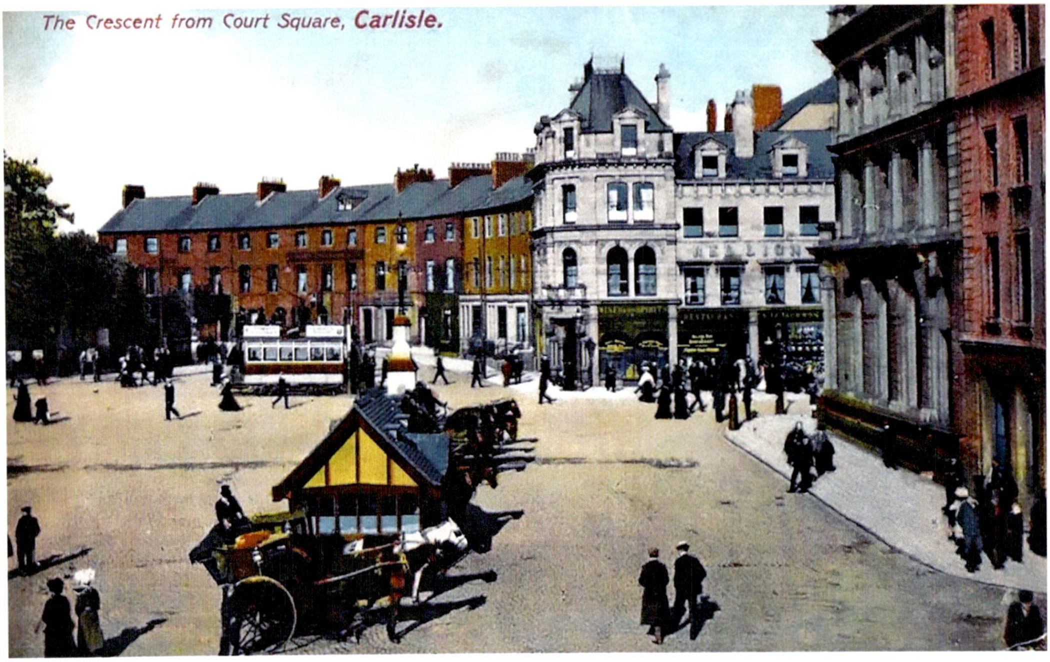

The Crescent

The Crescent runs from the junction of Lowther Street and Warwick Road to the junction of English Street and Botchergate in front of the Citadel and is approximately 102 yards long. The image is looking from Court Square Brow. The Red Lion Hotel can be seen on the right at the northern end of Botchergate. On the image below on the left can be seen the Eastern Tower of the Citadel.

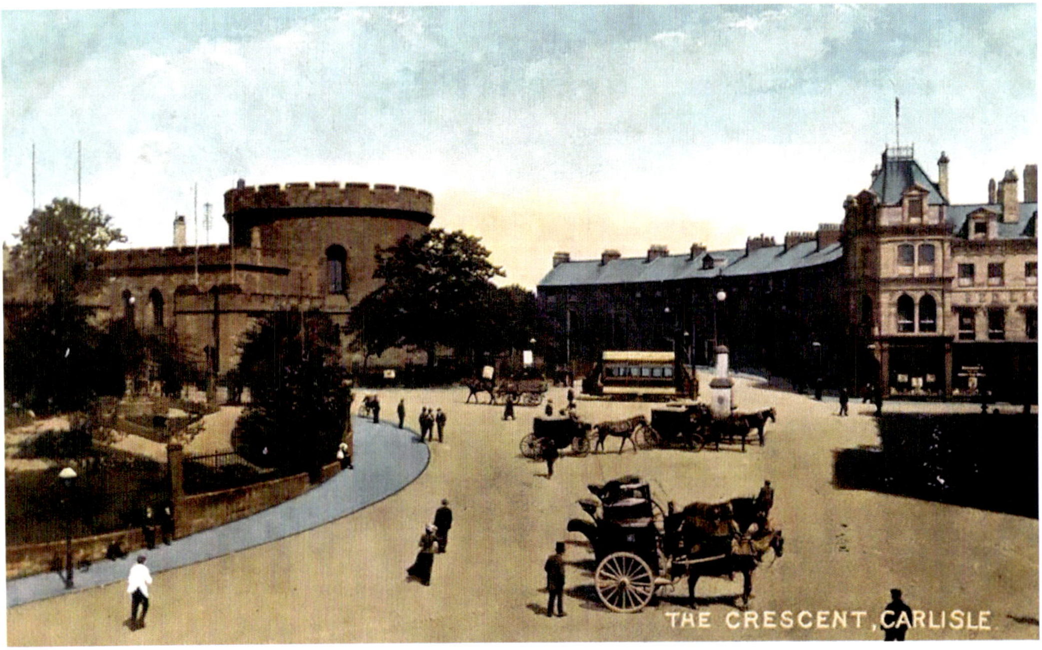

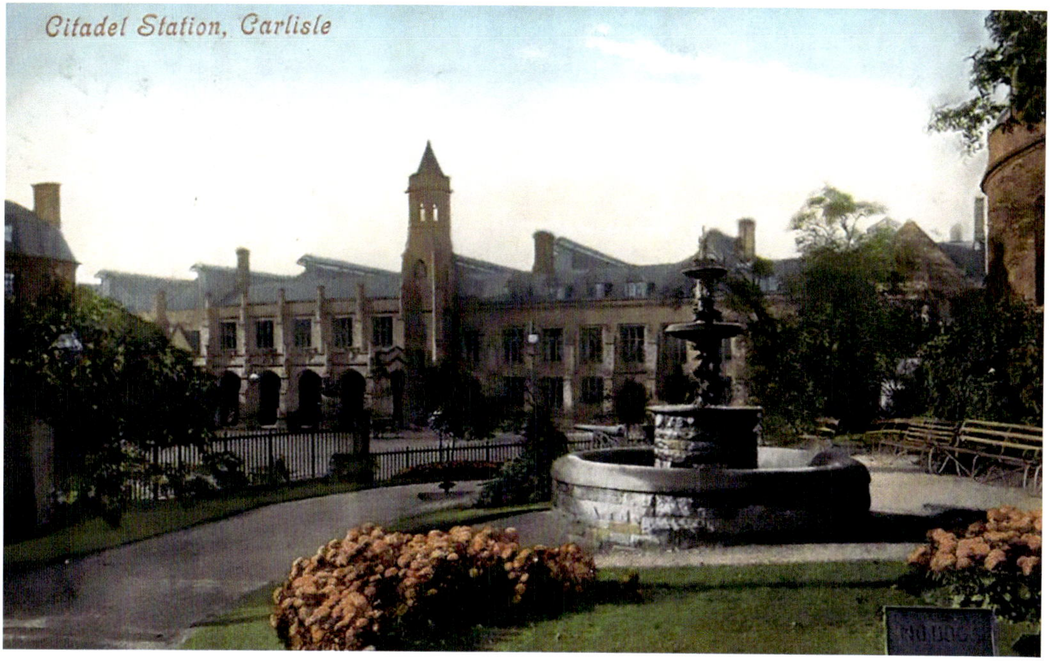

The Citadel Railway Station

Looking across Court Square from the Citadel. The County Hotel is on the left. The station, with its imposing facade, was designed in 1847 by Sir William Tite, who used a Tudor Gothic style to harmonise with the crenellated towers of the Citadel. The station had seven operating companies travelling over eight routes and was one of Britain's most important railway junctions.

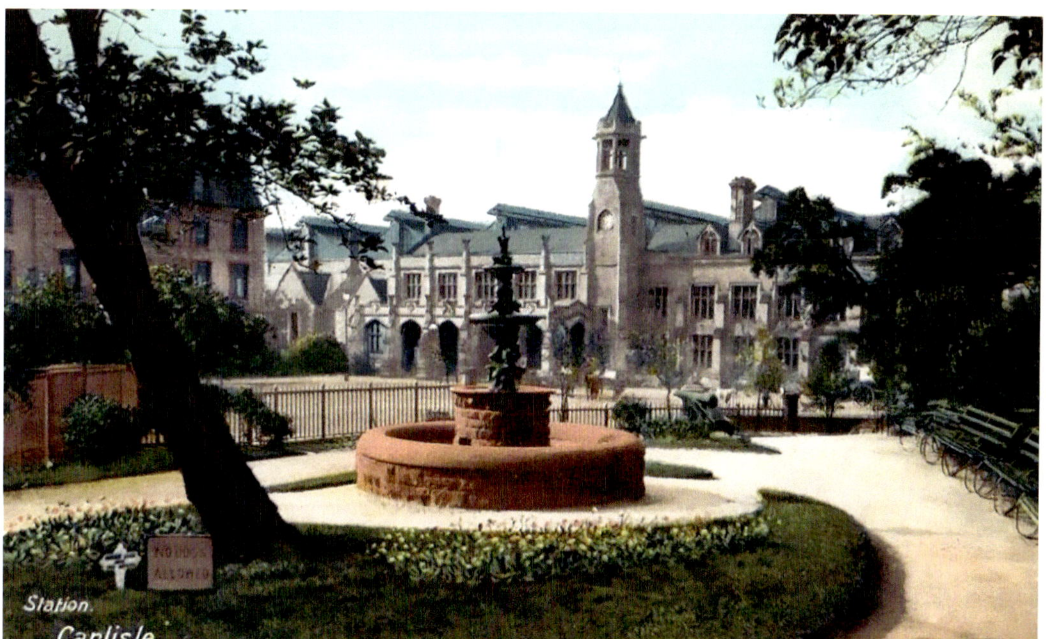

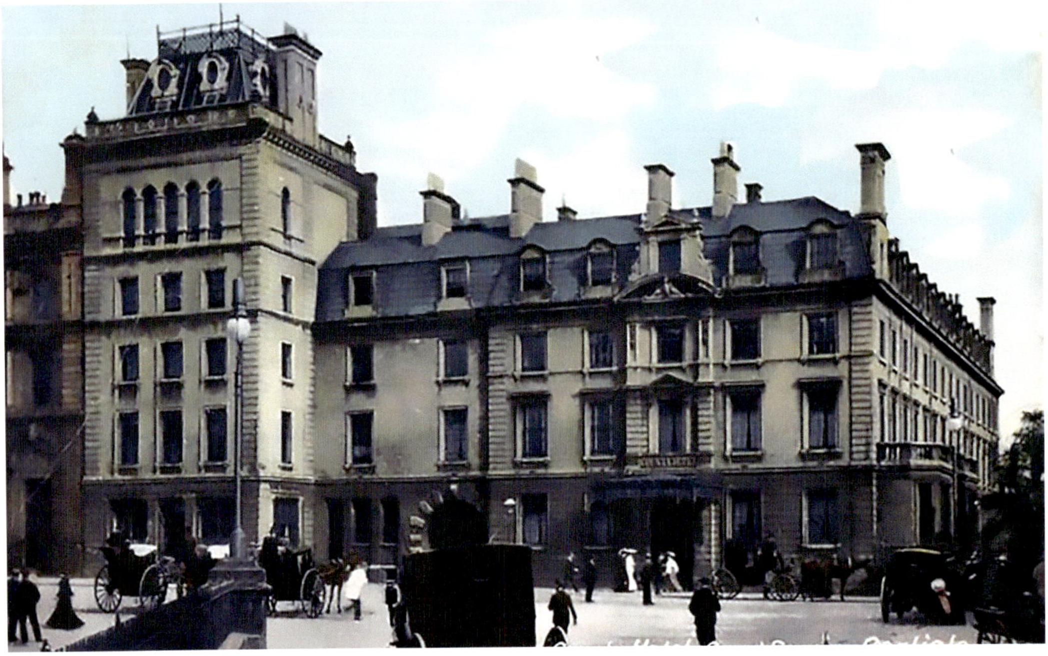

The County and Station Hotel

The hotel was built in 1852 for George Head Head, a Carlisle banker, and was designed by Anthony Salvin. Queen Victoria visited the hotel for a meal in 1853. The hotel was extended in 1866–8. It has had different names over the years, including The County Hotel, The Cumbrian Hotel, Hallmark Hotel and The Carlisle Station Hotel.

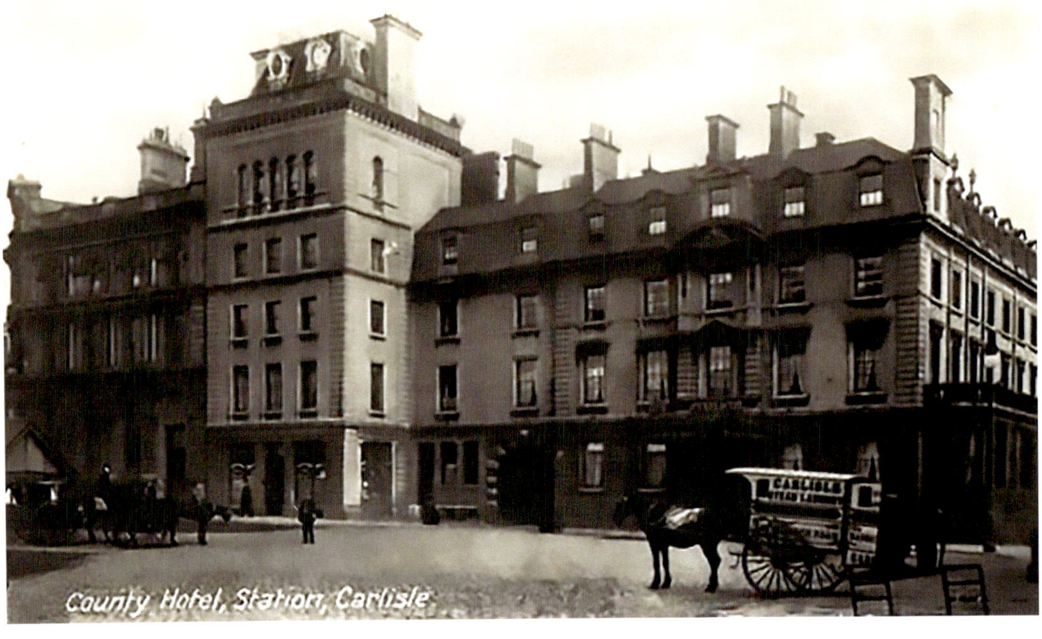

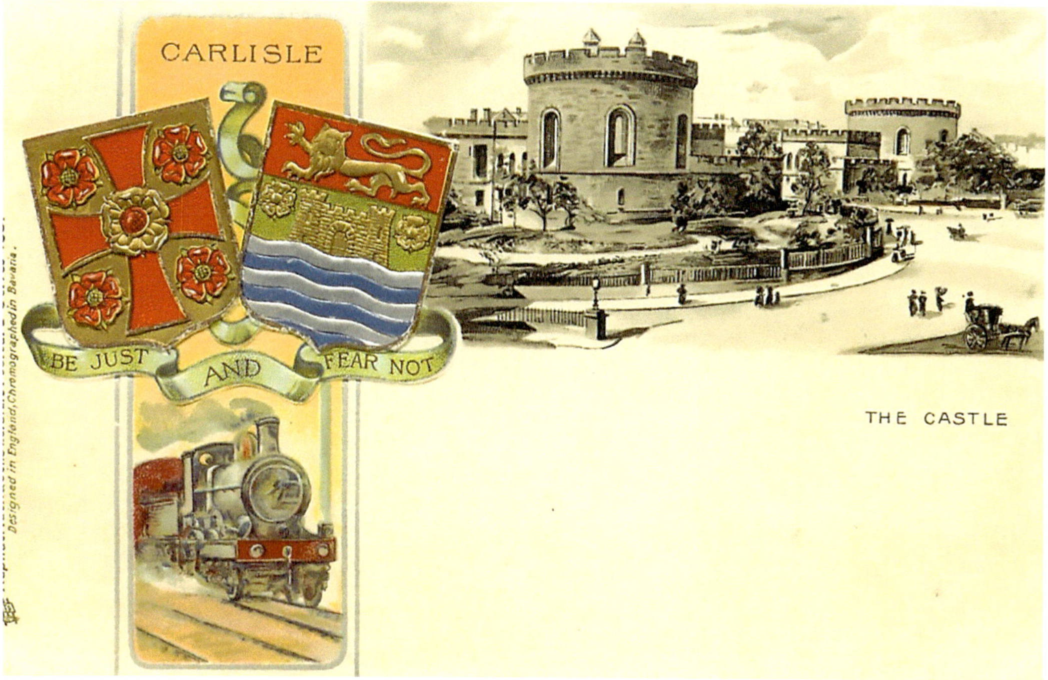

Heraldic Cards

These two cards are from a series showing images of important historical places in the city. These are of the castle and the cathedral.

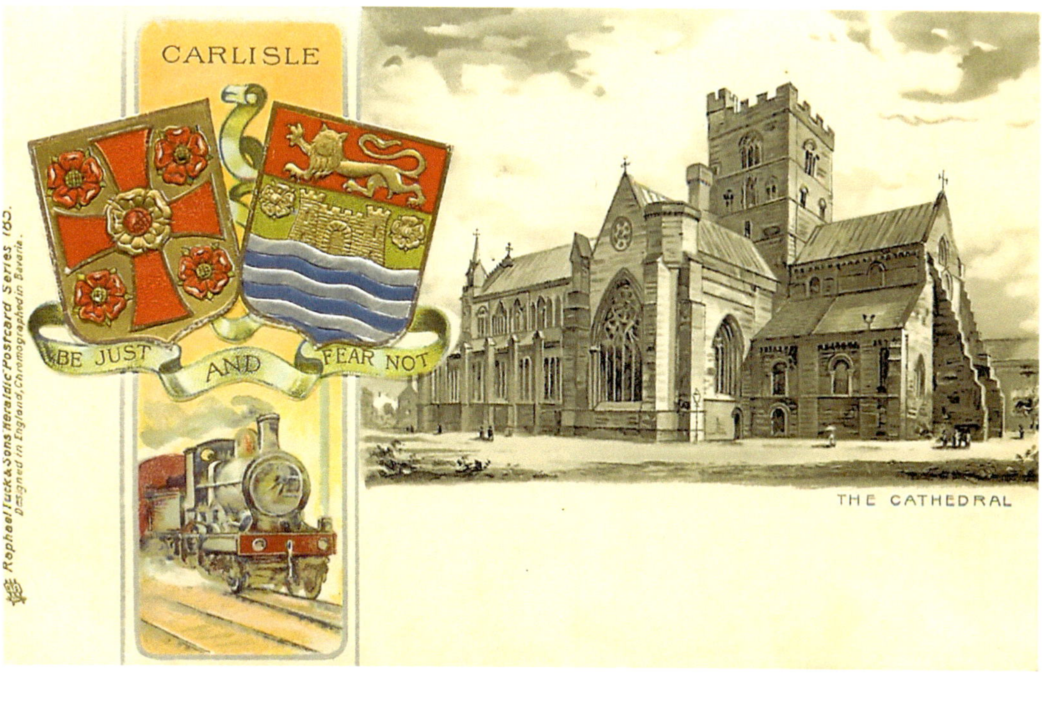

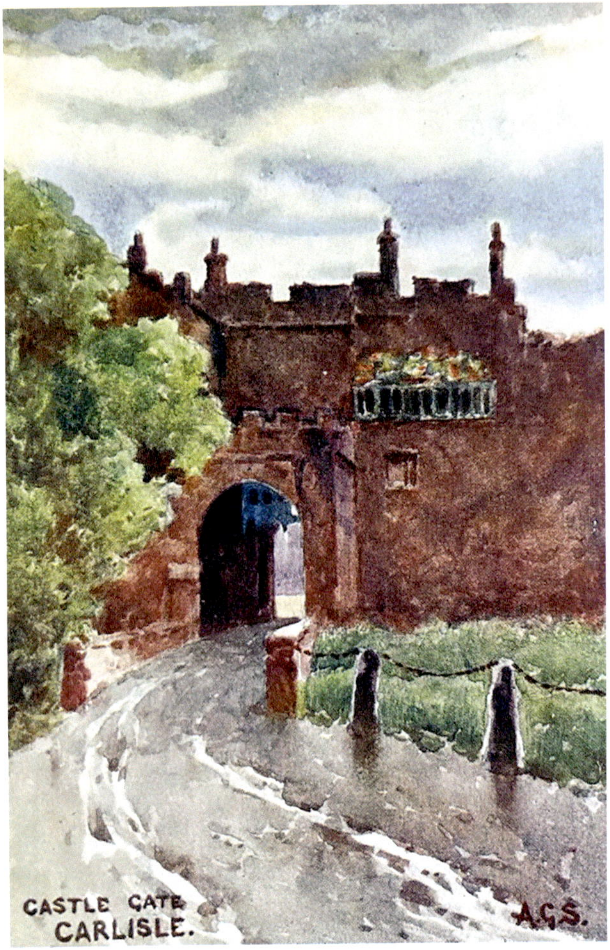

The Castle

The castle is located on Castle Way with the entrance drive to the gate adjacent to the northern end of Castle Street.This is a stone keep medieval fortress and is located near the ruins of Hadrian's Wall. First built during the reign of William II in 1092 and rebuilt in stone under Henry I in 1122. The castle played an extremely important part in the wars between England and Scotland (the Wars of Scottish Independence). It has been the centre of many wars and invasions. During the Jacobite Rising of 1745–6, Carlisle became the last English fortress to undergo a siege. These two images show the castle gate.

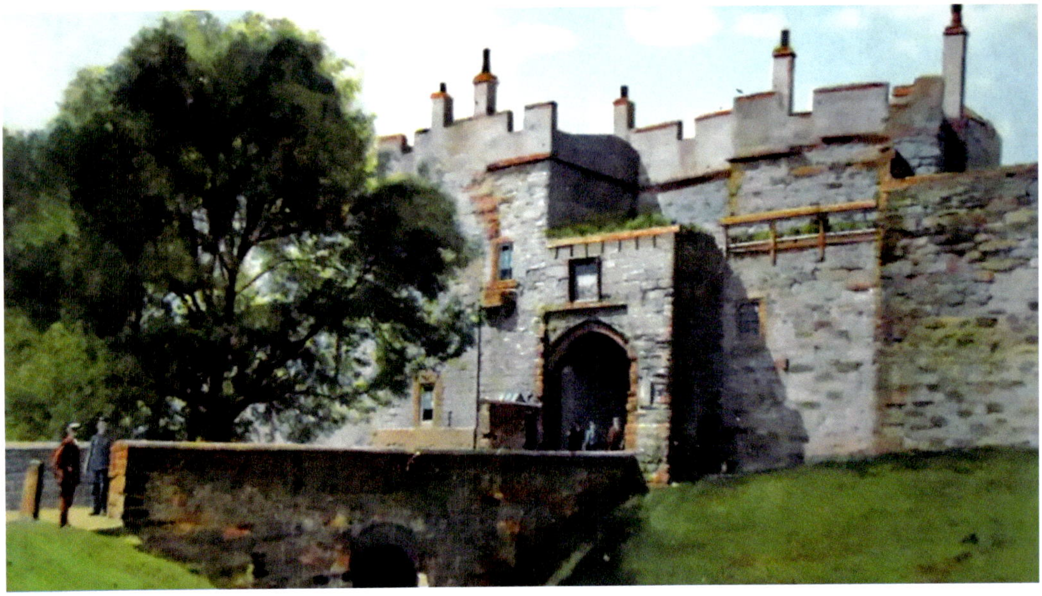

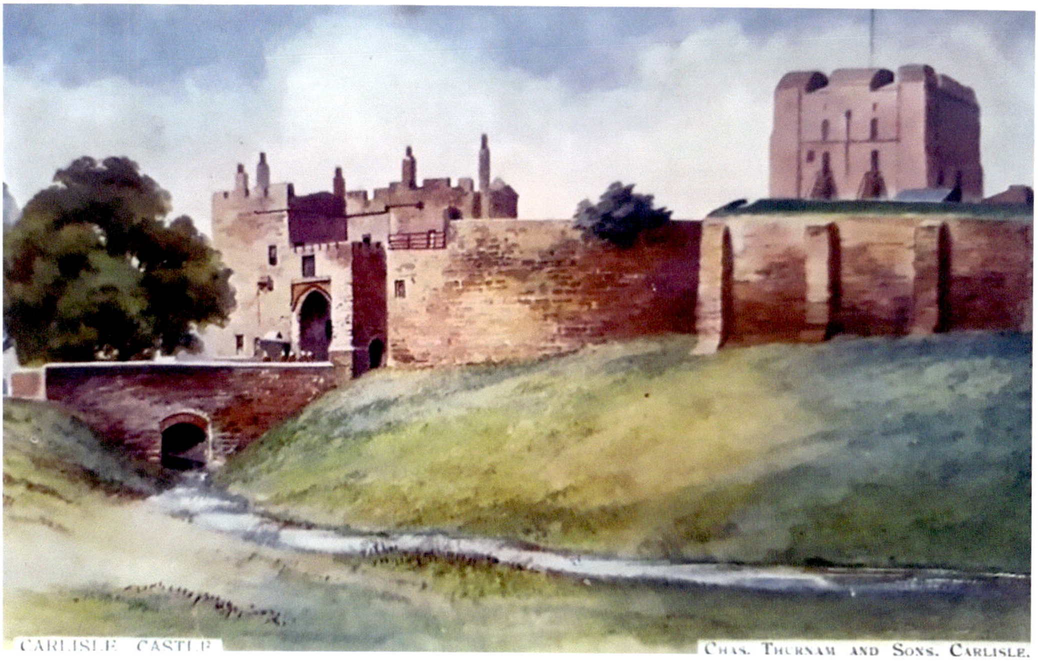

The Castle

The castle was first built during the reign of William II of England who was the son of William the Conqueror. At that time, Cumberland was still considered a part of Scotland. William II ordered the construction of a Norman-style motte and bailey castle in Carlisle on the site of the old Roman fort of Luguvalium, dated to AD 72. The two images show the southern walls of the castle.

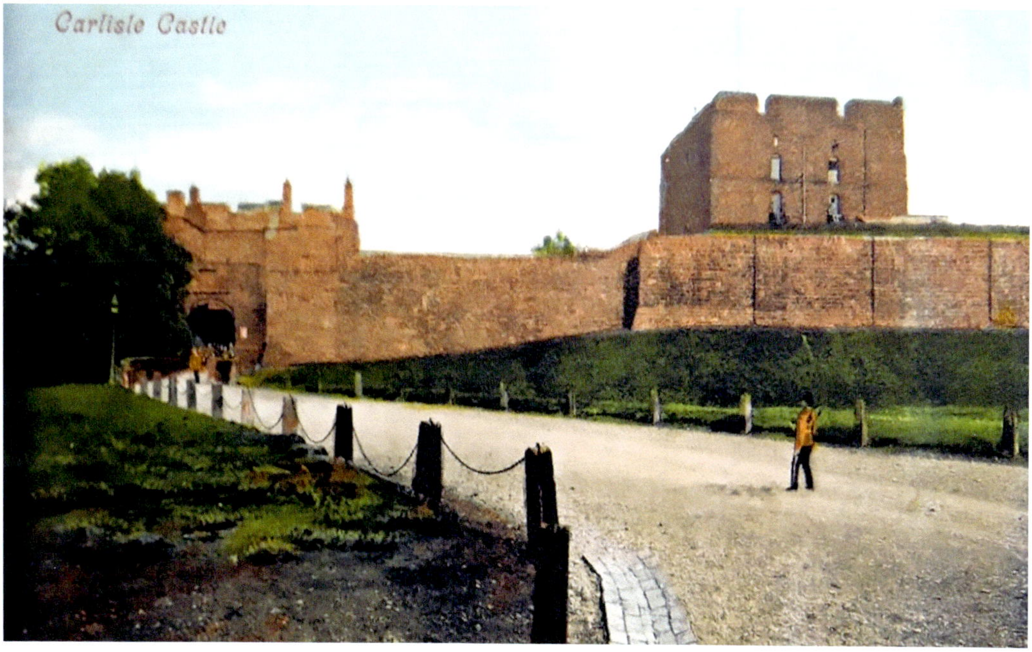

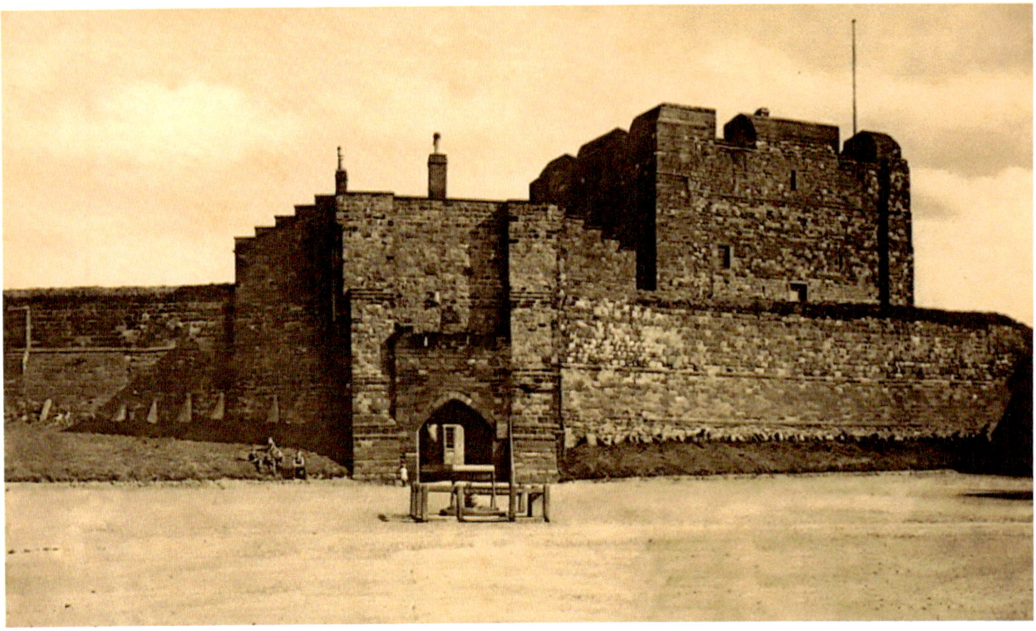

The Castle

The two images are taken within the grounds of the castle looking east and show the Captain's Tower and the keep. The Captain's Tower is the main gateway into the inner bailey of Carlisle Castle. The inner bailey is roughly triangular in shape, comprising north, south and west walls. Its walls date from the twelfth century and were partially rebuilt in the nineteenth century. The Captain's Tower dates from the thirteenth century, with fourteenth-century modifications and some later alterations.

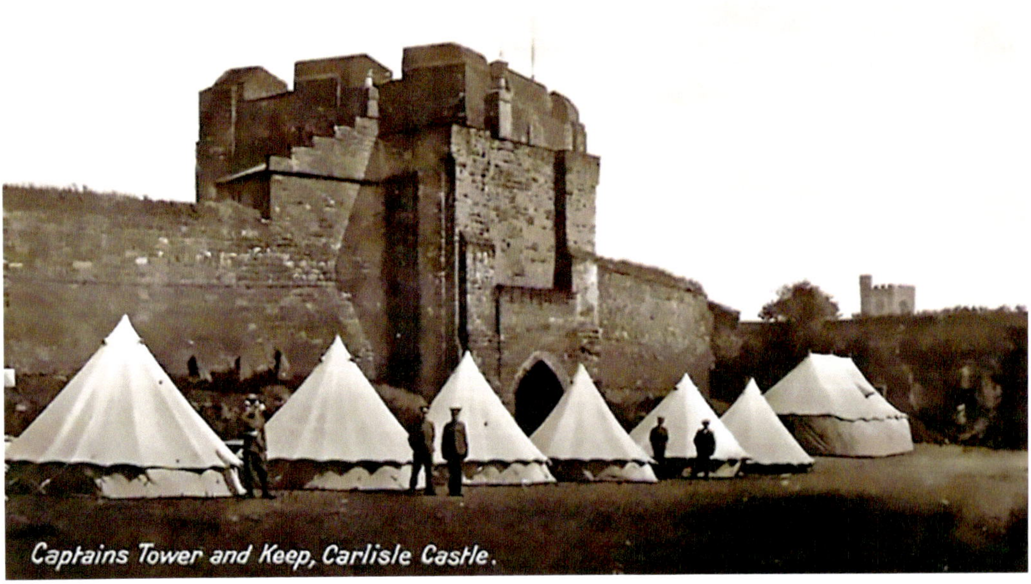

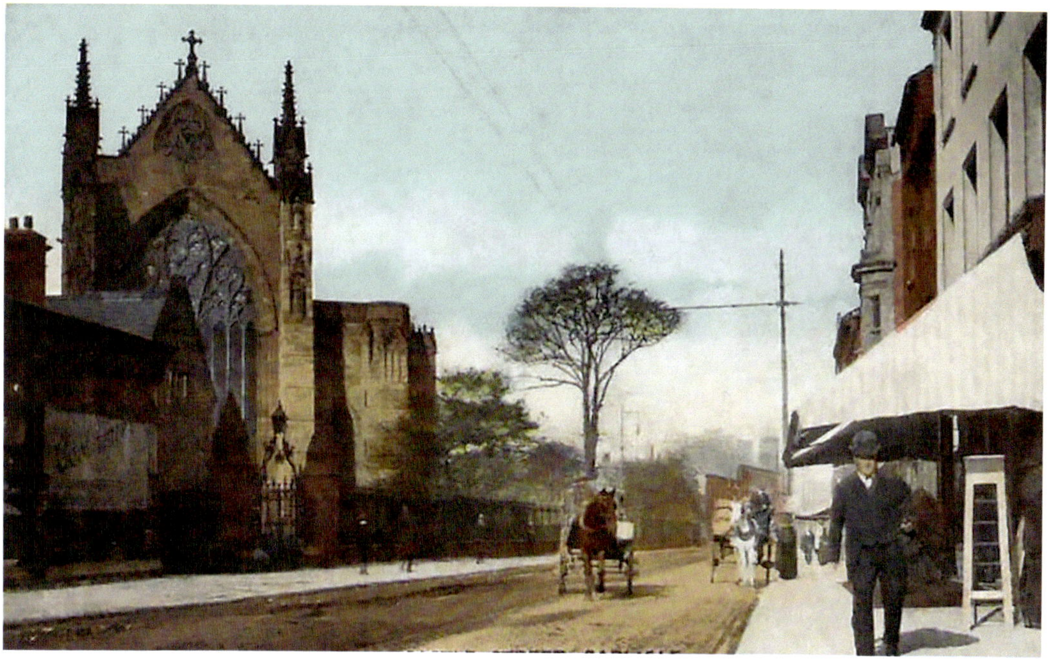

Castle Street

The street is approximately 320 yards long and runs from Fisher Street in a north-westerly direction to Castle Way. The images are taken looking towards Castle Way with the cathedral shown on the left. The transition of horse and cart to transport by the motor vehicle is noted.

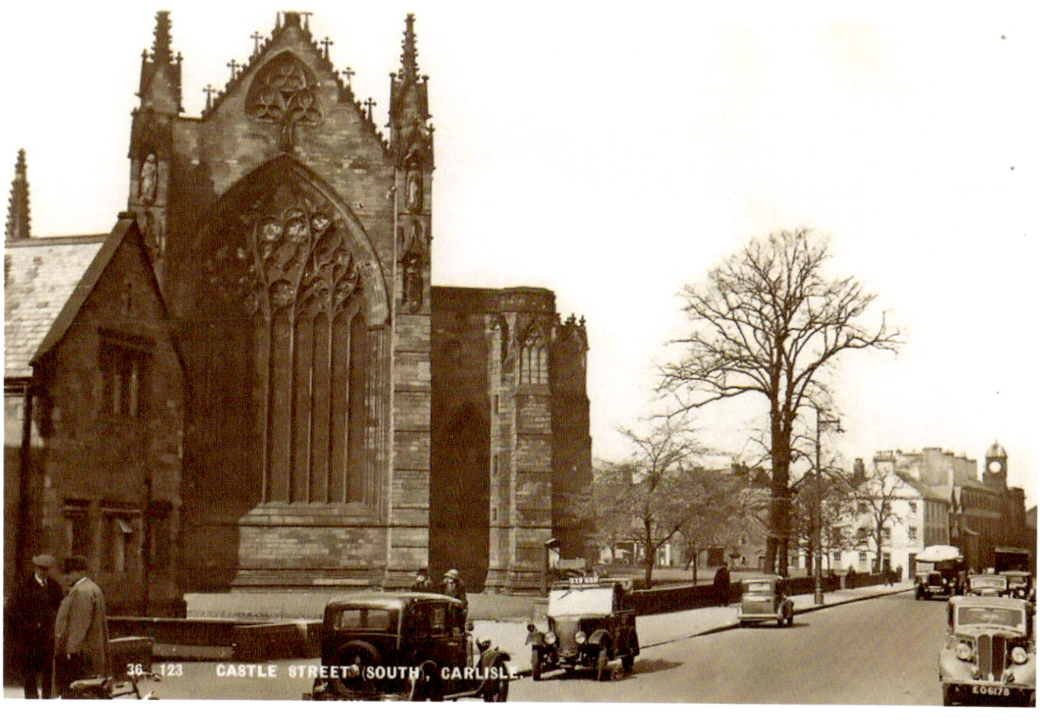

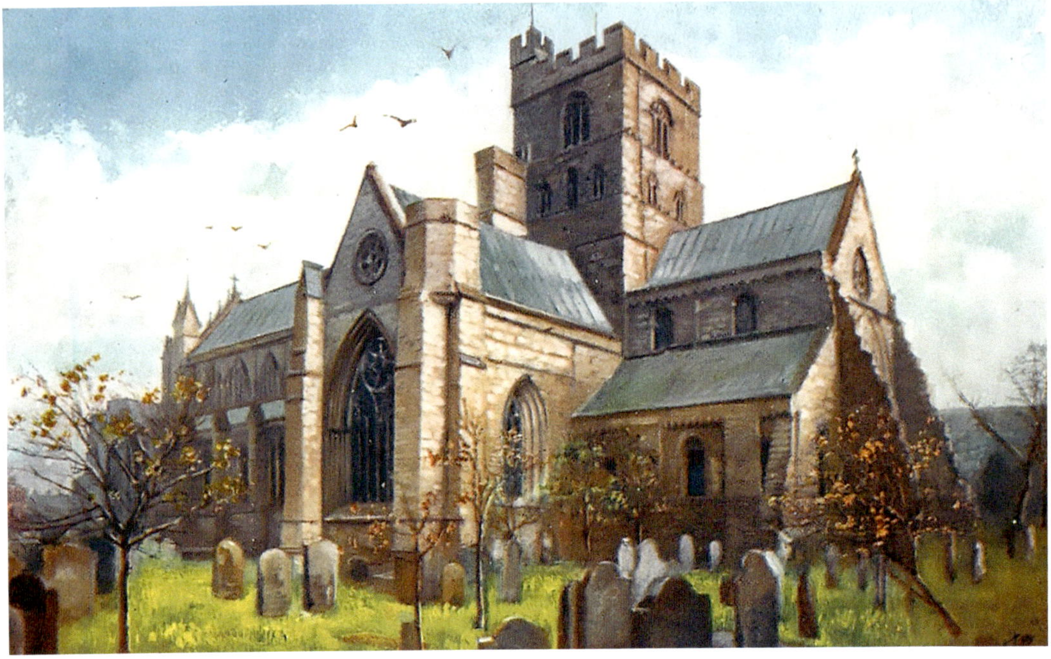

The Cathedral

The cathedral is located on Castle Street with the entrance opposite the southern end of St Mary's Gate. It was founded as a Norman Priory Church by King Henry I in 1122 and became a cathedral when the King created the diocese of Carlisle in 1133. The building is constructed of red sandstone. Parts of the nave had to be rebuilt after being destroyed by the Scots in the seventeenth century and a substantial restoration of the cathedral was carried out from 1853–7 by Ewan Christian. The images are looking from Paternoster Row and show the north facade.

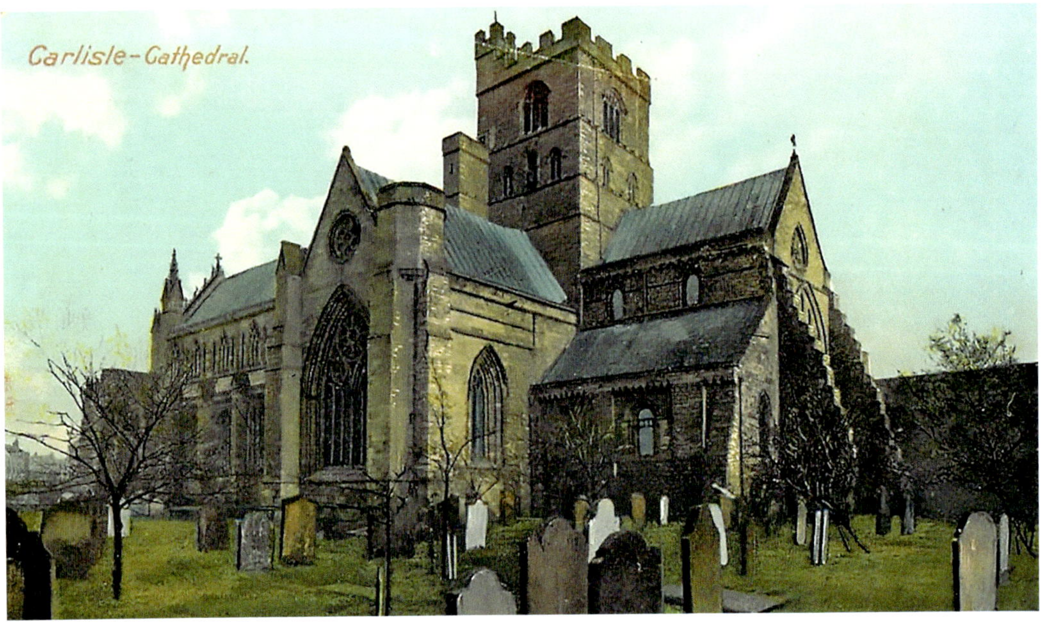

The Cathedral – East Window

The East Window is the biggest window in the cathedral at 58 feet tall. The top third is medieval glass from the fourteenth century and the only original glass left. It depicts the story of the last judgement. The lower nine panels were added in the Victorian period. These depict many stories from the Bible including the Nativity, miracles that Jesus performed, the Crucifixion and the Resurrection.

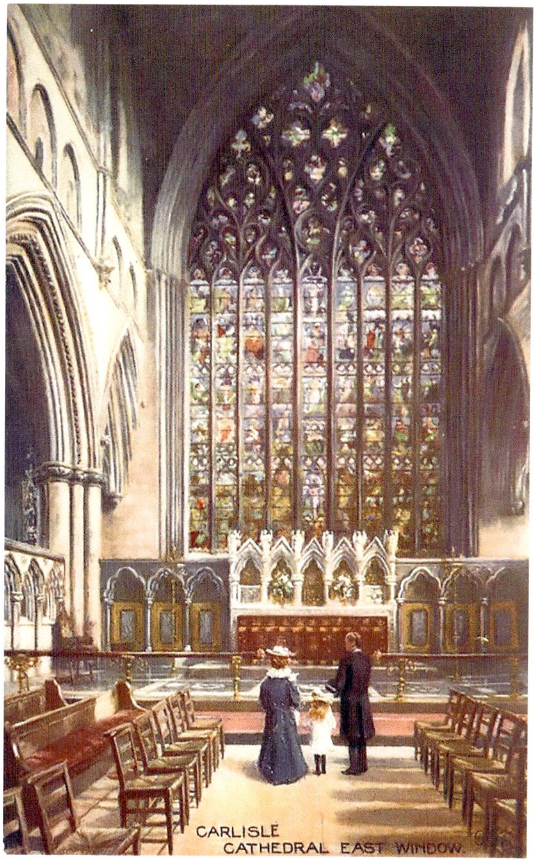

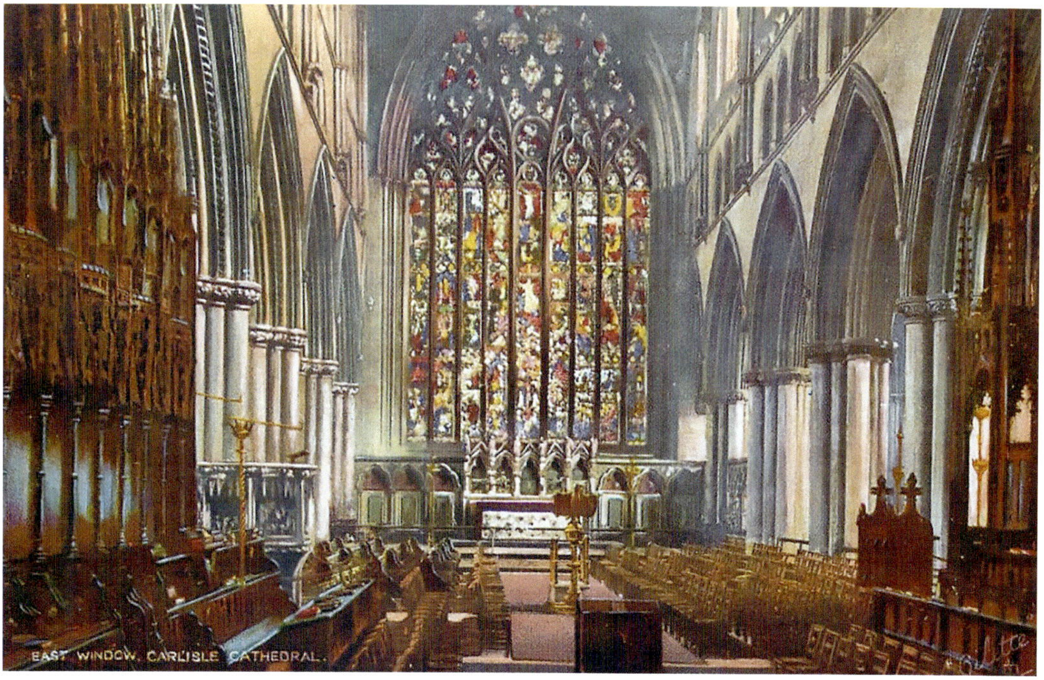

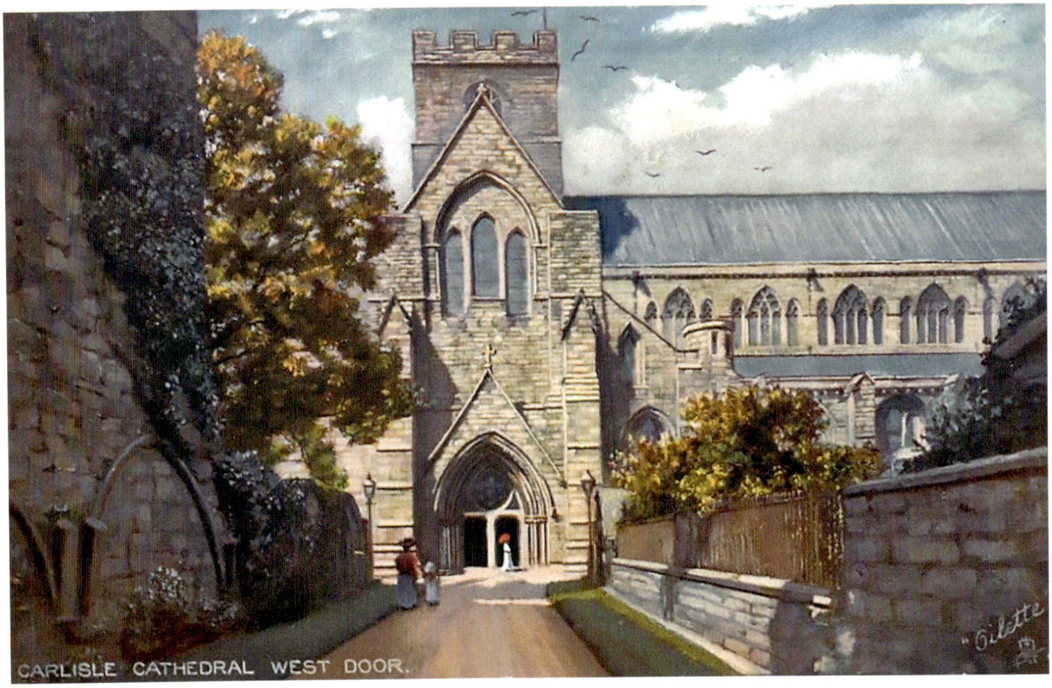

The Cathedral – West Door

Although annotated the West Door, this is clearly the South Door with the refectory shown on the left. The elaborately carved south doorway was part of the restoration work carried out by Ewan Christian in 1856.

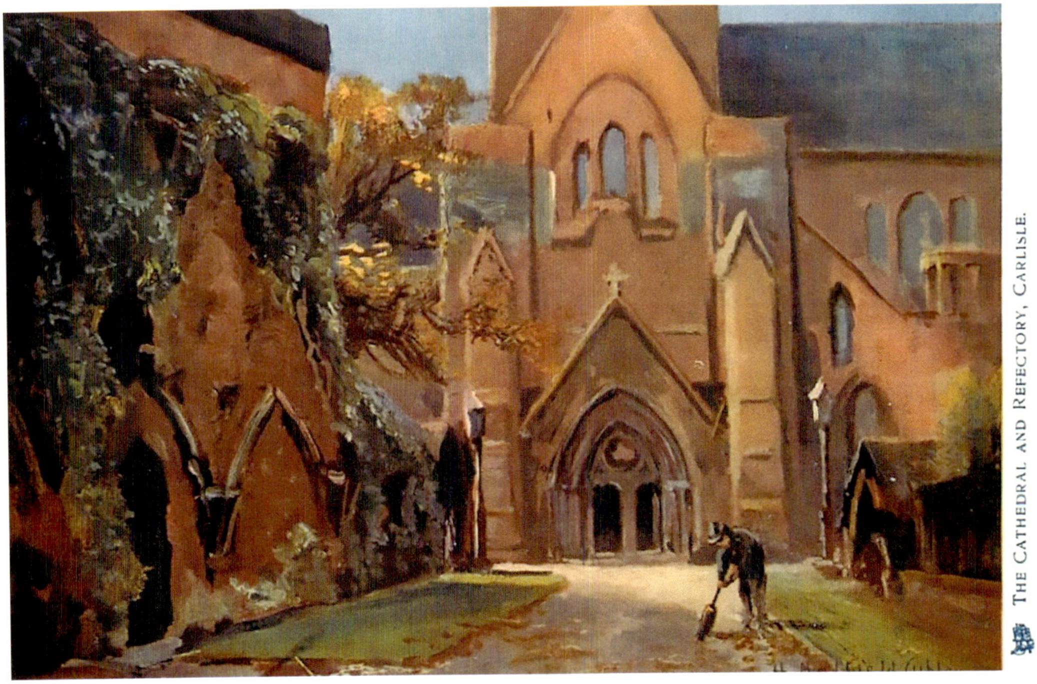

The Cathedral – Choir and Organ

Looking west away from the altar towards the entrance to the choir with the organ above. The north aisle is on the right and the south aisle on the left. Under the supervision of Dean Tait, one of the great organ-makers of the Victorian era, Henry Willis was approached to build a new instrument for Carlisle. The 'Willis' organ dates from 1856.

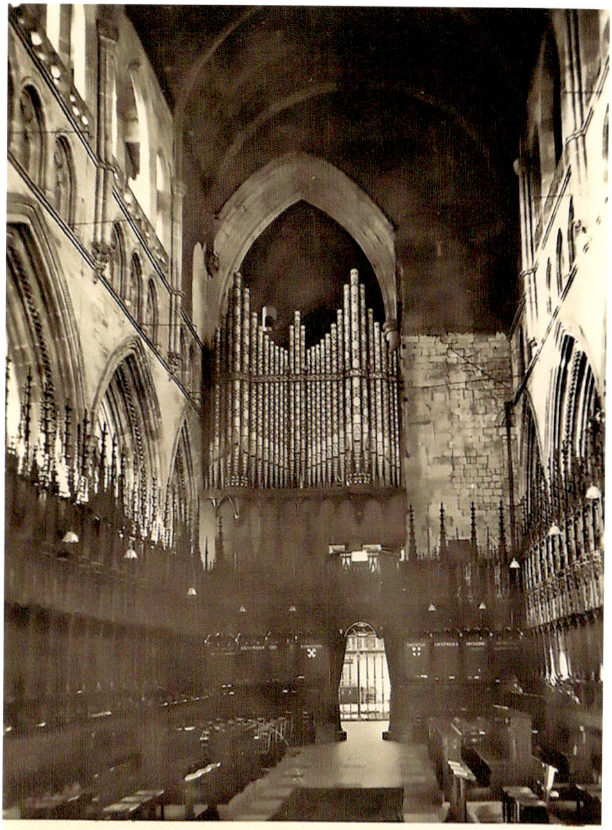

CARLISLE CATHEDRAL. CHOIR STALLS

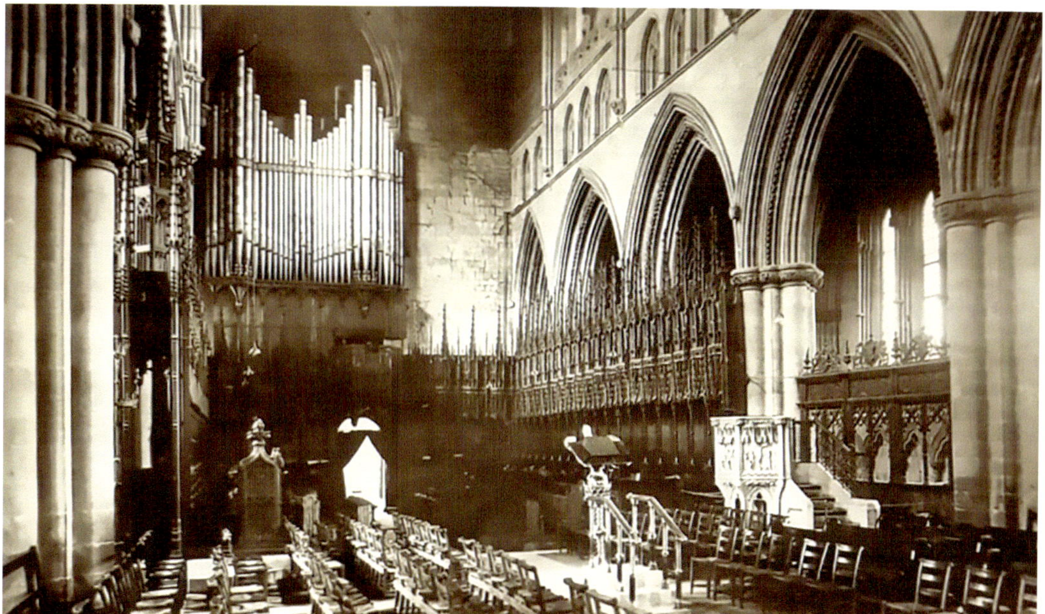

5 4355 CHOIR, W. CARLISLE CATHEDRAL

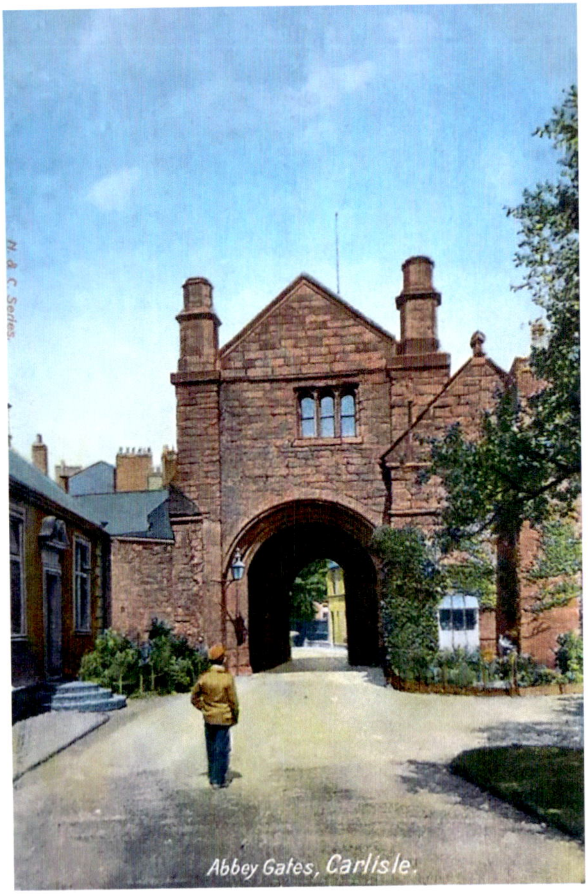

Abbey Gate

The gate is situated at the junction of Abbey Street, Paternoster Row and Dean Tait's Lane. The Gatehouse is dated 1528 and was built as the gate tower to St Mary's Priory. The gateway gives access to the cathedral precinct. Image left is looking south-easterly from Abbey Street with Paternoster Row on the left. The image below is from inside the precinct looking back to the Abbey Gate.

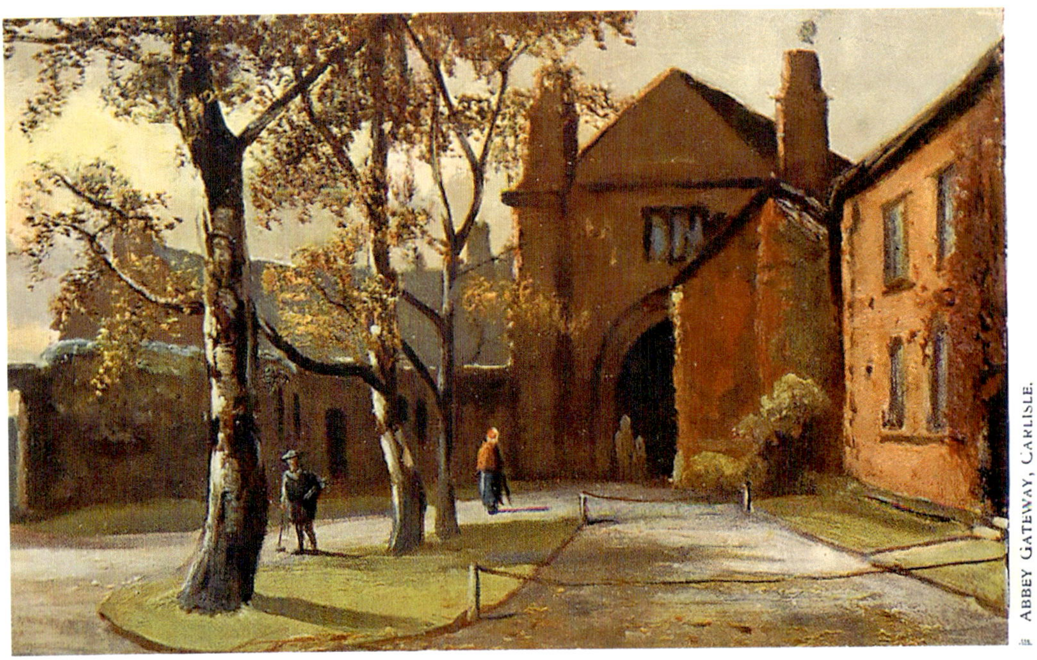

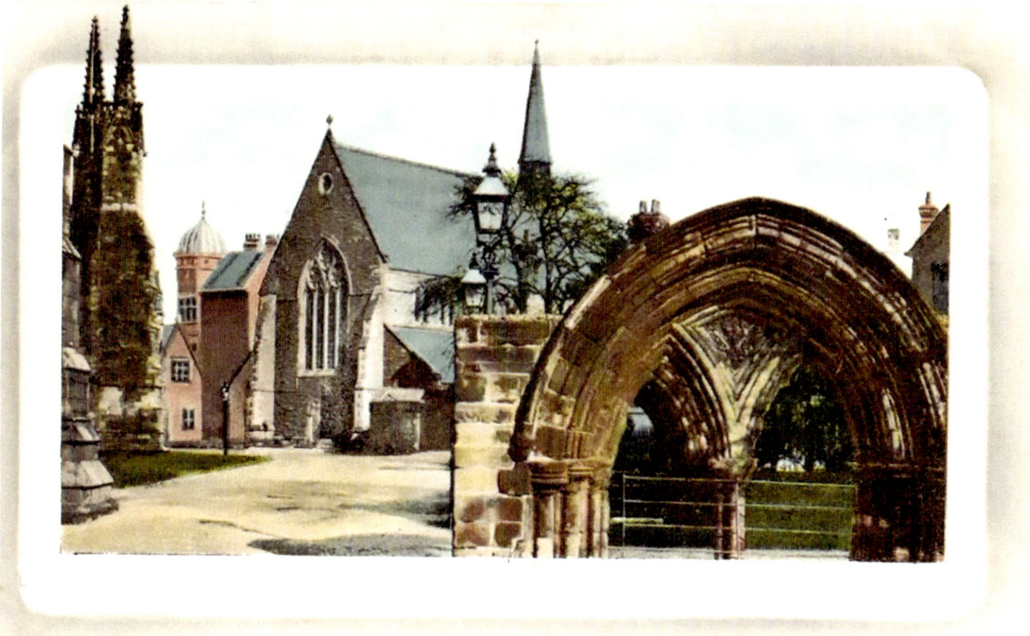

St Mary's Church Within the Abbey

The parish church of St Mary was within the nave of the cathedral and was used as such until 1870 when a new church of St Mary, as shown in the images, was built on the east of the cathedral close. It was demolished in 1954 and the area landscaped. The images are looking east with the South Door to the cathedral on the left.

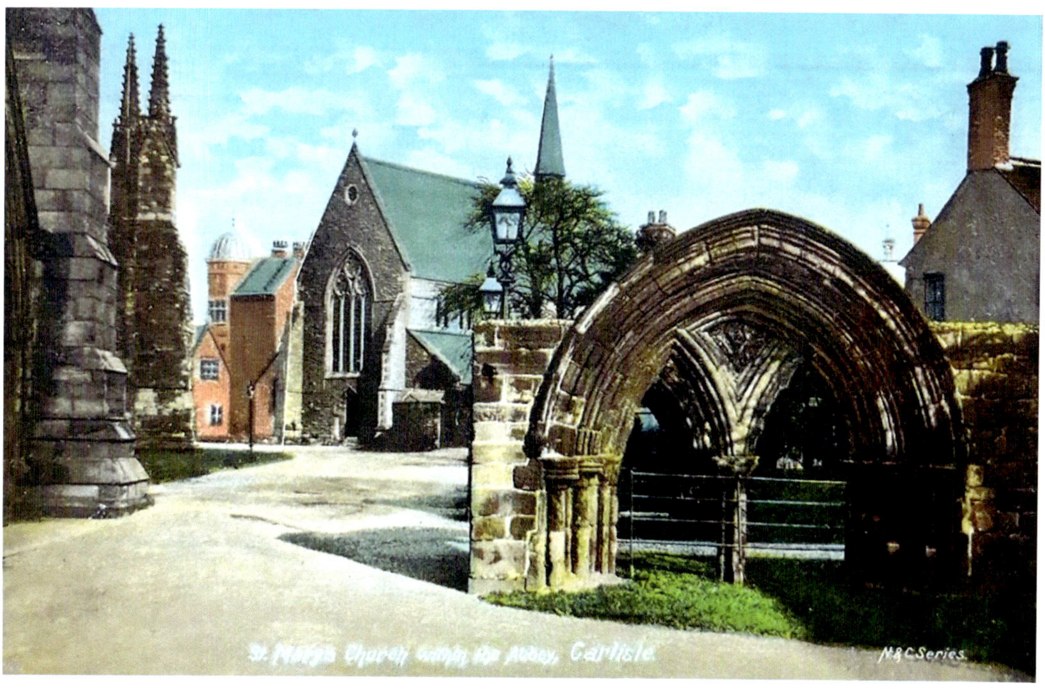

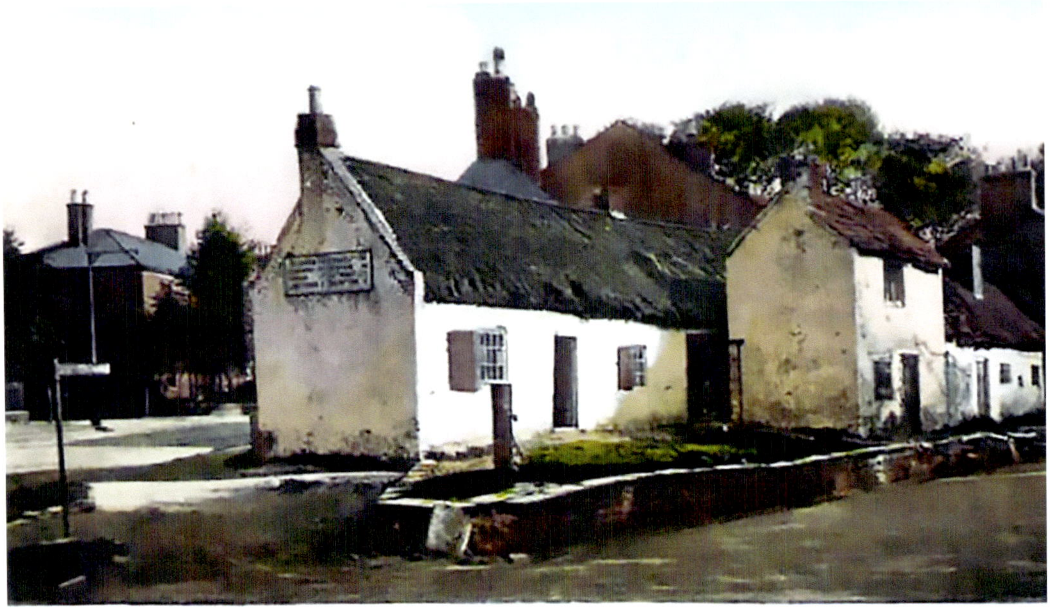

OLD THATCHED COTTAGES ON STANWIX BANK CARLISLE
THE COBWEBB'D COTTAGE WITH ITS RAGGED WALL OFF MOULDERING MUD.

Stanwix Bank – Thatched Cottages

On the junction with Devonshire Terrace (formerly Stanwix Bank) to the left and Brampton Road (formerly Albert Place) to the right. They were demolished in 1904. Note the water pump in the centre foreground. The board on the end of the house gives mileages to various places.

Old Thatched Cottages, Stanwix Bank, Carlisle.

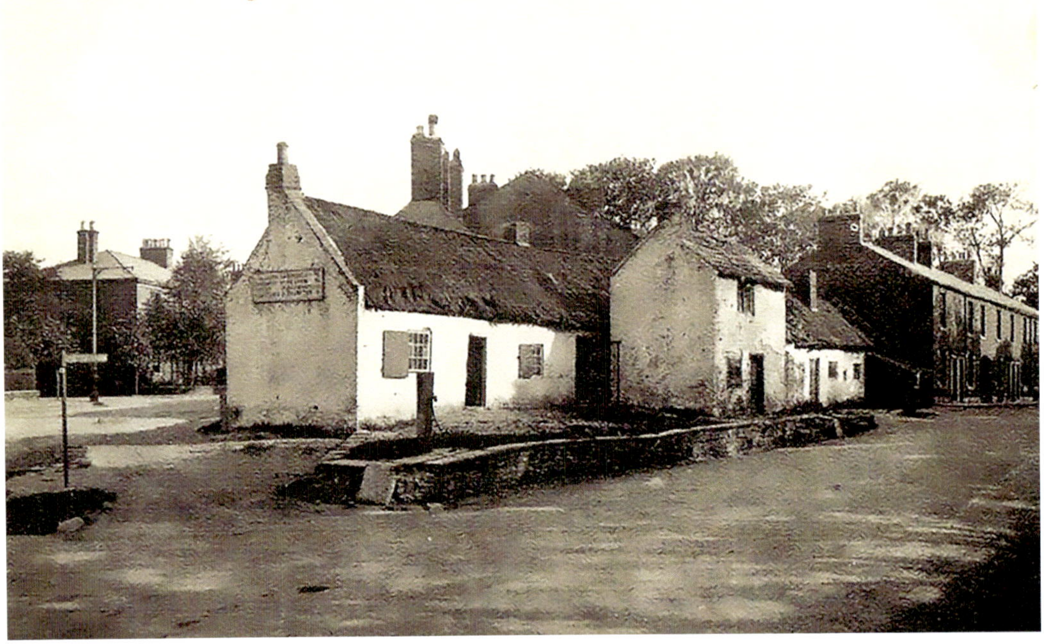

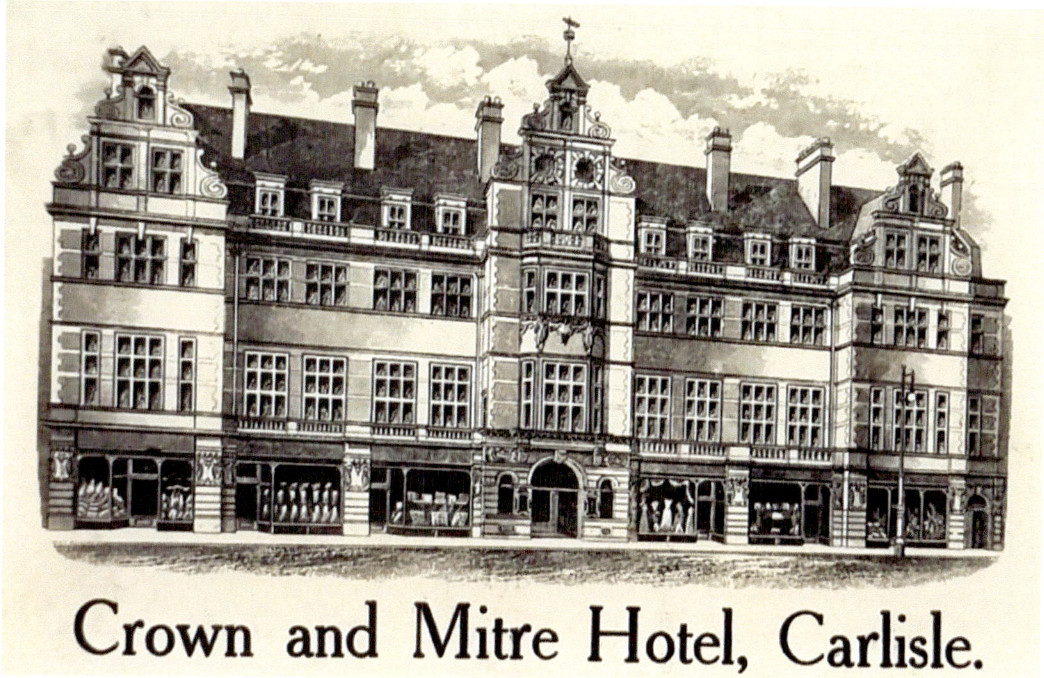

Crown and Mitre Hotel

Located at 54 Castle Street, the Crown and Mitre Hotel was built between 1903 and 1905 for Walter Scott, by George Dale Oliver of Carlisle. It was on the site of the original Crown and Mitre coffee house.

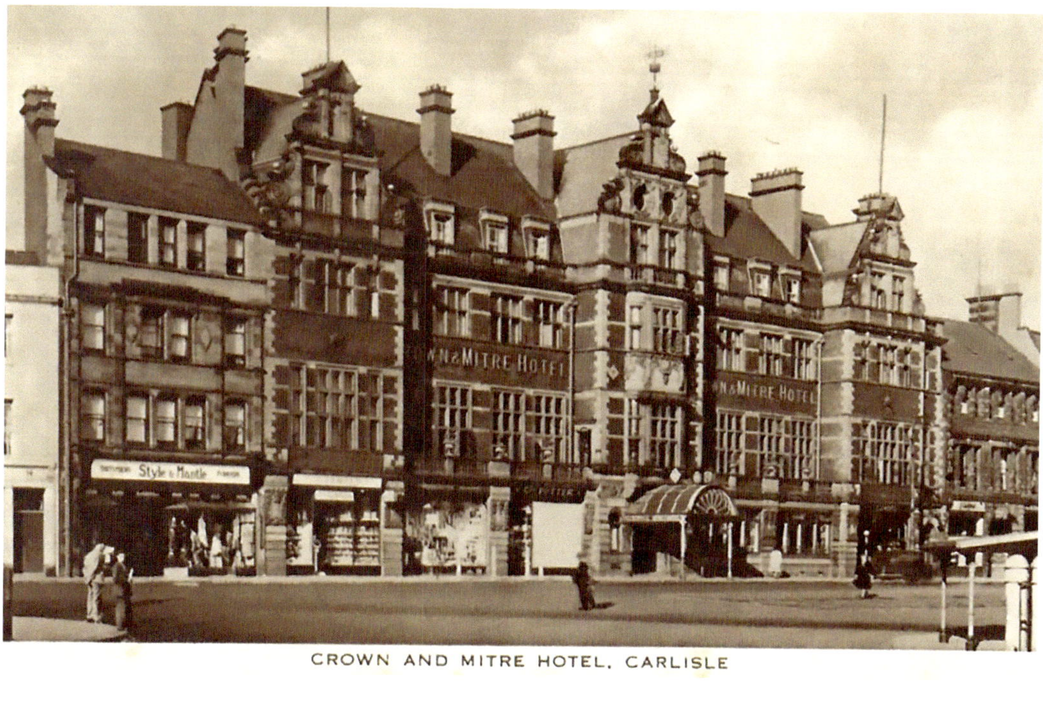

CROWN AND MITRE HOTEL, CARLISLE

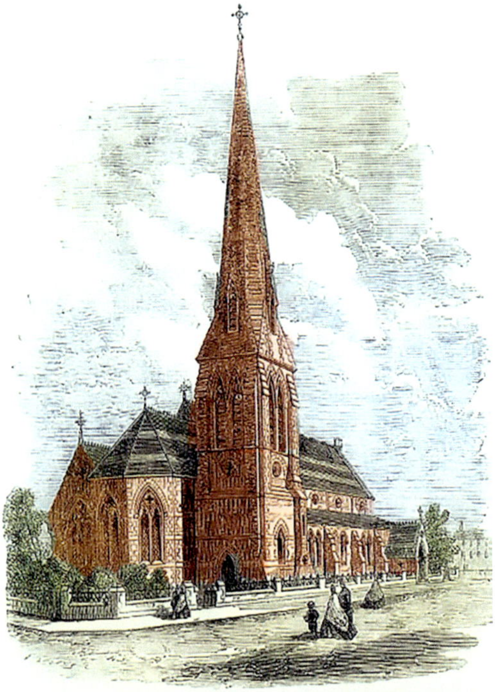

CHURCH OF ST. STEPHEN, CARLISLE.

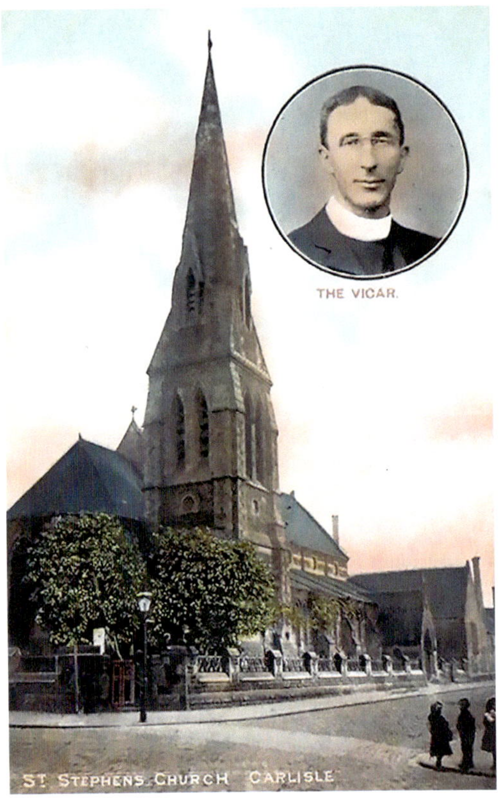

St Stephen's Church

St Stephen's Church was located between Hewson Street and St Stephen's Street and fronted onto James Street. The church was funded by Miss Angela Burdett-Coutts, a Victorian philanthropist, the daughter of Sir Francis Burdett, 5th Baronet and Sophia, formerly Coutts, daughter of banker Thomas Coutts. In 1837 she became one of the wealthiest women in England when she inherited her grandfather's fortune. The foundation stone was laid on 2 March 1864, and the church was consecrated on 31 May 1965.

The church was impressive with its red sandstone and stone dressing and was built in the geometric Gothic style with a curved chancel, a nave of four bays, aisles and a tower with a spire. The spire contained eight bells.

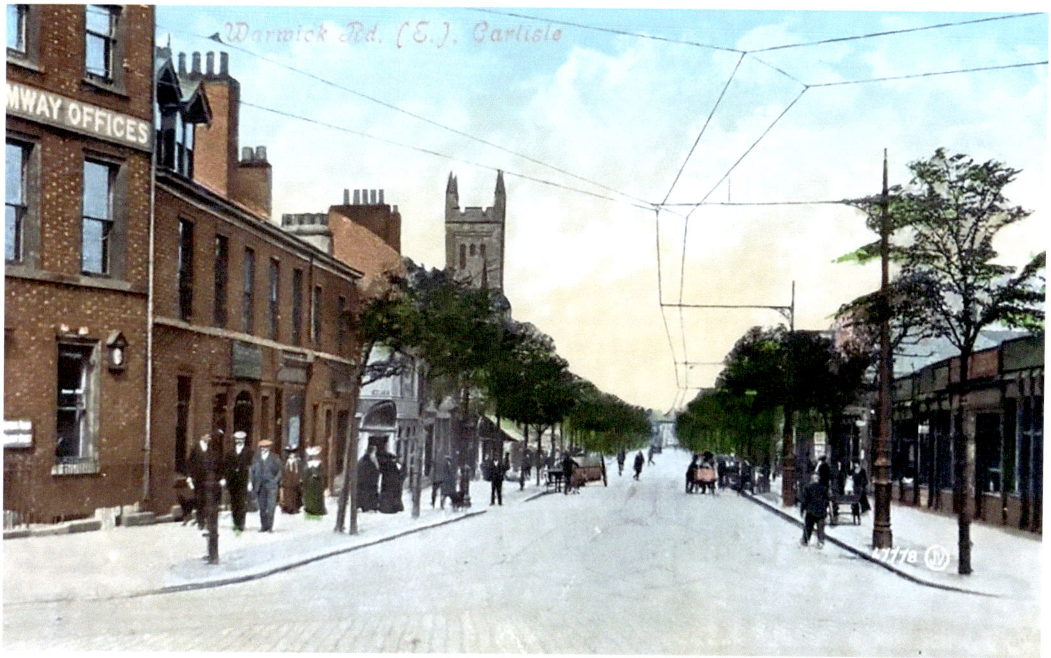

Warwick Road

The images are looking west from the junction of Lowther Street and The Crescent. Tramlines can be seen in the road and the Tramway Offices are on the corner of Lowther Street and Warwick Road. The tower of the English Presbyterian Church, built in 1862–63, can be seen on the junction with Earl Street. This section of Warwick Road was formerly Henry Street.

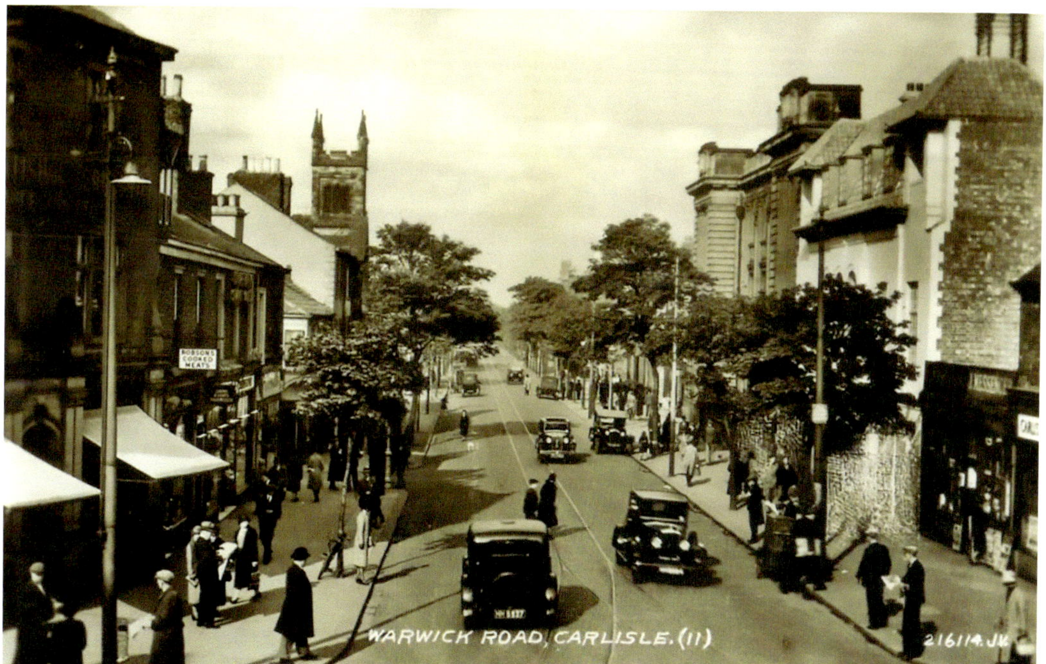

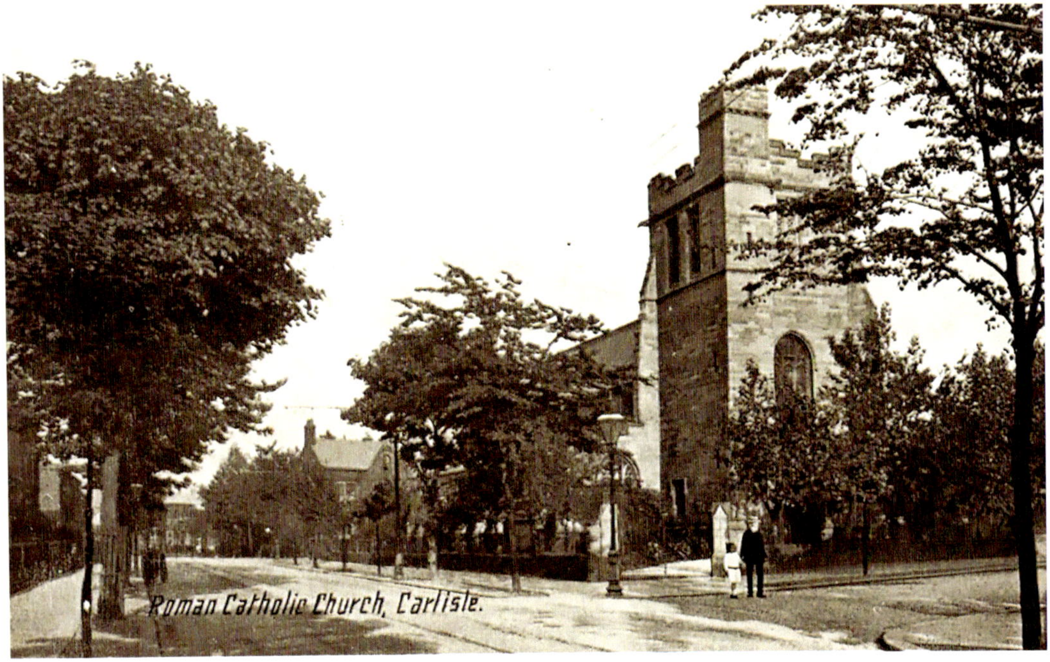

Warwick Road – Our Lady and St Joseph's Church

This church was built in 1891–93 and is situated on the junction of Warwick Road and Warwick Square. The image above is looking east along Warwick Road with Warwick Square on the right. The image below is looking north-westerly from Warwick Square. The foundation stone was laid on 18 May 1891 and the church was opened in 1893. It was designed by Archibald Matthias Dunn, his son Archibald Manuel Dunn and Edward Joseph Hansom.

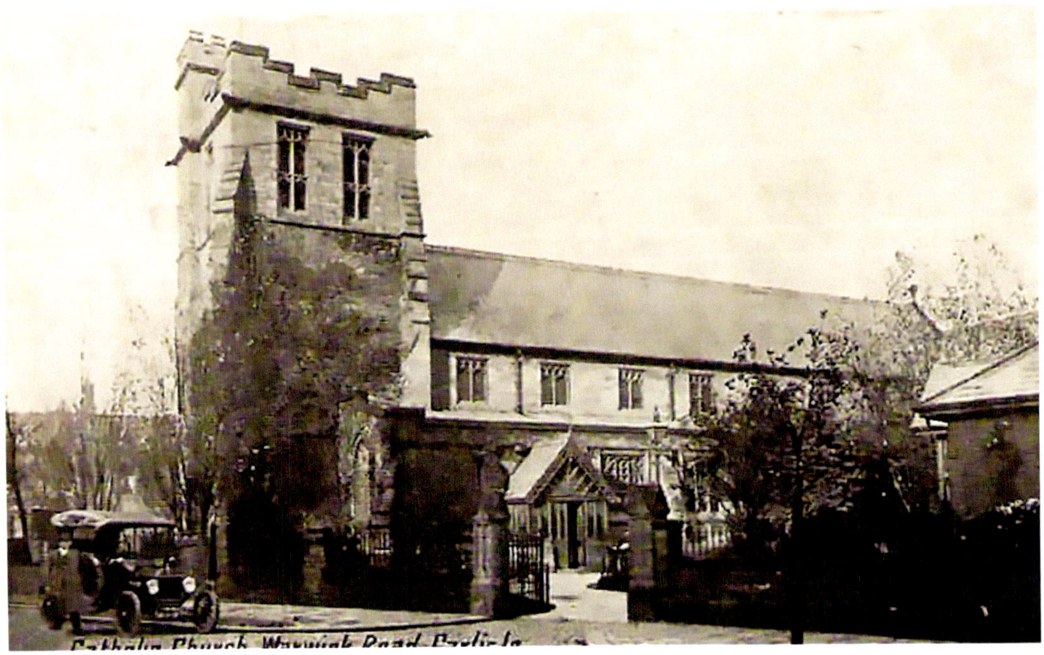

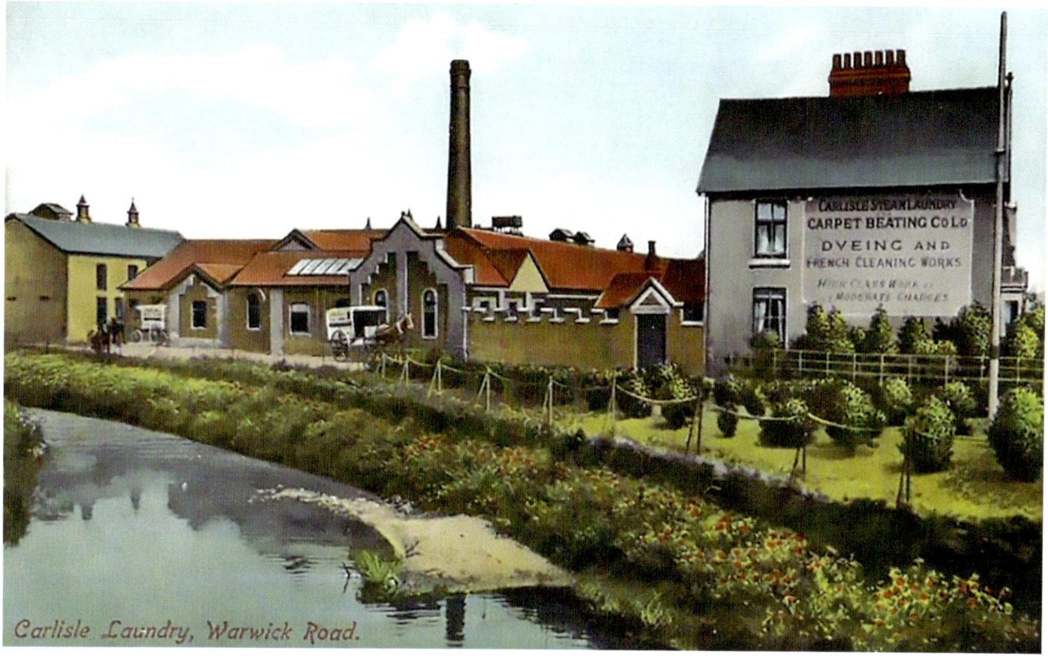

Carlisle Laundry, Warwick Road.

Warwick Road – Steam Laundry

The steam laundry was located north of Botcherby Bridge on Warwick Road by the River Petteril. It was constructed in 1892. The advertisement on the side of the building says 'Steam Laundry and Carpet Beating Co. Ltd. Dyeing and French Cleaning Works. High class work at moderate charges'.

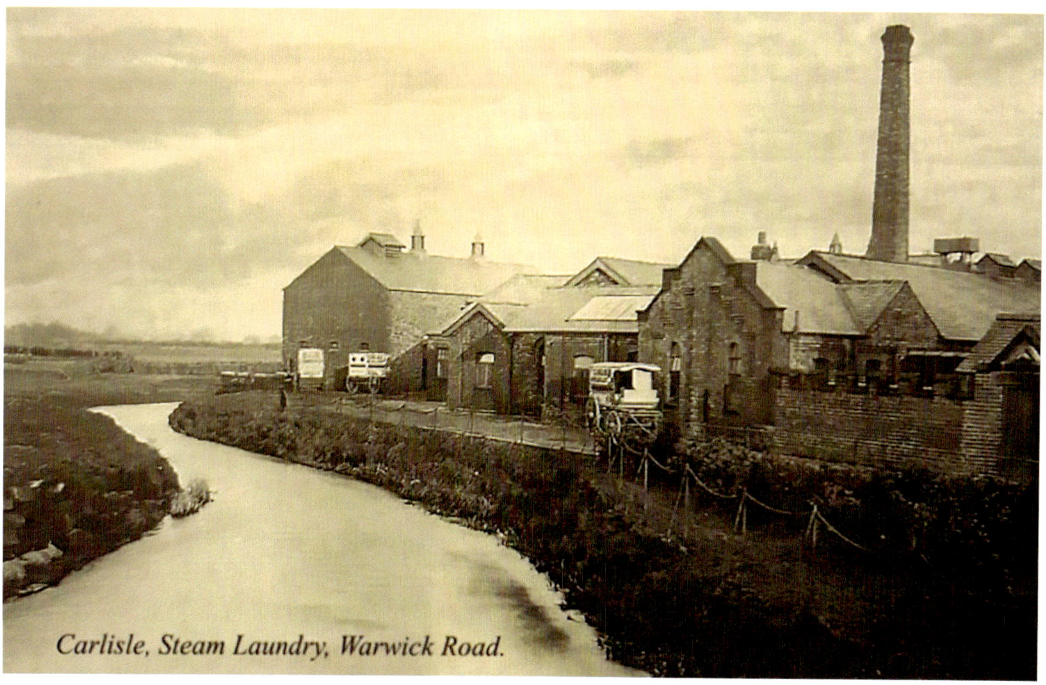
Carlisle, Steam Laundry, Warwick Road.

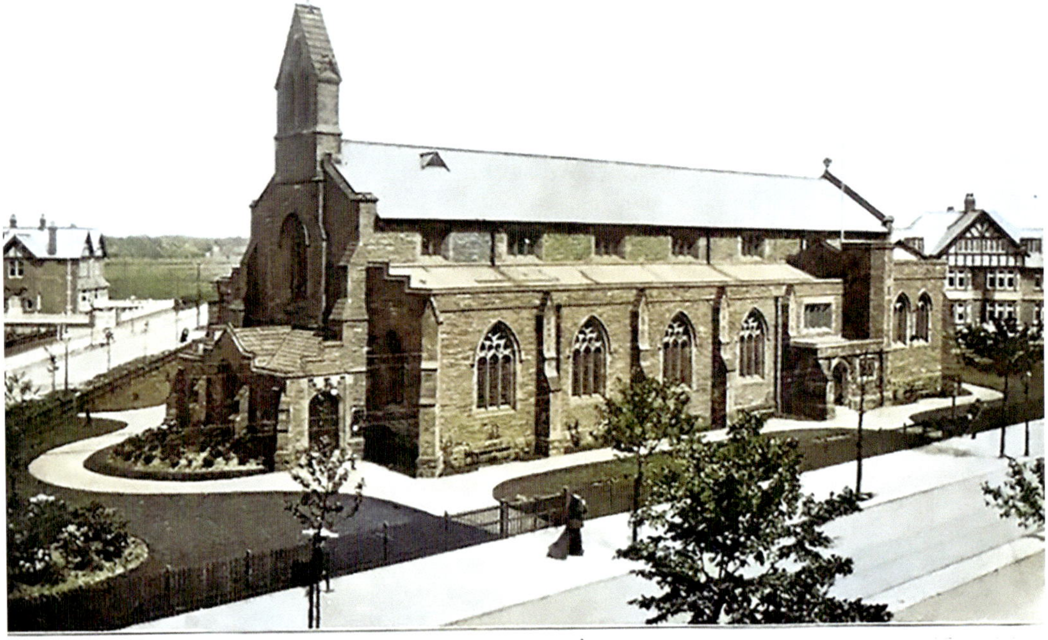

Warwick Road – St Aidan's Church

This image is looking easterly along Warwick Road with St Aidan's Road to the left. This Church of England church is a late example of a Gothic Revival church building. This large church and its attached hall were built at the same time and was designed by C. J. Ferguson. The foundation stone was laid on 8 September 1899, and the building was completed in 1902.

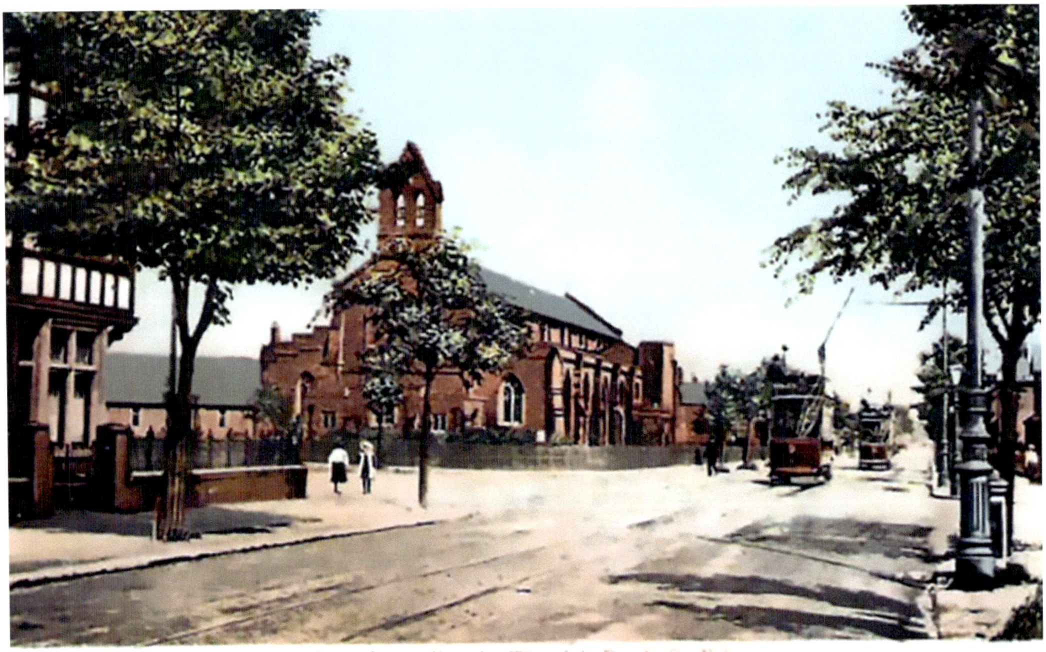

St. Aidan's Church, Warwick Road, Carlisle

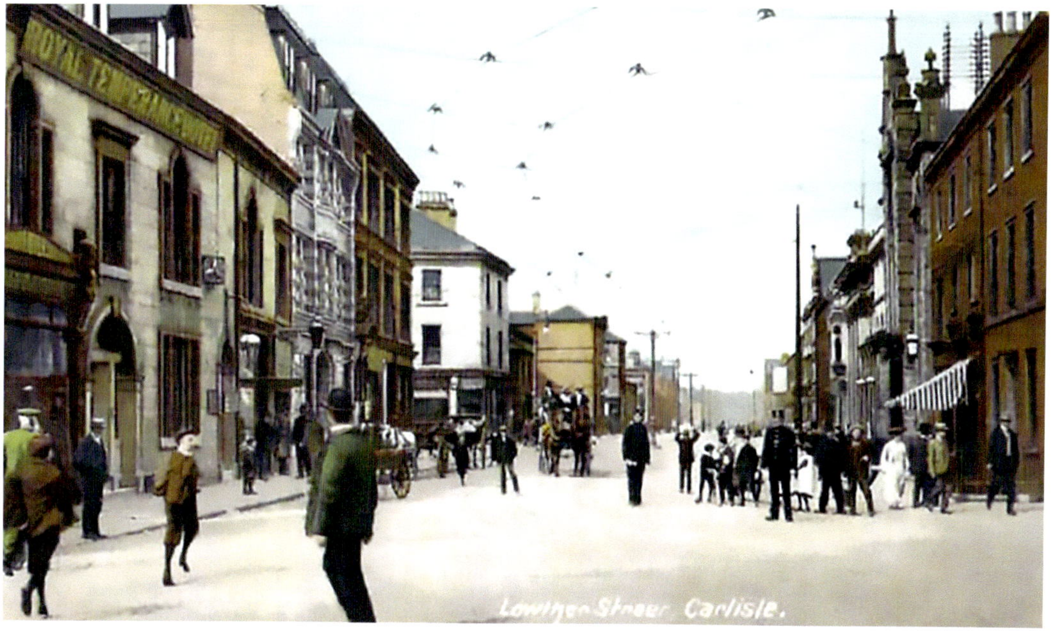

Lowther Street

The street runs in a northerly direction from the junction of Henry Street and The Crescent towards Hardwicke Circus and is approximately 620 yards long. These images are looking north from near the junction with Henry Street. The Royal Temperance Hotel is on the left and the Lowther Arcade, built in 1904, is just beyond it. Devonshire Street is on the left by the white building and opposite that is the General Post Office which was opened in 1863 and extended in 1874. The Congregational Church, completed in 1843, is on the right with the tall facade.

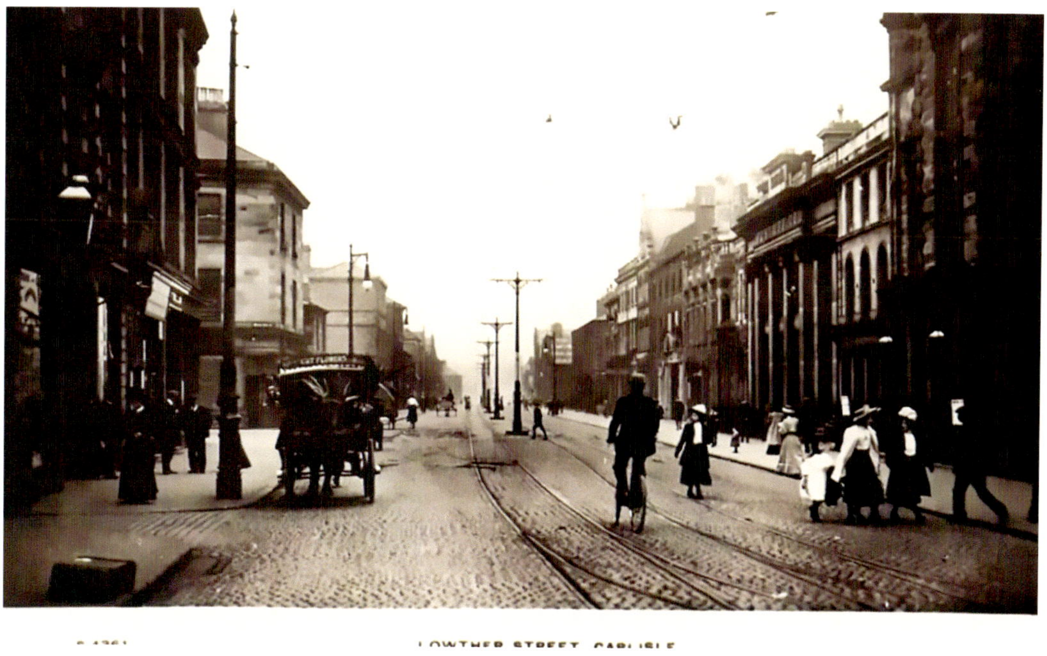

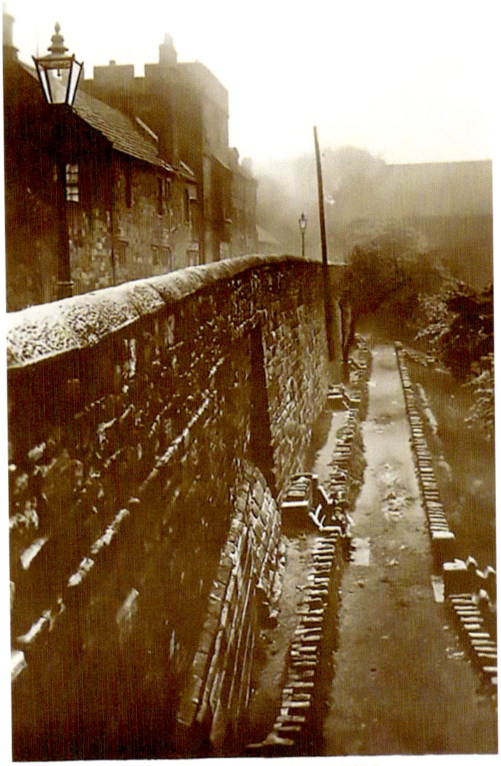

S.10483. THE OLD WEST WALLS, CARLISLE

The West Walls

A part of the medieval city walls can be seen in these two images which are looking along the West Walls with the deanery to the cathedral on the left. The sally port and the sally port steps are at the far end of the section of wall shown and were added in 1813 to provide easy access from the base of the walls area above. A sally port is a small secure entrance or exit in a fortified wall which can be easily defended or used to exit and attack the enemy. At the time of these images the entrance is blocked up.

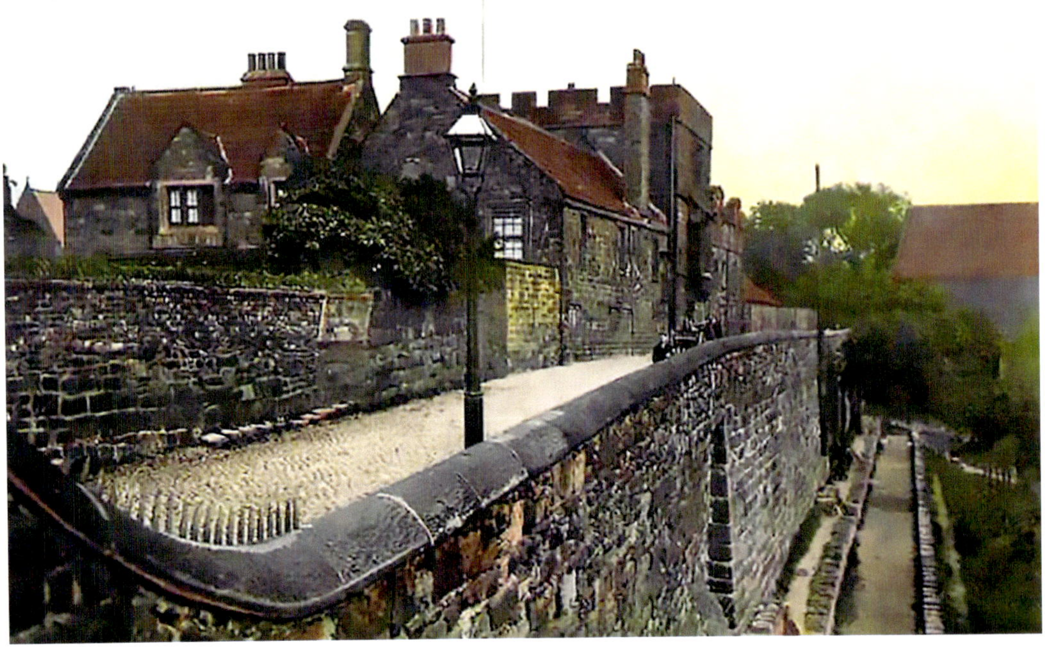

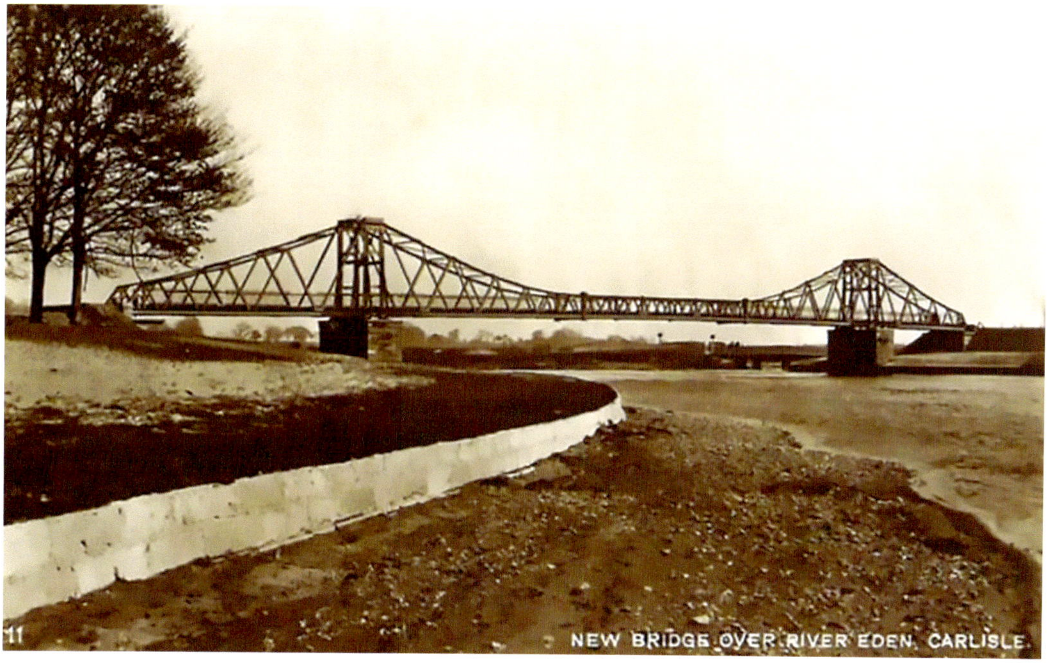

Rickerby Park Bridge

The Rickerby Park suspension footbridge over the River Eden was constructed in 1922 by Redpath Brown & Co., Construction Engineers and was financed by the Carlisle Citizens League in memory of those who died in the Great War between 1914 and 1918. The bridge was opened on 25 May 1922 by the Earl of Lonsdale. Note in the image below the children using it for bathing. Images are looking north-westerly from the river.

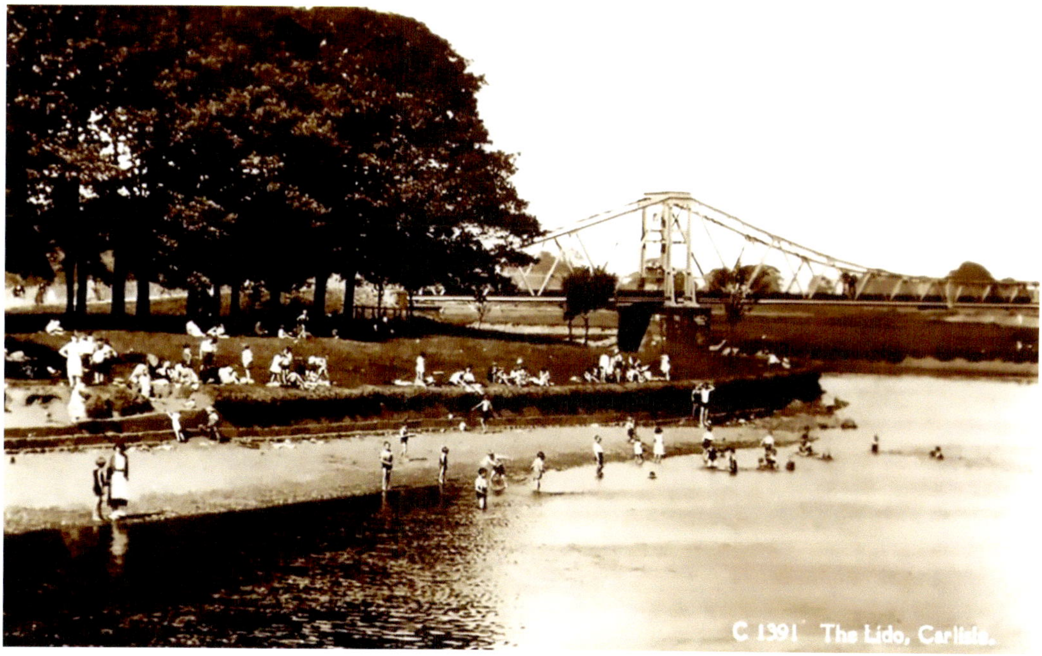

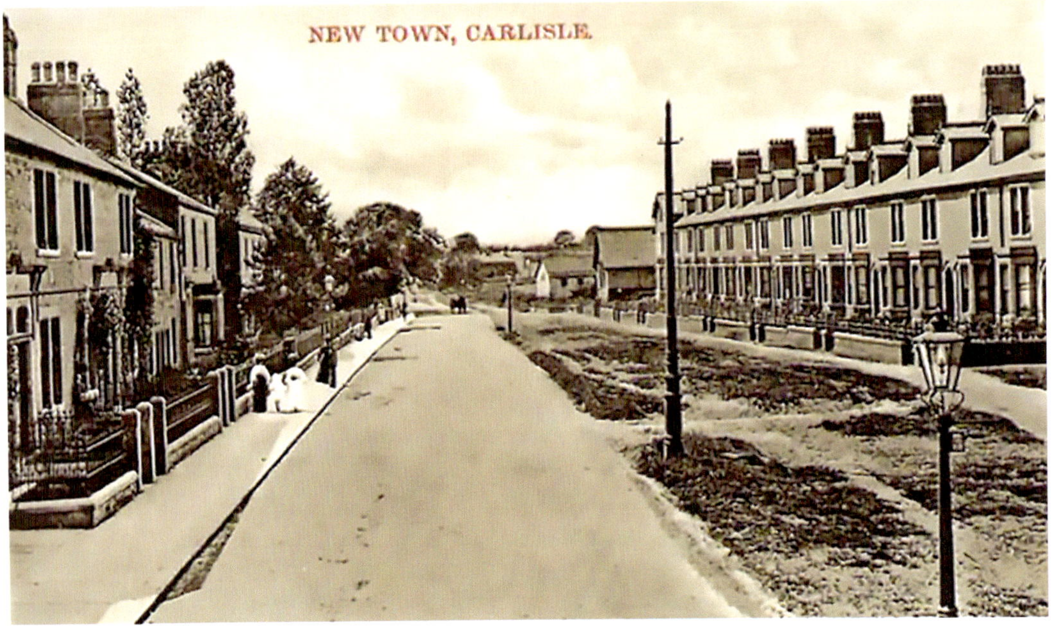

New Town

Two different views of Newtown Road. The image above is looking westerly from just up from Shadygrove Road. On the right at the end of the row of houses is St Barnabas Church Mission Hall, built in 1898, and just beyond that is the old Smithy. In the far distance on the right is St Mary's Home for Fallen Women. The image below is looking westerly from just below Bower Street which is on the left. Lawson Street is further up on the right. In the centre distance can be seen the gable end of the Green Dragon Inn.

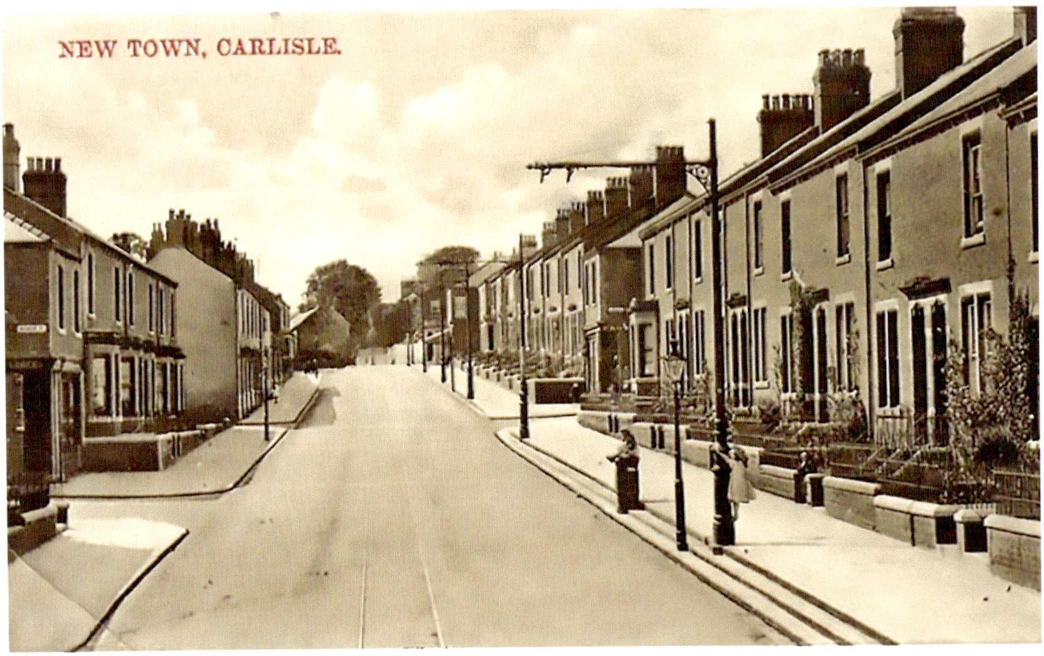

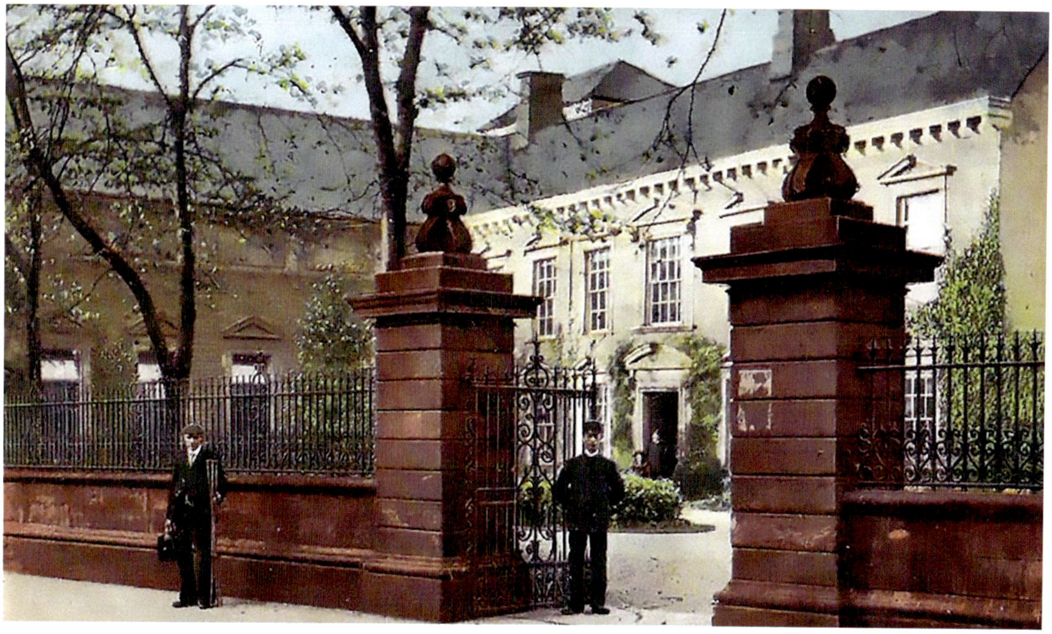

Tullie House Museum

Images looking north from Abbey Street. Tullie House is a Jacobean mansion house which can be traced back to the sixteenth century. The Tullie family occupied the building until the nineteenth century. A museum was opened in the house by the Carlisle Corporation in 1893, after extensions had been added to the original house. At first the building contained the museum and also a library, an art school and a technical school. The two schools were moved in the 1950s and the library later.

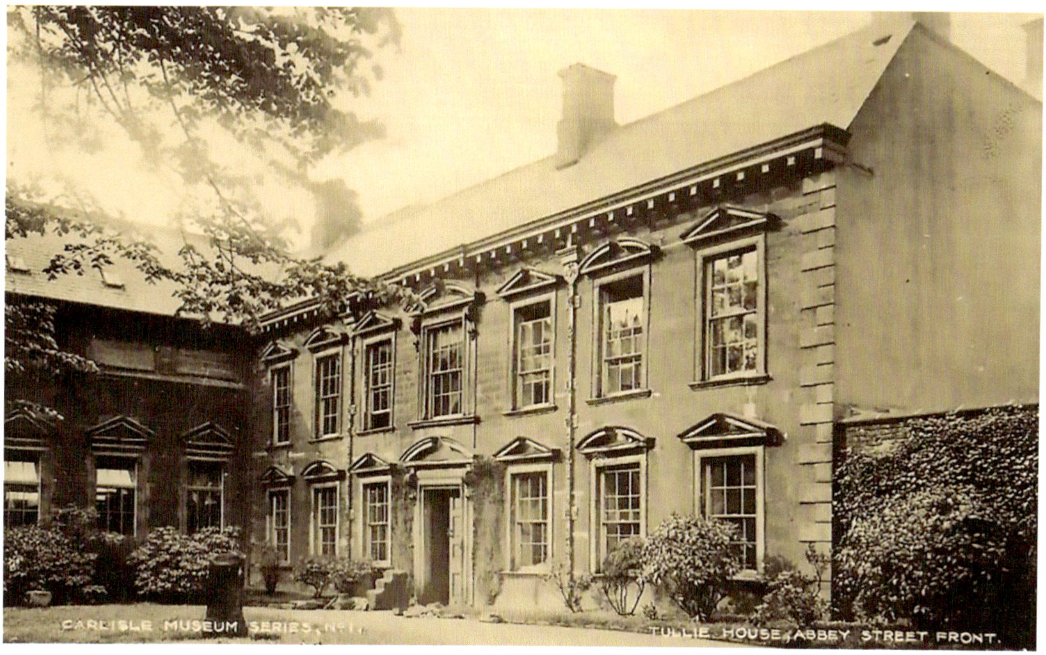

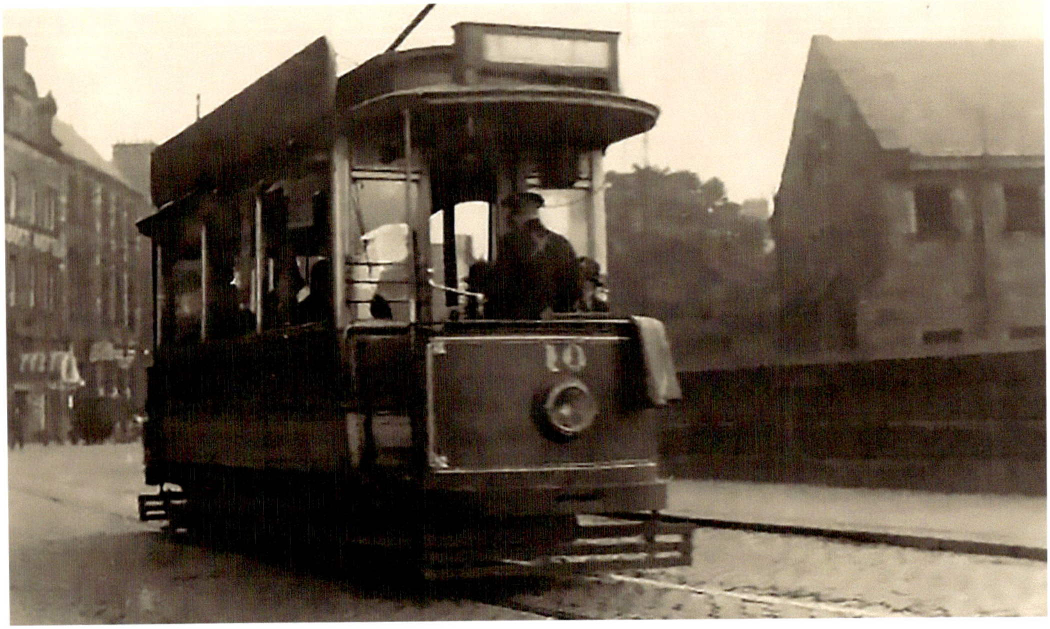

Trams

The tramway system comprised six lines radiating from Carlisle railway station to Newtown, Stanwix, along Warwick Road to Petteril Bridge, London Road, Boundary Road and Denton Holme. The tramway operated by the City of Carlisle Electric Tramways Co. Ltd opened for public service on 30 June 1900 and closed on 21 November 1931. The above image shows tram No. 10 making its way over the viaduct to Denton Holme. The image below shows tram No. 4 en route to Newtown with Castle Street on the left and Green Market on the right where the shops of Sawyer the Chemists and J. Huthart & Co., General Drapers can be seen.

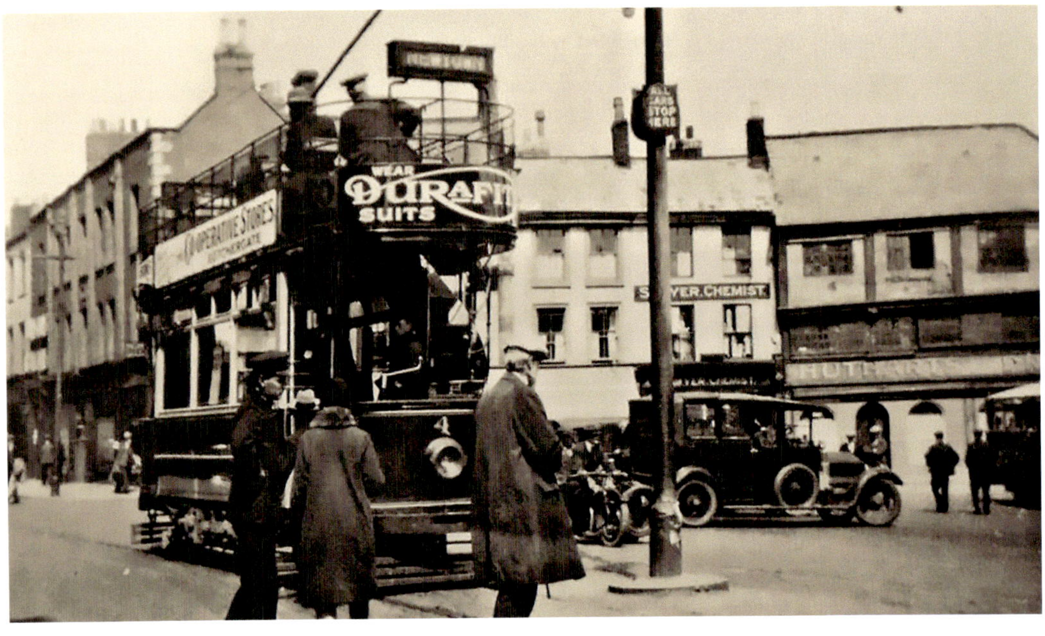

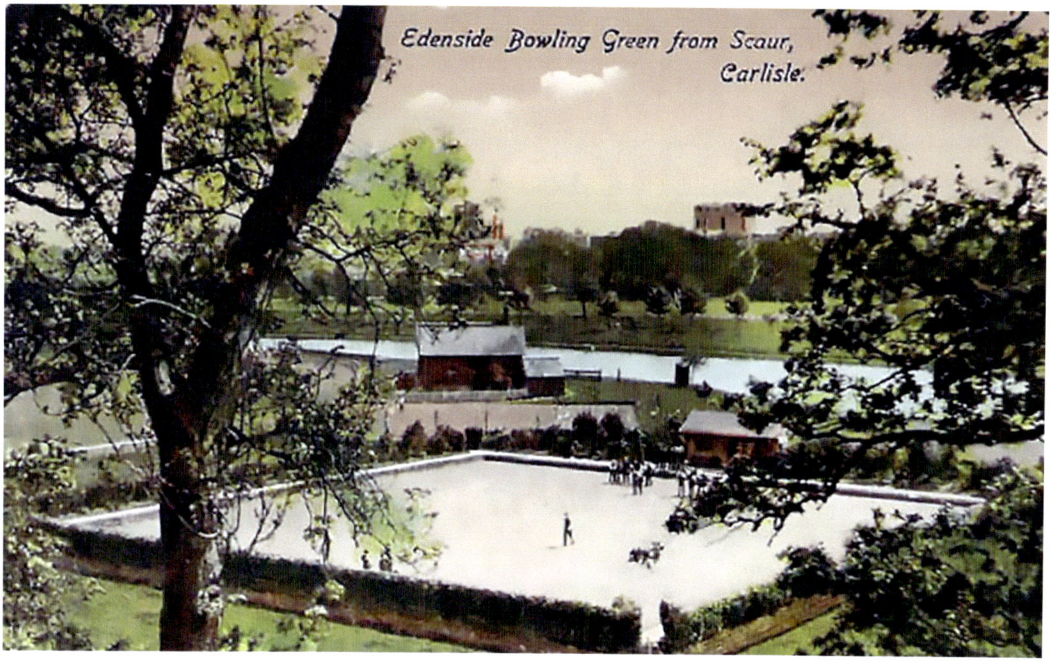

Edenside Bowling Green and Cricket Ground

The above image shows the Edenside Bowling Club from the Scaur with the cricket ground to the left. The pavilions for both facilities are shown. The bowling club was formed around 1899. The bottom image shows the cricket ground and its pavilion with the bowling green partially shown on the right. Both images show the tower of the castle and the cathedral in the background across the River Eden.

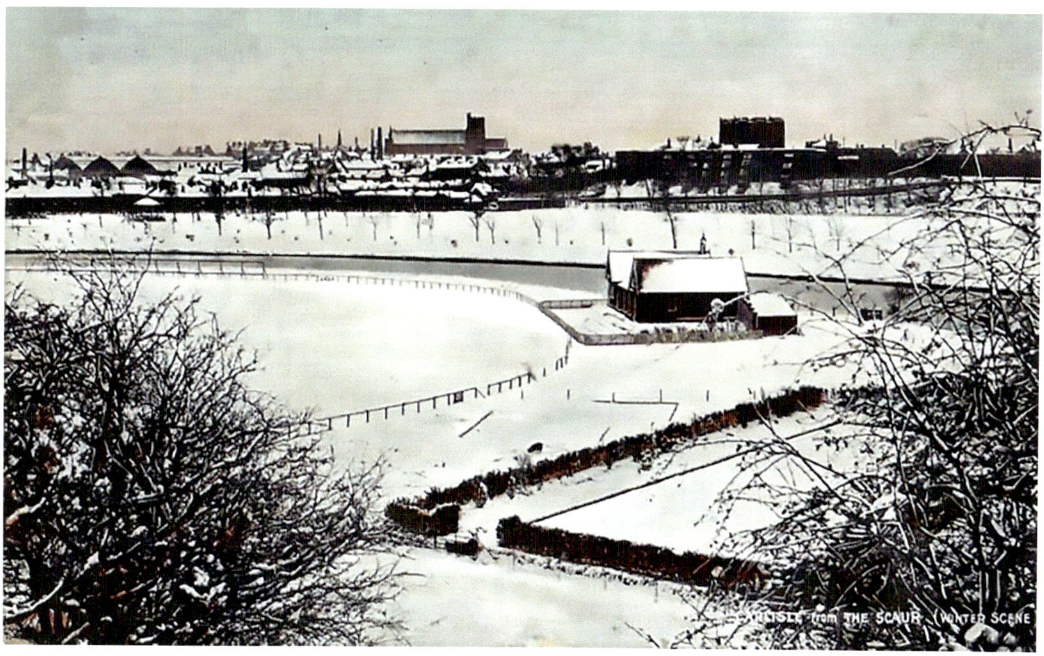

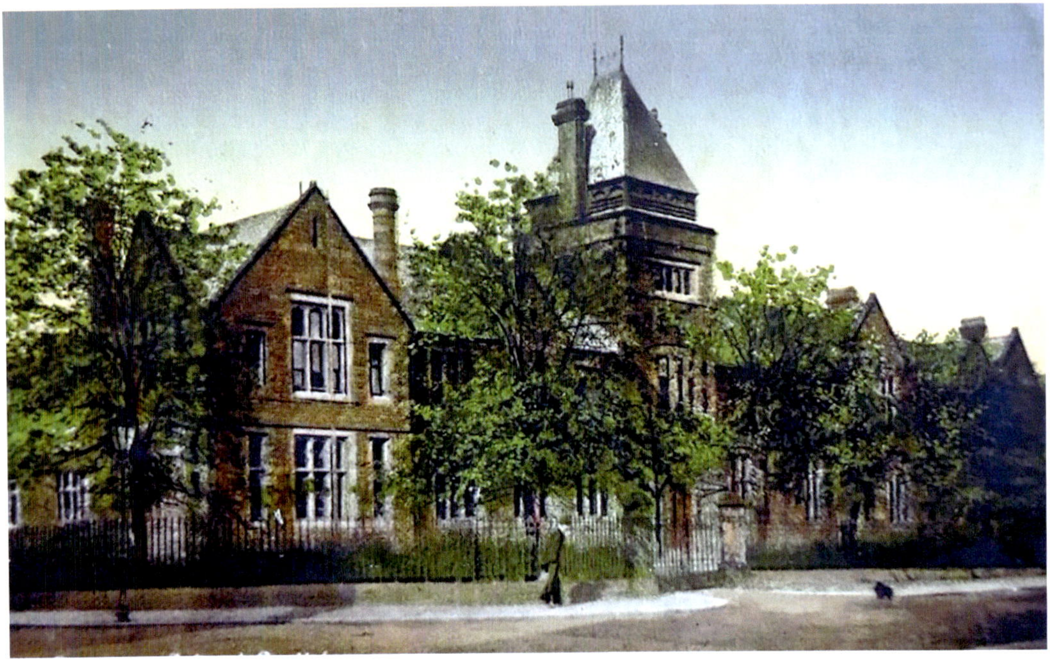

Grammar School

In 1545 The Dean and Chapter of Carlisle Cathedral took on responsibility for the school in the Cathedral Close. The school occupied buildings on the West Walls. In 1883 this school became Carlisle Grammar School and moved to Strand Road. It later became the Trinity School. Strand Road is to the right and Spring Gardens Lane to the left.

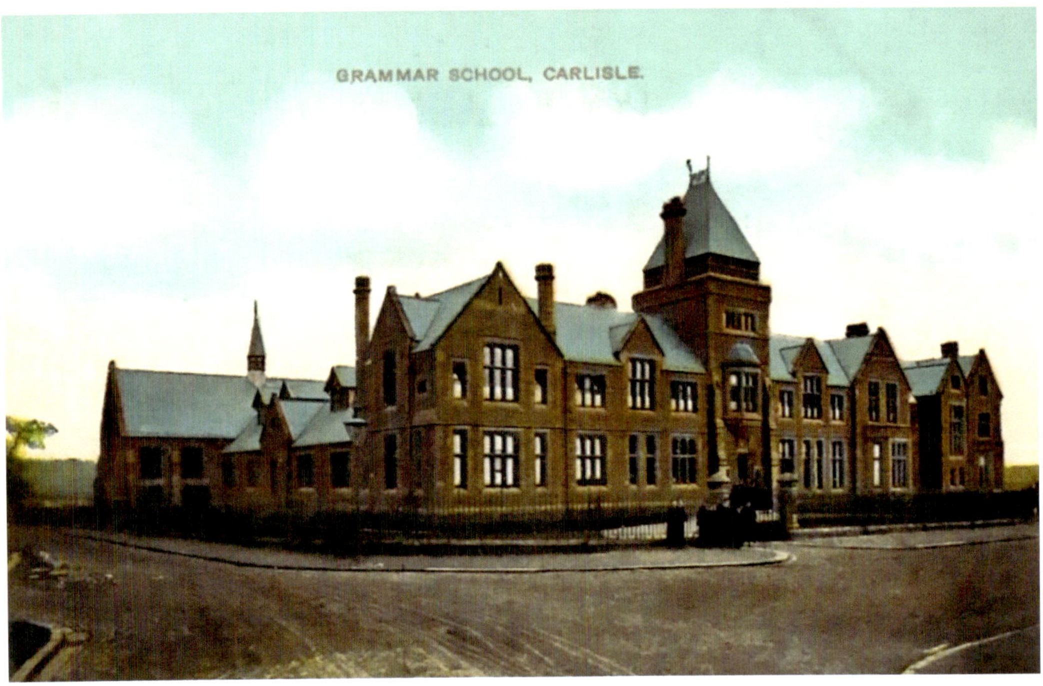

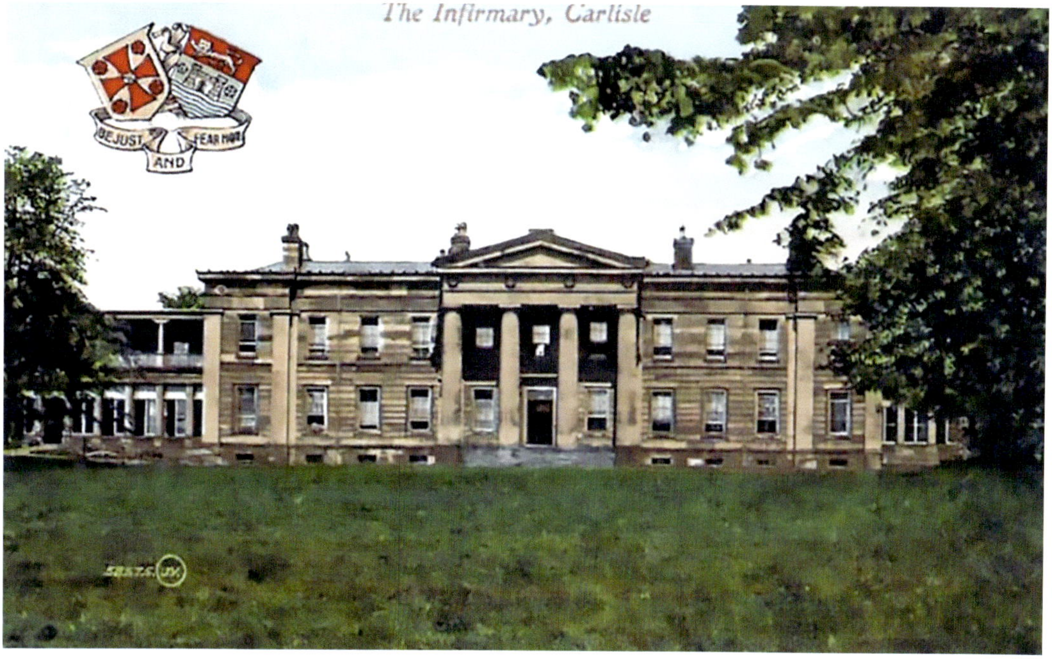

Infirmary

Located in Newtown Road, the infirmary was designed by Richard Tattersall and constructed by Messrs Robinson and Bennet, contractors of Preston, between 1830 and 1832. It was funded by wealthy benefactors and made available for charity patients. A new wing was opened by the Countess of Lonsdale in October 1911.

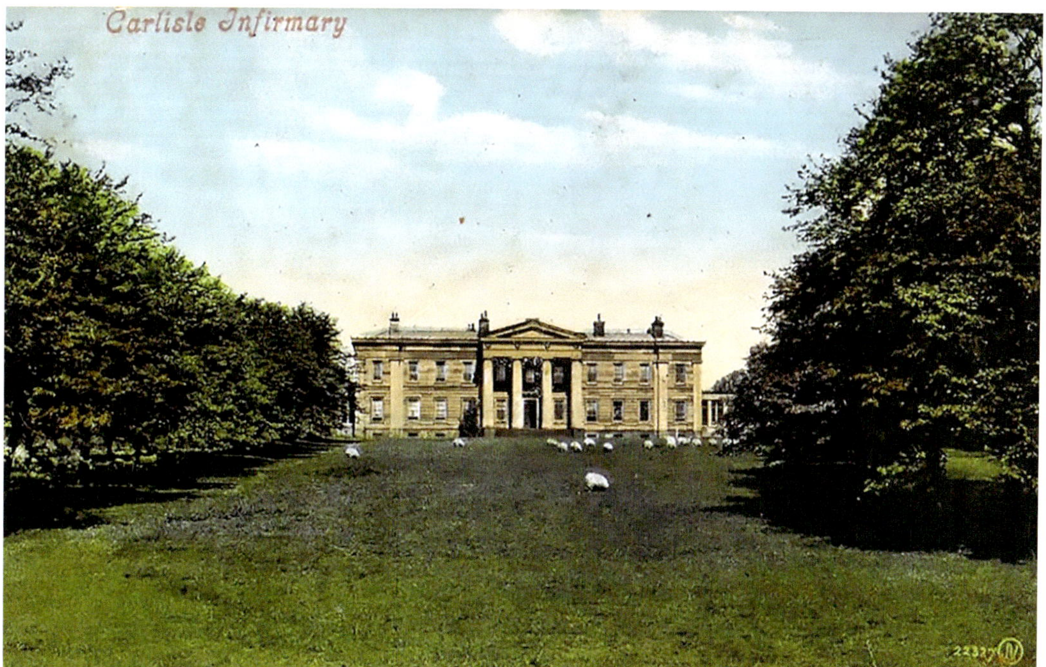

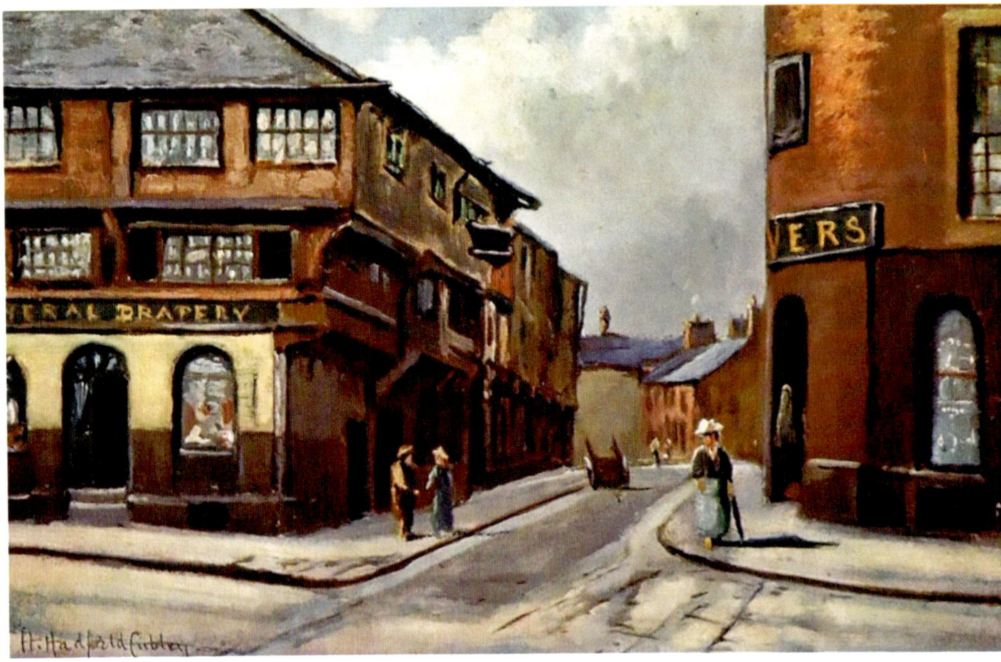

THE GUILDHALL, CARLISLE.

The Old Guildhall

The Old Guildhall was located on the corner of Fisher Street and Greenmarket. It was built by Richard de Redness, probably between 1396 and 1407 – it is thought that it was built after a fire in 1391 that destroyed many buildings in Carlisle. On the above image J. Huthart & Co., General Drapers occupy the Old Guildhall and Sawyers the Chemists is on the right on the corner of Fisher Street. The image below is a representation of how it might have looked in the time of Bonnie Prince Charlie around the mid-eighteenth century.

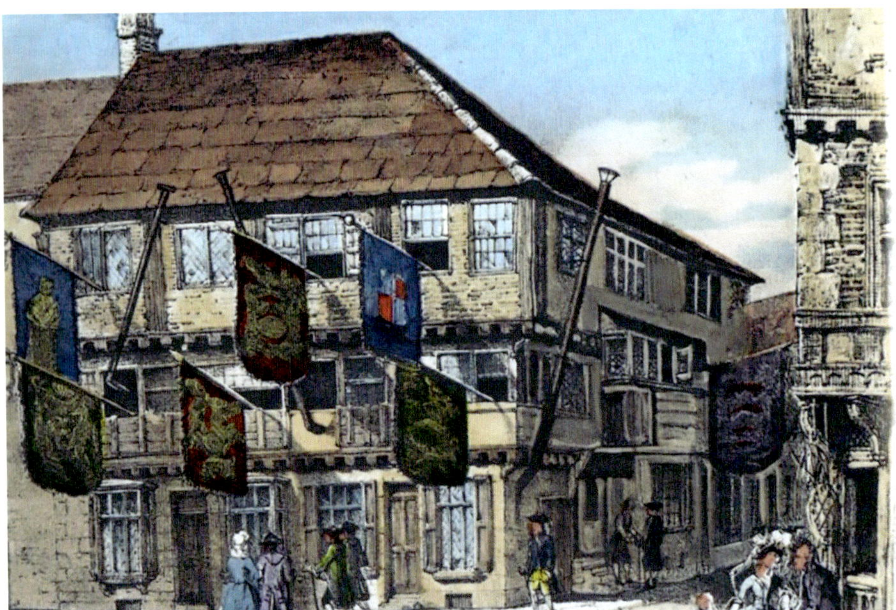

Old Guild Hall, Carlisle, in the times of Prince Charlie.

N. & C. Series.

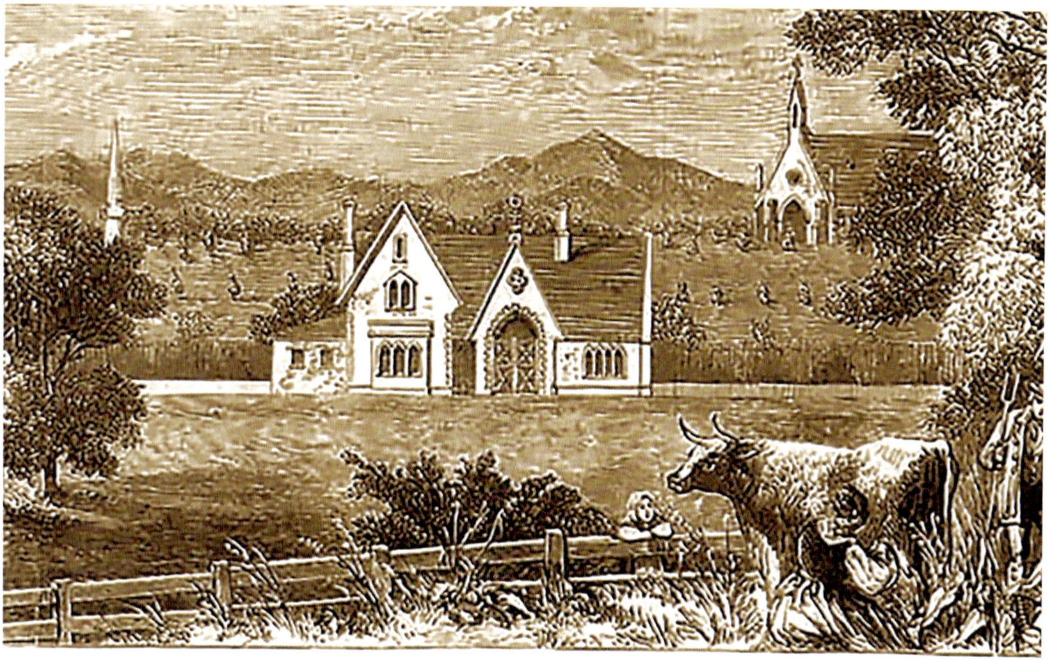

Cemetery

This cemetery was located on Dalston Road with an entrance on Richardson Street, as shown on the images. It was one of three opened to address the overcrowding situation of the cemeteries already in the city. It was originally laid out in 1855 with offices, chapels, and lodges designed by J.W.H. & J.M. Hay of Liverpool. The cemetery covers an area of over 60 acres.

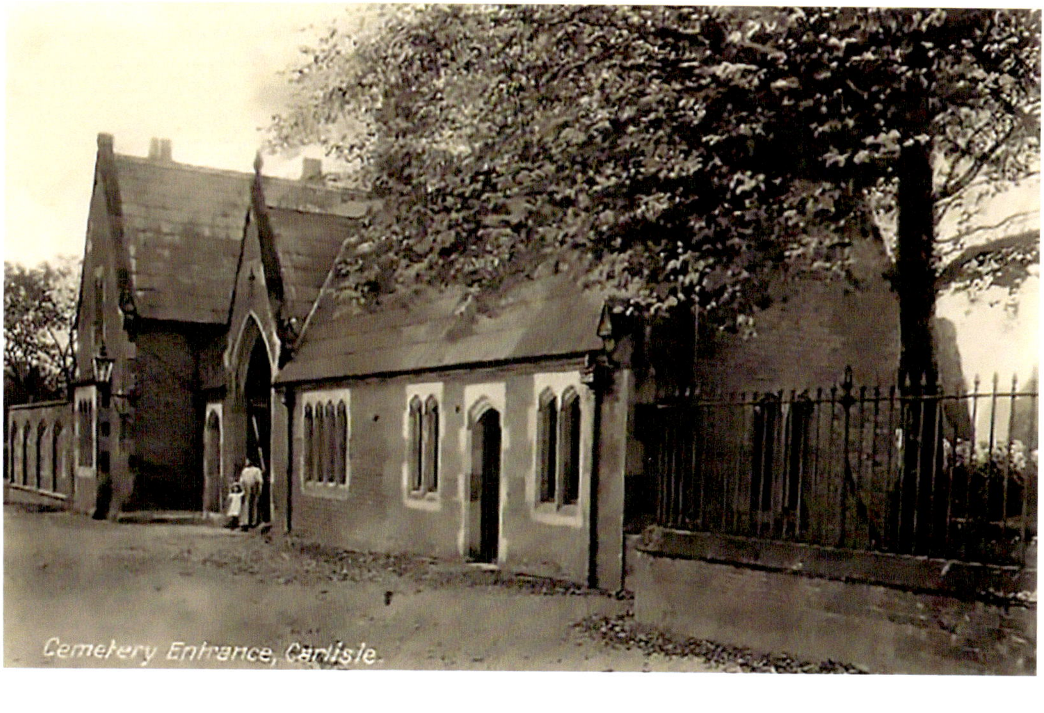

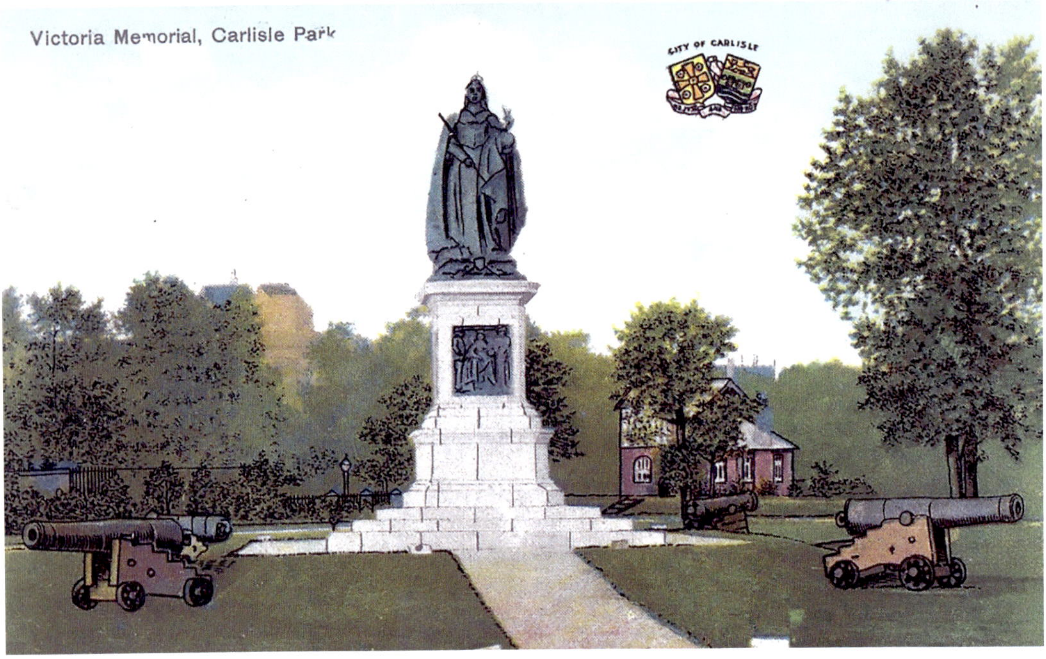

Bitts Park Including Victoria Park – Victoria Memorial

Bitts Park was the very first public park to be established in the county and city. The 'bitts' were thought to be small parcels of land that were once used for grazing livestock. Victoria Park is within the Bitts Park area between the River Eden and the castle. It contains formal gardens, landscaped walks and a bandstand. The two images show the Victoria Memorial located in the Victoria Park section of Bitts Park. The monument was erected in 1902 and was designed by Sir Thomas Brock RA.

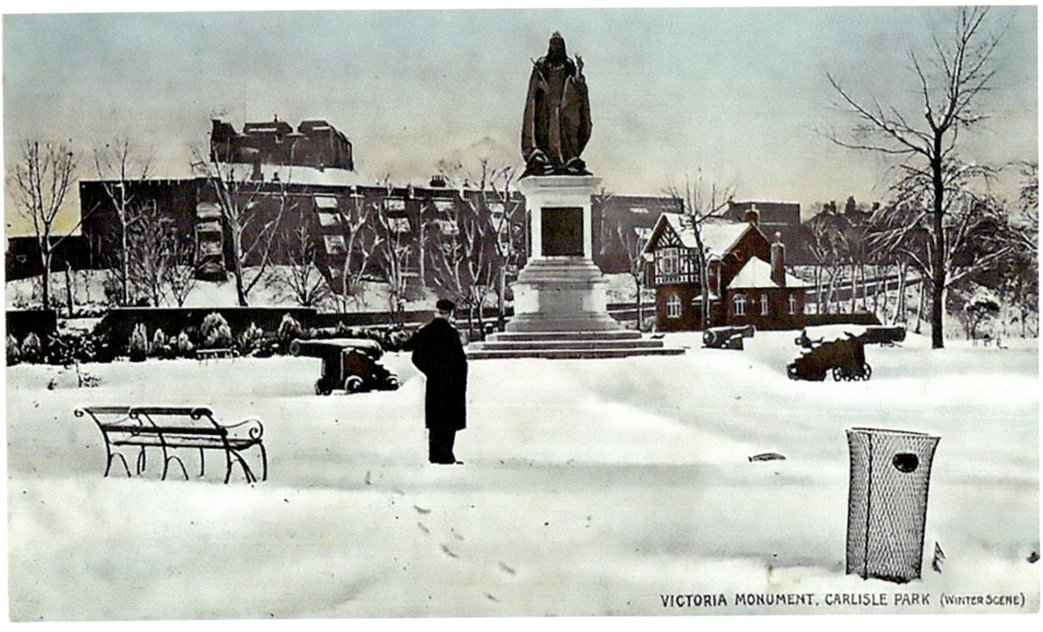

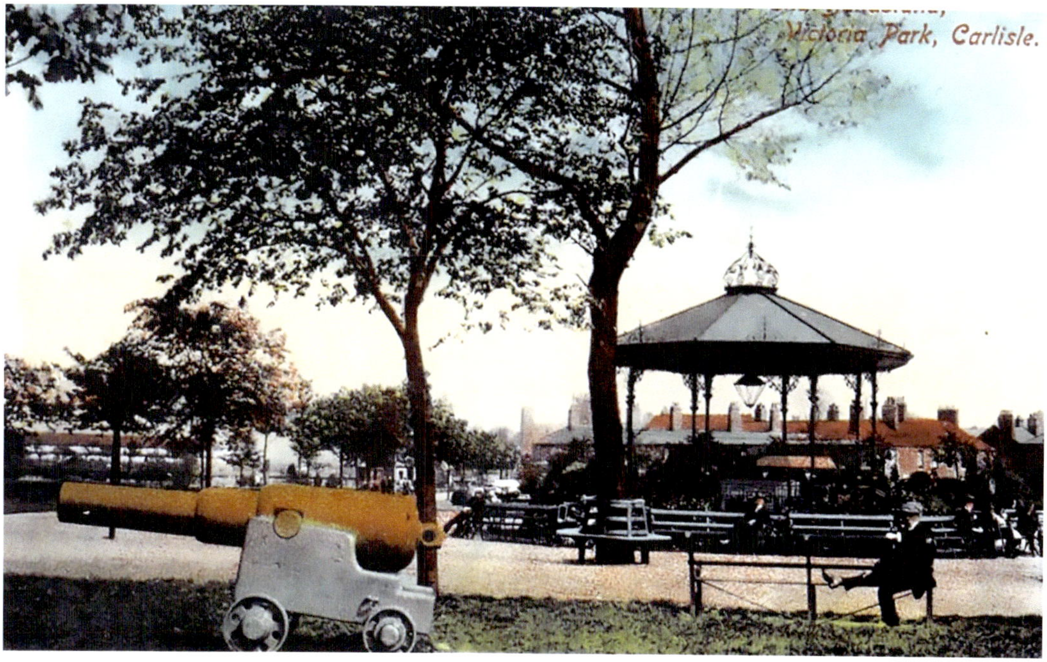

Bitts Park Including Victoria Park – Bandstand

The bandstand was erected in the park in March 1890 and quickly became a popular place for people to congregate and socialise. During the summer evenings and holidays it was used by a range of local bands. From 1920 the bandstand was also home to the open-air school which was attended by children who were thought to be too frail for full-time education. The cannons were used at the Siege of Sebastopol and were brought to this country after the capture of that city by the British in 1855.

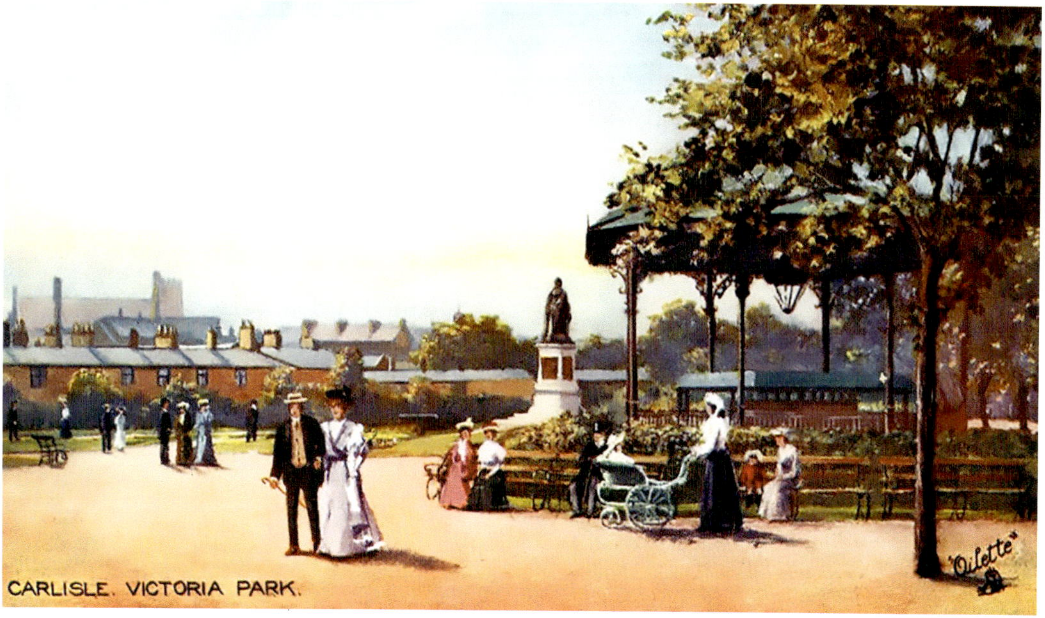

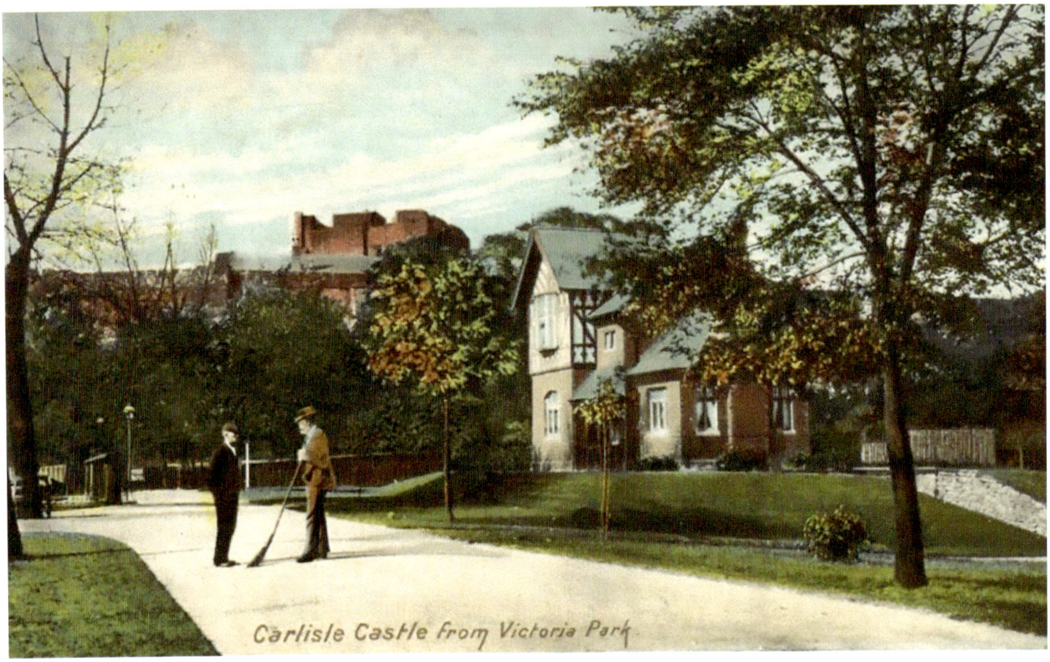

Bitts Park Including Victoria Park – The Lodge

Looking southerly towards Dacre Street on the left and Dacre Road on the right with the castle in the background. The Edwardian Battail Holme Gatekeepers Lodge on the right was built *c.* 1905. Note the park keeper with his 'witches' broom' stopping for a chat.

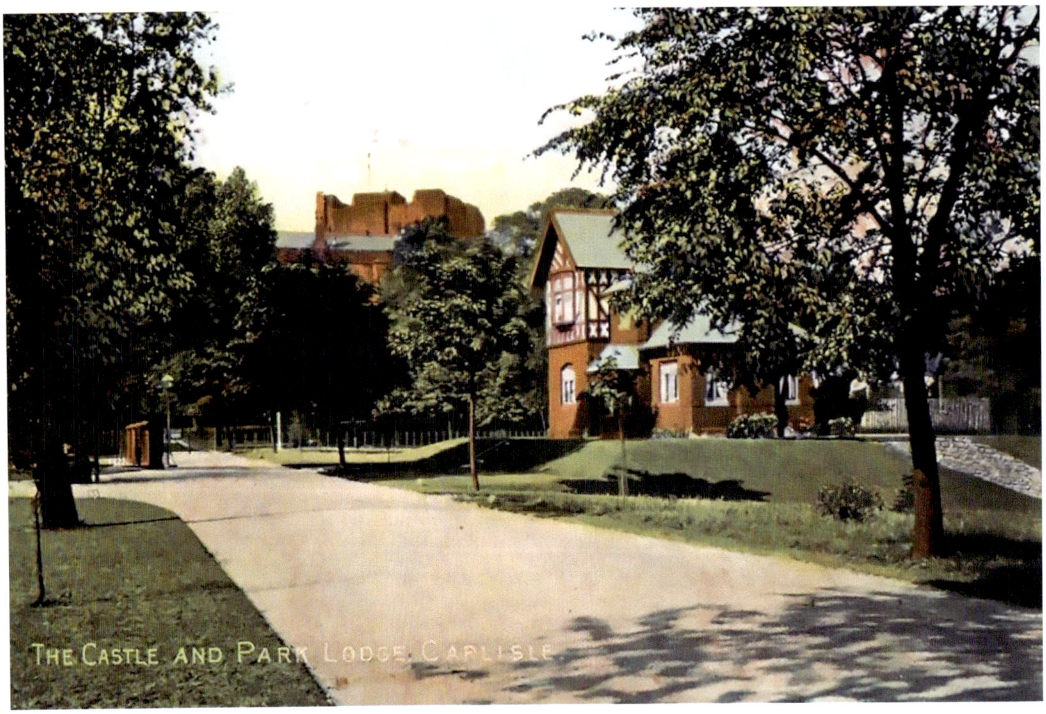

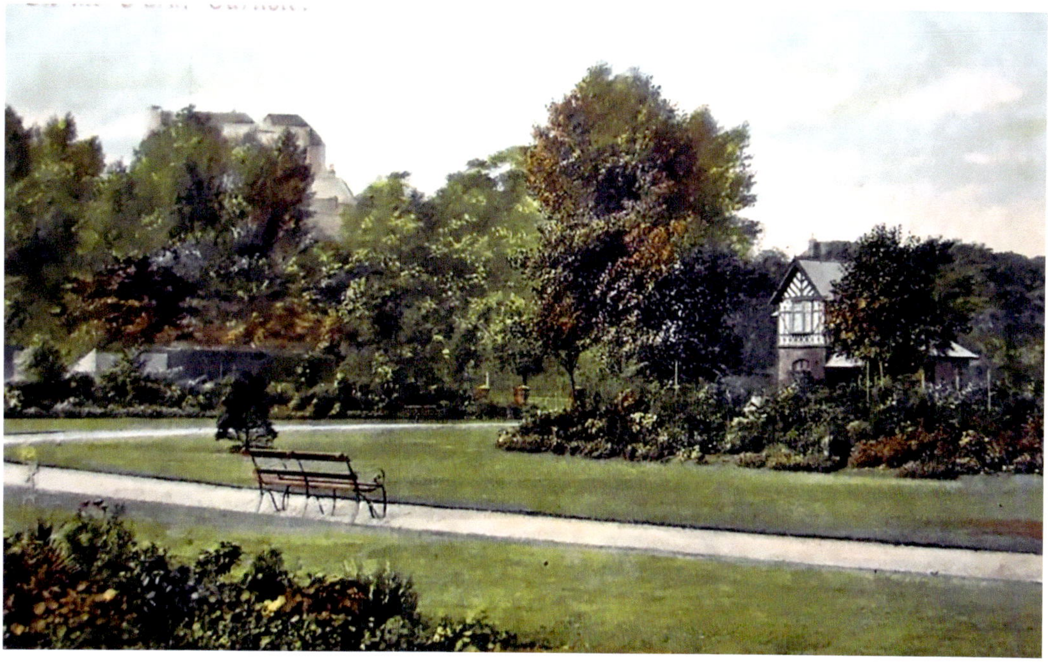

Bitts Park Including Victoria Park – Gardens

Looking across the gardens to the lodge. The above image is looking in a westerly direction and the image below, which also shows the Queen Victoria memorial, is taken further along the path and looking in a south-westerly direction. The walls of the castle can be seen in the background.

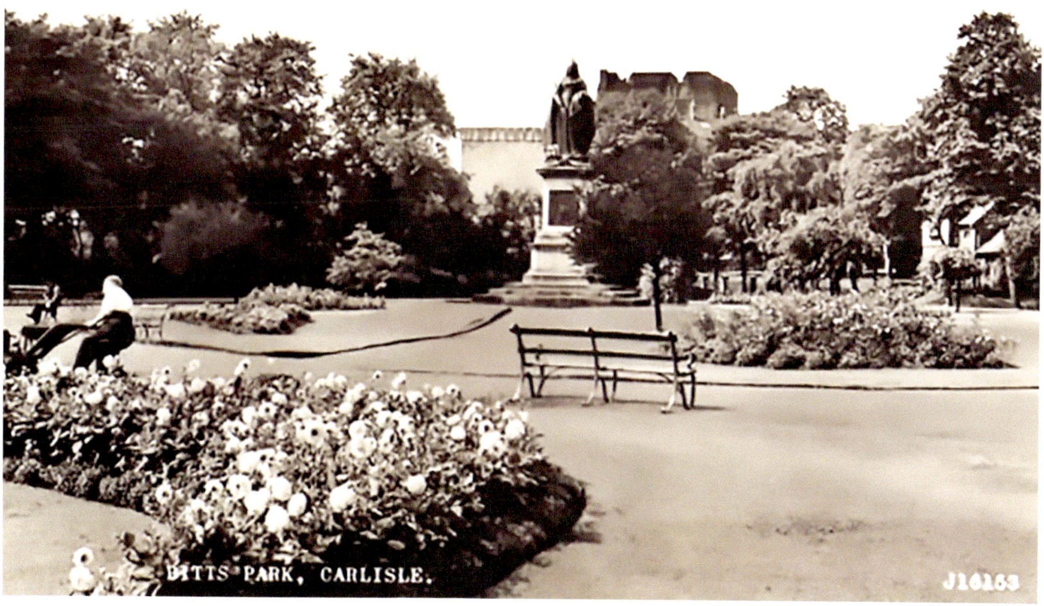

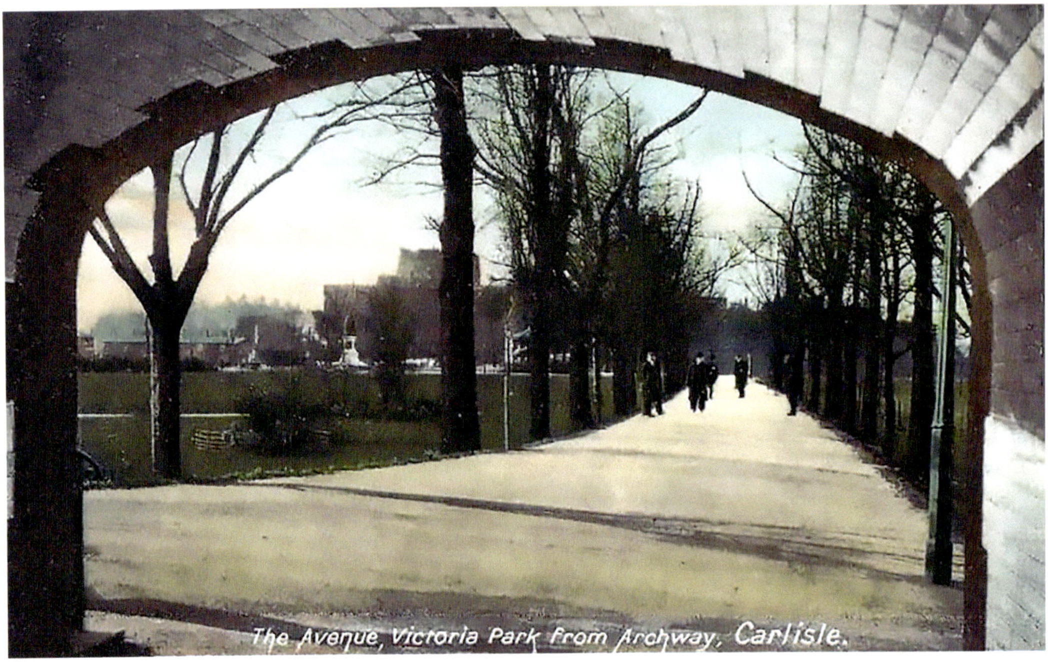

Bitts Park Including Victoria Park – The Avenue

The Avenue runs alongside the River Eden and may follow the course of one of the paths dating back to 1818 that were built by unemployed weavers to form a riverside walkway. The top image is looking in a south-westerly direction from under one of the arches of the Eden Bridge. The snowy scene below is looking in the opposite direction.

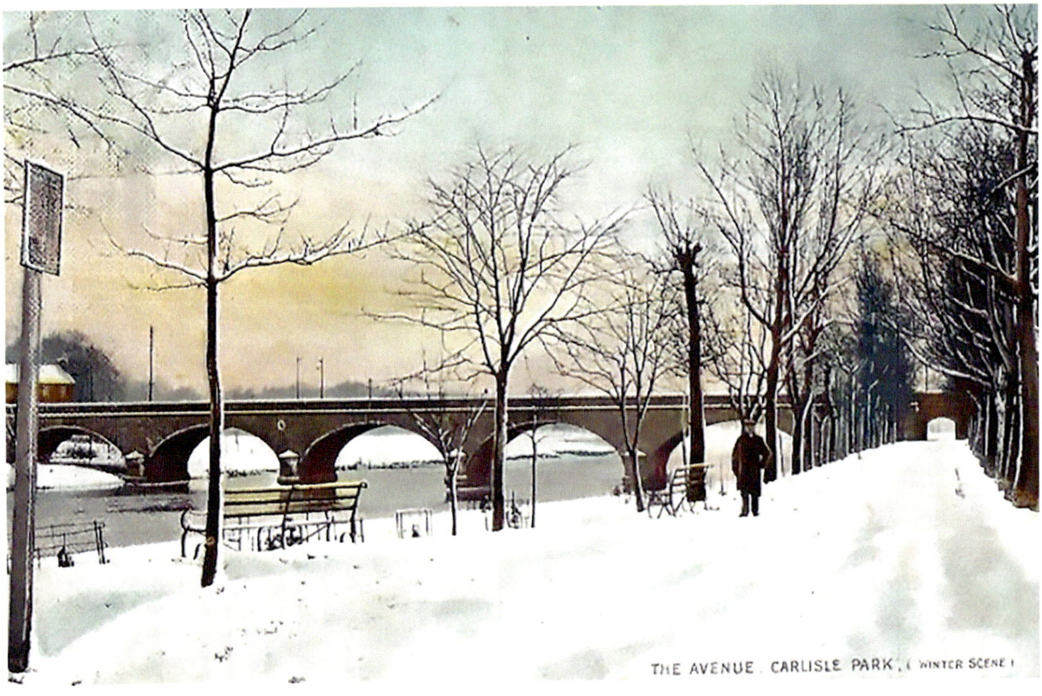

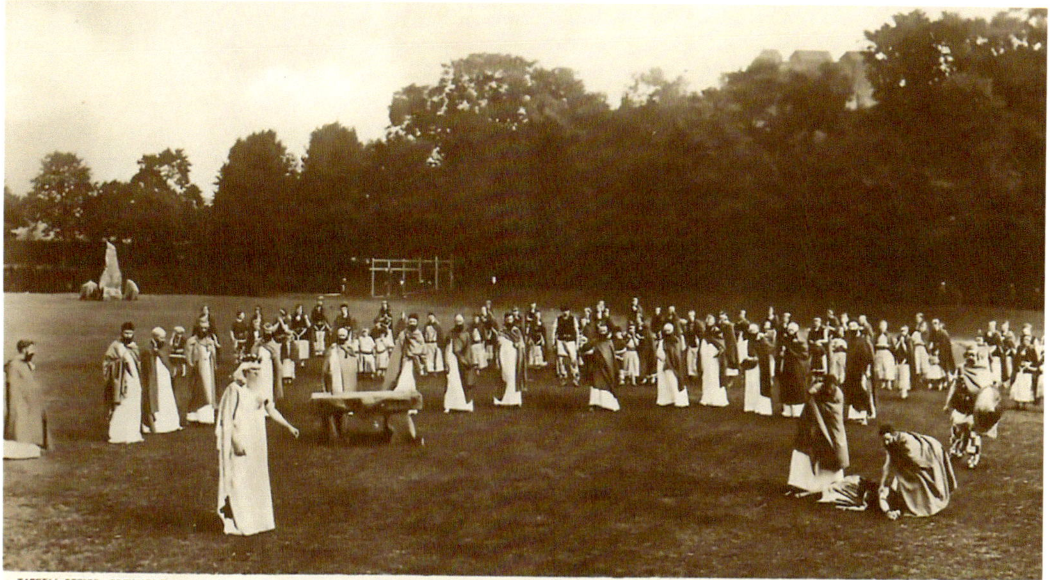

TASSELL SERIES. COPYRIGHT.

THE DRUIDS ABOUT TO MAKE A HUMAN SACRIFICE. EPISODE I. NO. 2

CARLISLE HISTORICAL PAGEANT.

Bitts Park – Historical Pageant

The pageant was held in the north-west area of the park called the Sauceries. It took place from Monday 6 August 1928, when it was opened at 2.45 p.m. by Lord Lonsdale, to Saturday 11 August 1928. The pageant was presented in nine episodes with these two images showing scenes from episodes 1 and 4.

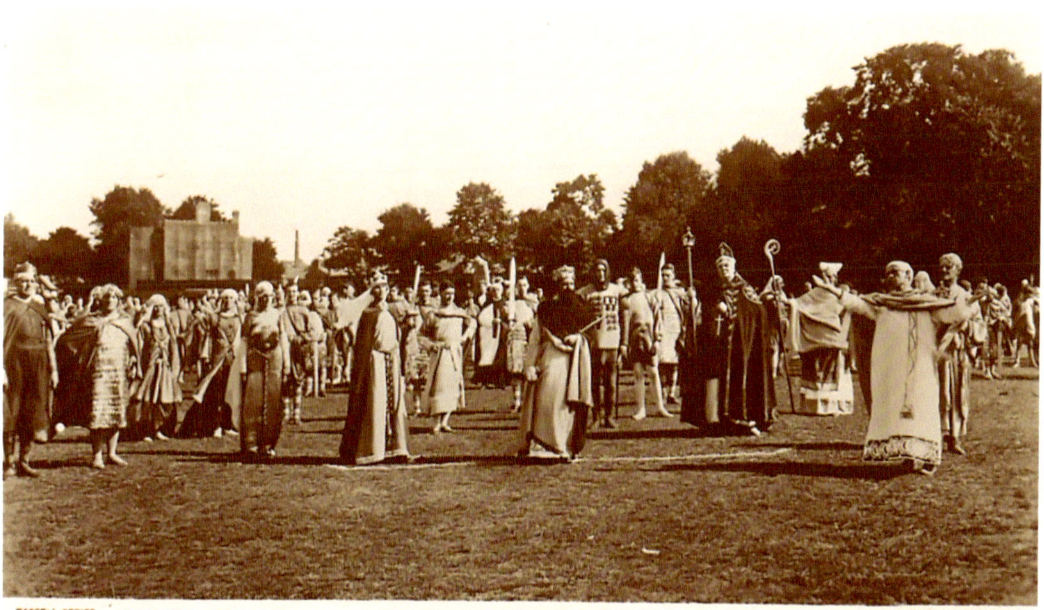

TASSELL SERIES. COPYRIGHT.

WALTER THE PRIEST TAKES THE OATH OF ALLEGIANCE TO KING HENRY I. A.D. 1132. EPISODE IV NO. 23.

CARLISLE HISTORICAL PAGEANT.

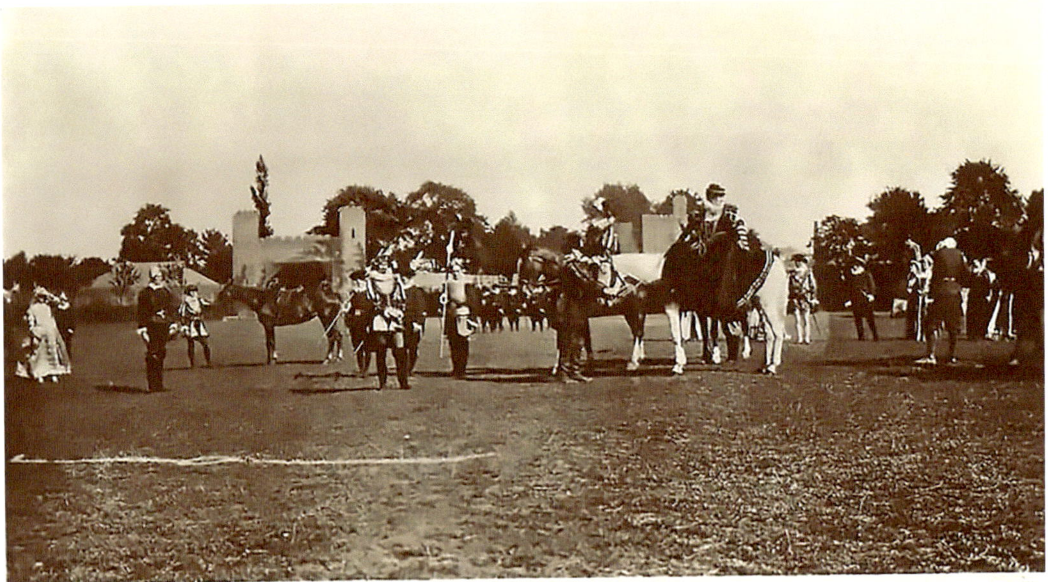

TASSELL SERIES. COPYRIGHT MARY, QUEEN OF SCOTS ARRIVES AT CARLISLE. A.D. 1568. EPISODE VI. NO. 9.

CARLISLE HISTORICAL PAGEANT.

Bitts Park – Historical Pageant

These two images show scenes from episodes 6 and 9. The full list of episodes is as follows: Episode I. Hadrian and the Roman Wall, *c.* AD 120. Episode II. King Arthur and the Picts, AD 500. Episode III. St Cuthbert, AD 685–875. Episode IV. Carlisle and the Norman Kings, 1092 and 1132. Episode V. King Edward I, 1307. Episode VI. Mary, Queen of Scots, 1568. Episode VII. Kinmont Willie, 1596. Episode VIII. The 45, 1745. Episode IX. Carlisle and Gretna Green, *c.* 1797.

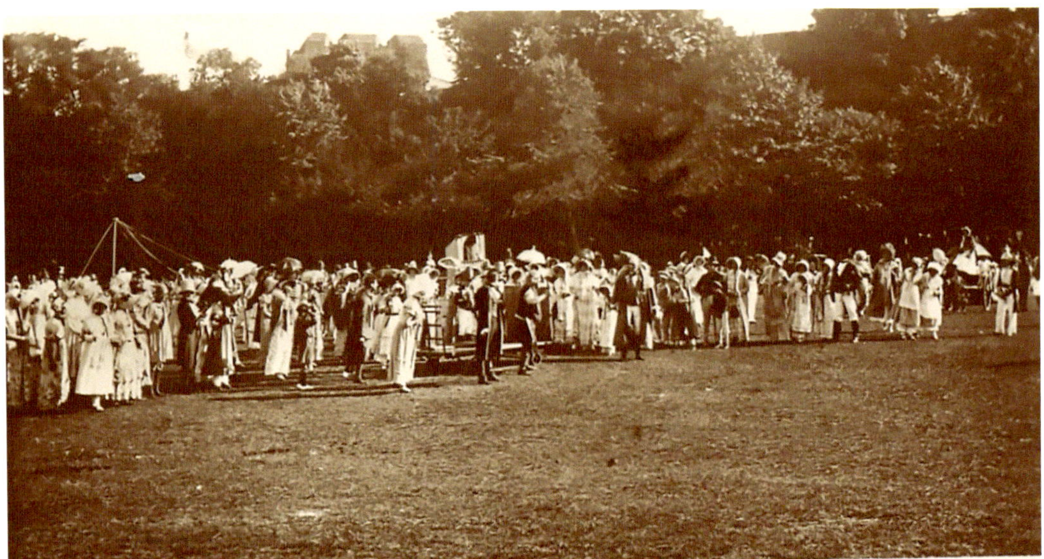

TASSELL SERIES. COPYRIGHT SCENES OF OLD GRETNA GREEN. THE BLACKSMITH DEFENDS HIS CLIENTS FROM THEIR ANGRY PARENT. EPISODE IX.

CARLISLE HISTORICAL PAGEANT.

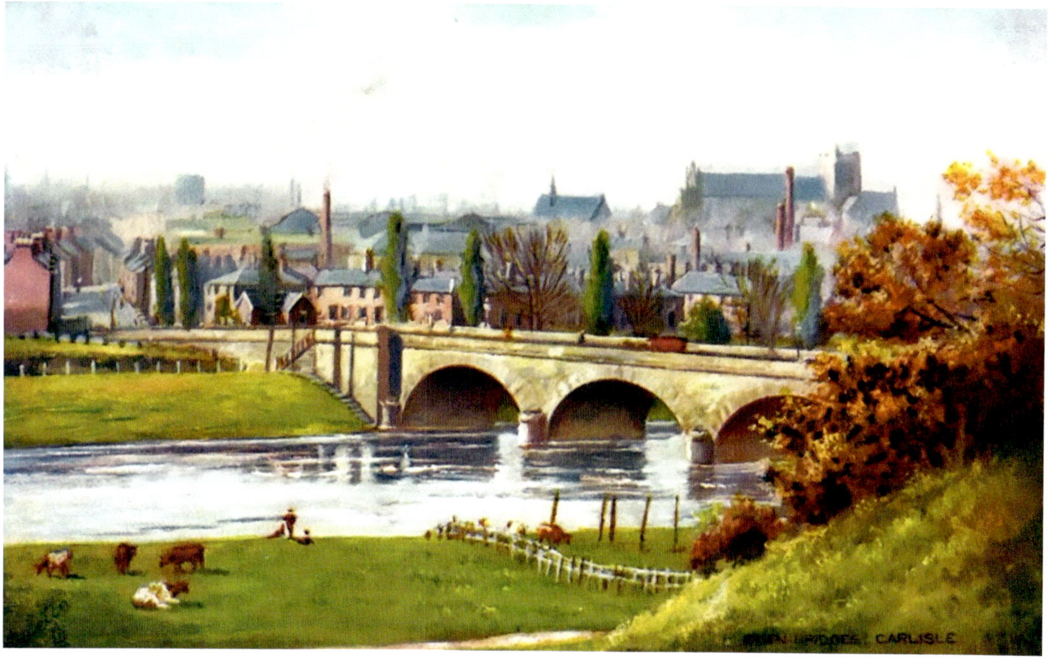

Eden Bridge

Eden Bridge is approximately 230 yards long and was built between 1812 and 1815 for the County of Cumberland by Robert Smirke. It is constructed as five segmental arches of double width. In 1932 it was widened by Percy Dalton, the City Engineer. Fixed onto the bridge parapet are various bronze plaques giving a brief history and a central one recording the widening.

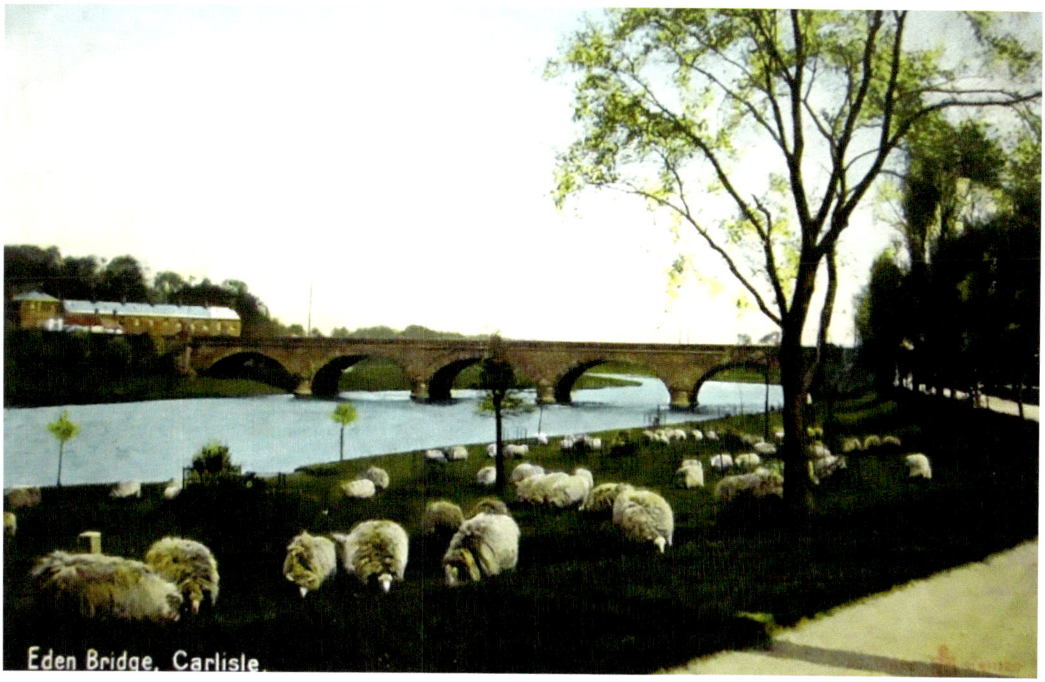

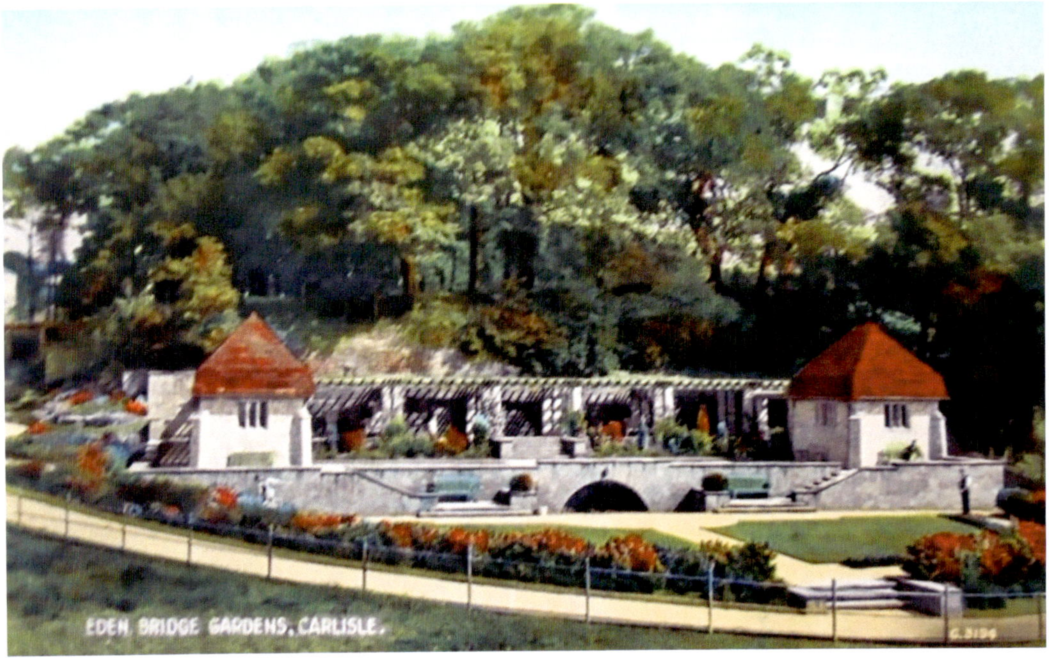

Eden Bridge Gardens

Situated on the north bank of the River Eden just off Eden Bridge, the gardens were designed by the internationally renowned landscape architects Thomas H. Mawson & Sons. Built using unemployed labourers in the depression of the 1930s, under the supervision of City Engineer Percy Dalton, the gardens were opened in 1933 by City Mayor Councillor E. B. Gray.

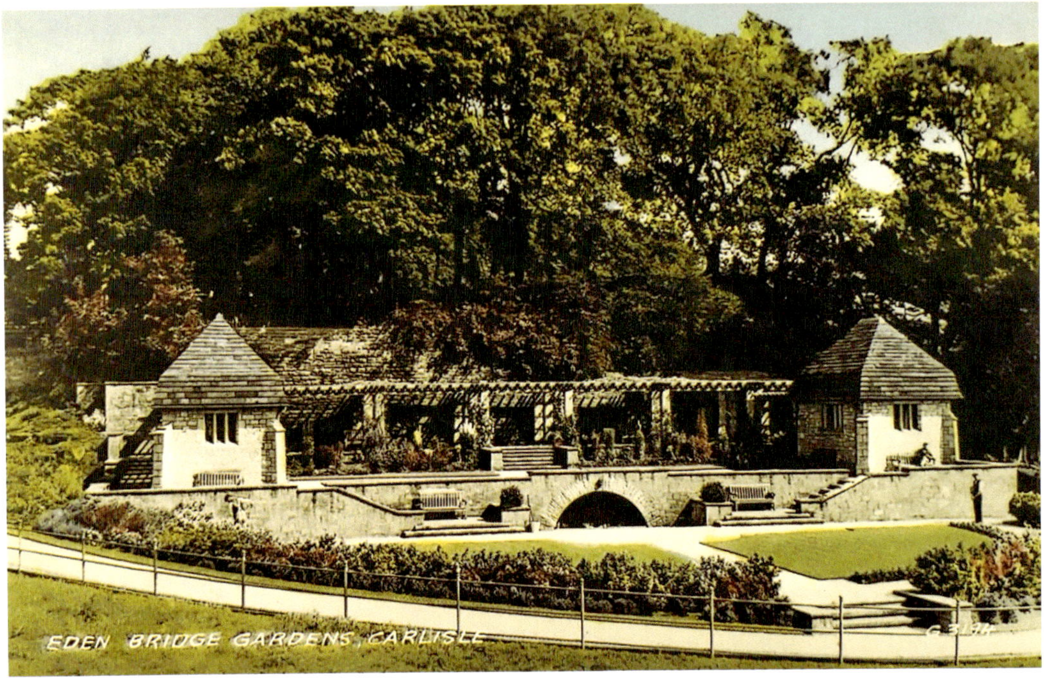

Burgh Monument to Edward I

The monument marks the place on Burgh Marsh, by the Solway Firth, where King Edward I of England died at the age sixty-eight on 7 July 1307 after developing dysentery. The red-sandstone monument is located around a mile north of Burgh by Sands in Cumbria. It was originally built in 1685 and rebuilt in 1803 following a collapse, and was restored and fenced in 1876. Edward I, sometimes called the 'Hammer of the Scots', was on his way north during conflict with Scotland.

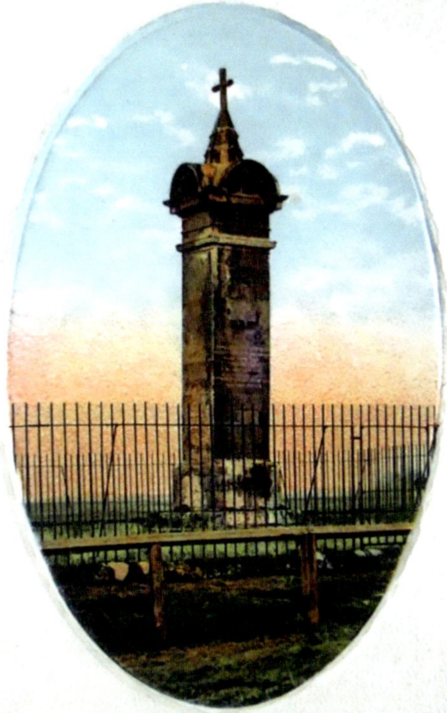

BURGH MONUMENT NEAR CARLISLE.
MARKING THE SPOT ON WHICH KING EDWARD I DIED

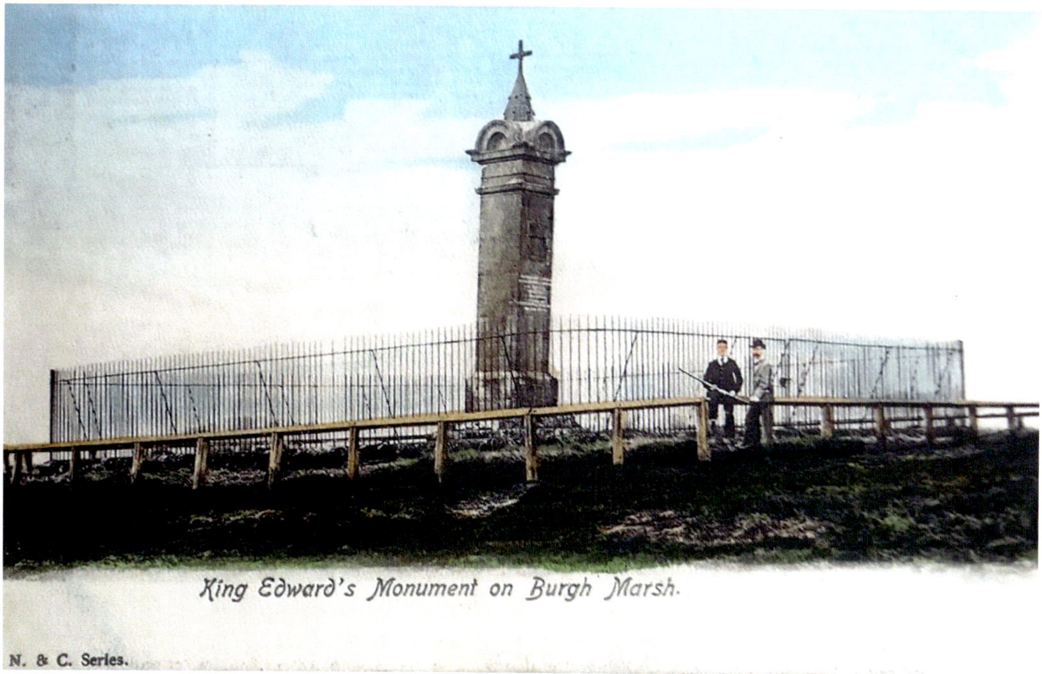

King Edward's Monument on Burgh Marsh.

N. & C. Series.

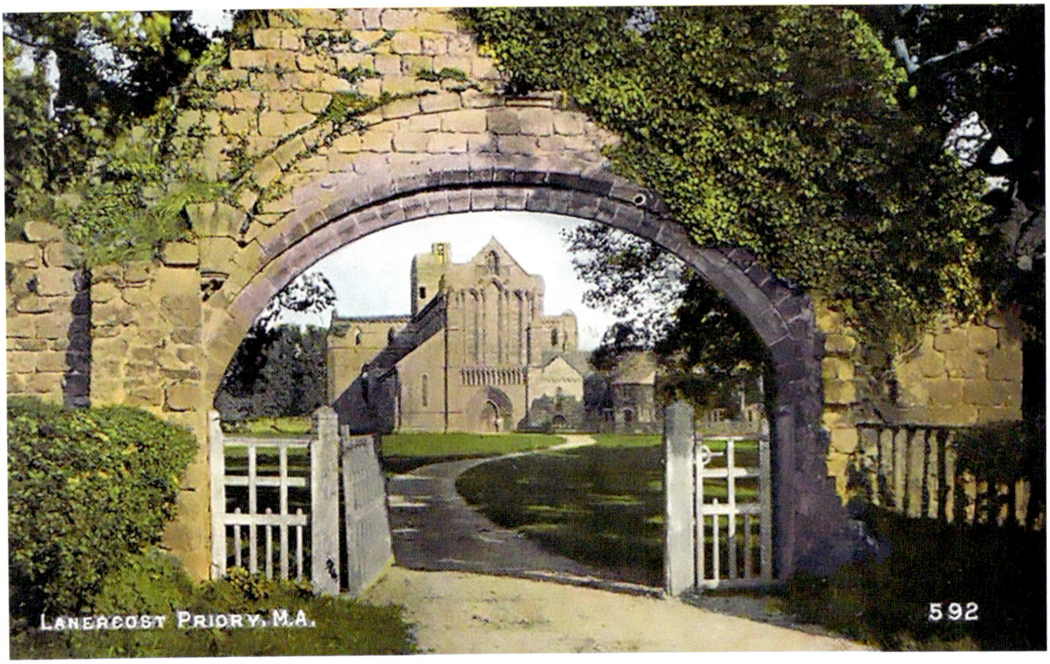

Lanercost Priory – Gateway

Lanercost Priory was founded by Robert de Vaux between 1165 and 1174, the most likely date being 1169, to house Augustinian canons. The priory is situated in the village of Lanercost, within sight of Naworth Castle, with which it had close connections. At the time of the images the nave is used as the parish church and the west end buildings as parish rooms. The east side buildings are in ruins.

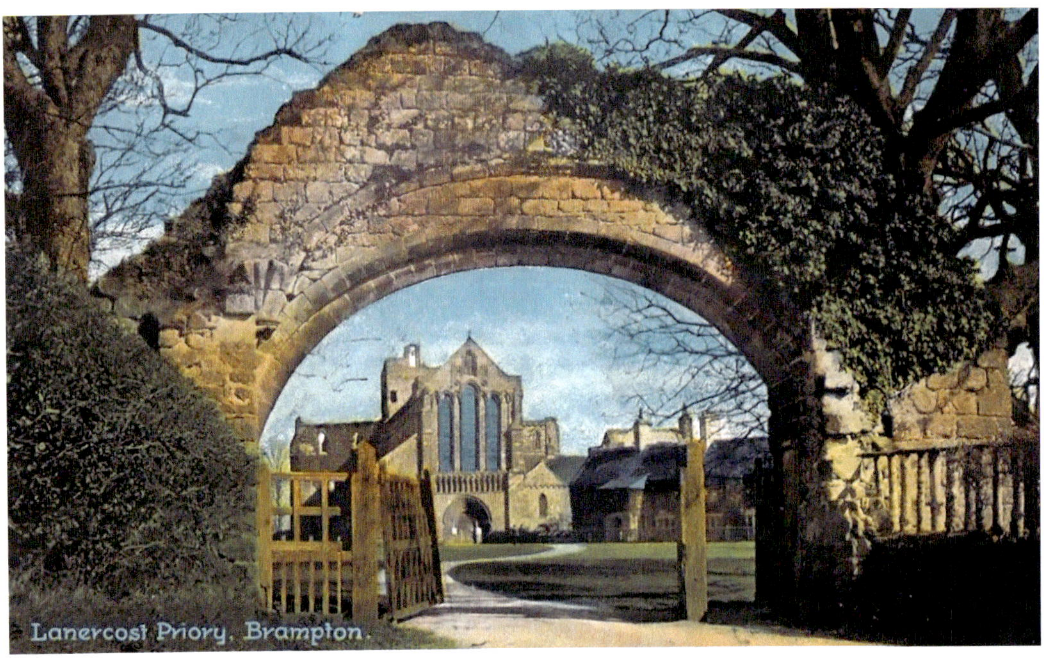

Lanercost Priory – Ruins

Lanercost Priory was dissolved in 1538 by Henry VIII and its buildings were stripped of their roofs, except for the church building which continued in use as the parish church. In 1747, the nave was re-roofed, but by 1847 the priory was in a state of disrepair to the extent that the east end roof collapsed. In 1849, the church was in use again after a major restoration by Anthony Salvin. In the 1870s, there was further restoration by the Carlisle architect C. J. Ferguson.

At the Dissolution, ownership had passed to the Dacre family, and then in the early eighteenth century to the Howards. In 1929, the priory ruins were put into public ownership

The two images taken in the north transept show the tomb of Sir Humphrey and Lady Mabel Dacre.

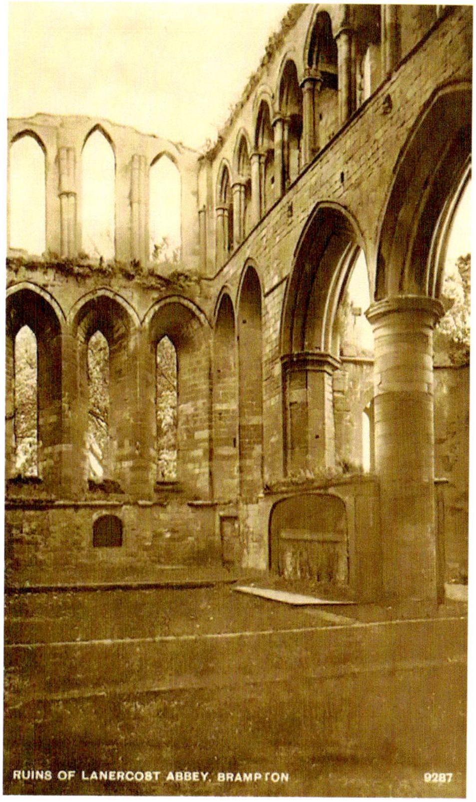

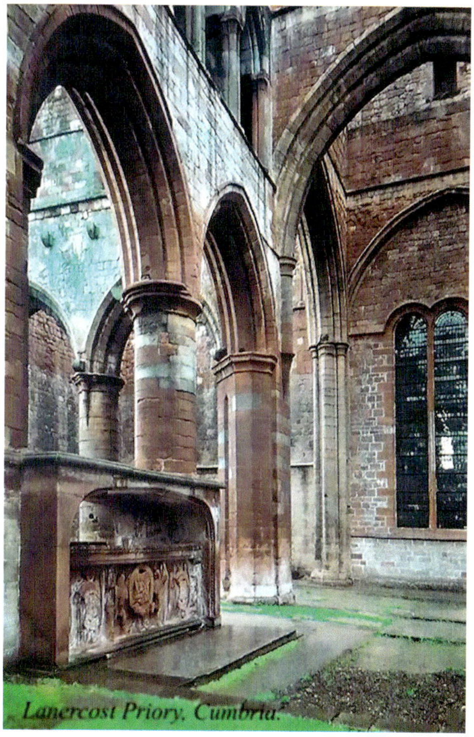

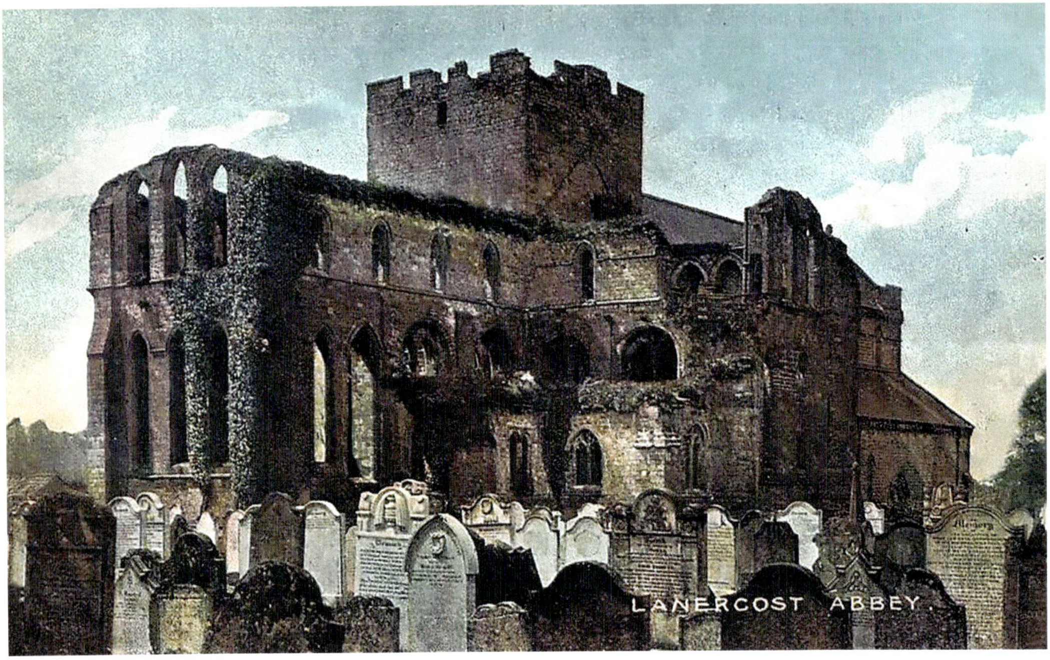

Lanercost Priory – View

The above image looking south-westerly from the graveyard shows the nave on the right which remained in use for parish worship. At one time the north aisle in the right foreground was also used for this purpose. The lower image is looking south-easterly and shows the nave and the north aisle to the right and front foreground.

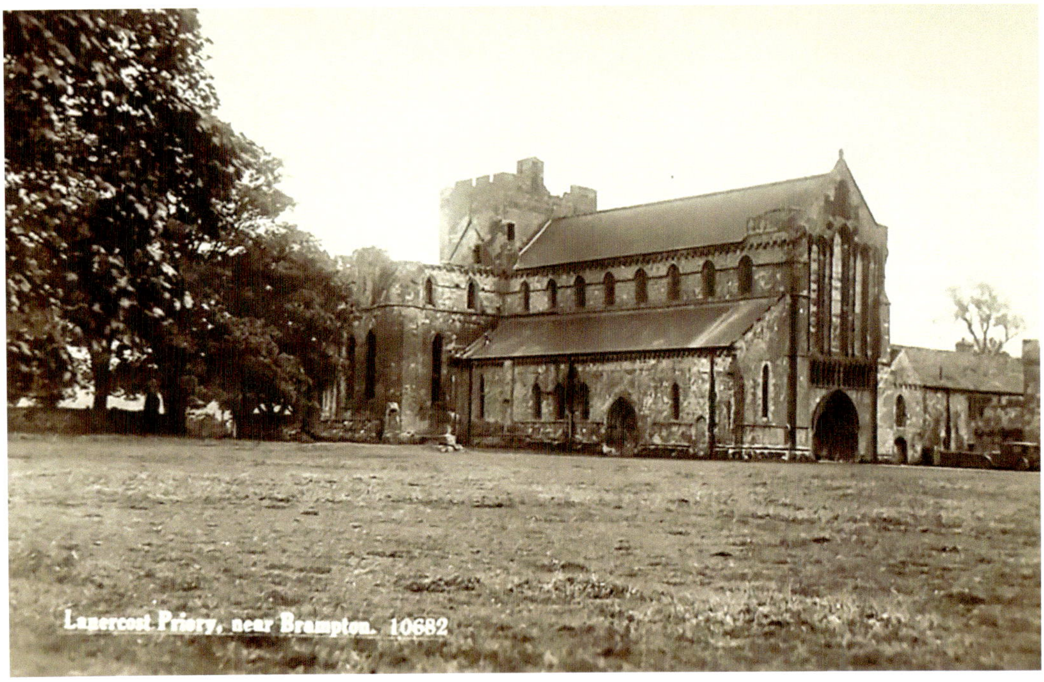

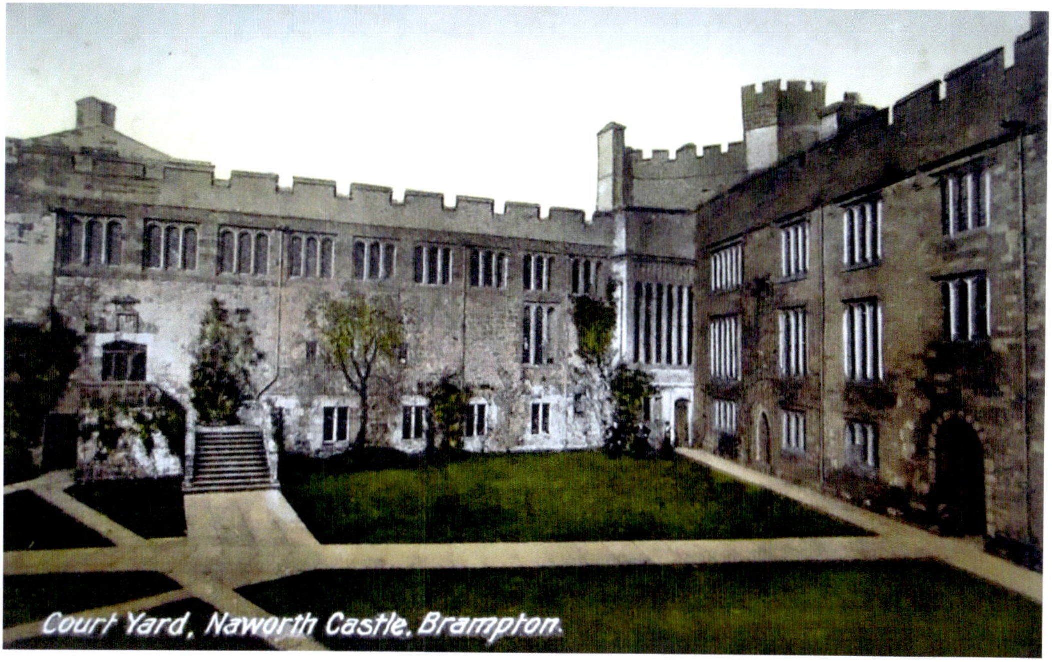

Naworth Castle, Brampton – Courtyard

Naworth Castle was originally a thirteenth-century fortified manor house or stone tower house founded by de Multon family. In 1335, Ranulph de Dacre founded the stone castle, when granted a licence to crenellate. He added the Dacre Tower and parts of the curtain wall. The castle was remodelled in the sixteenth and seventeenth centuries.

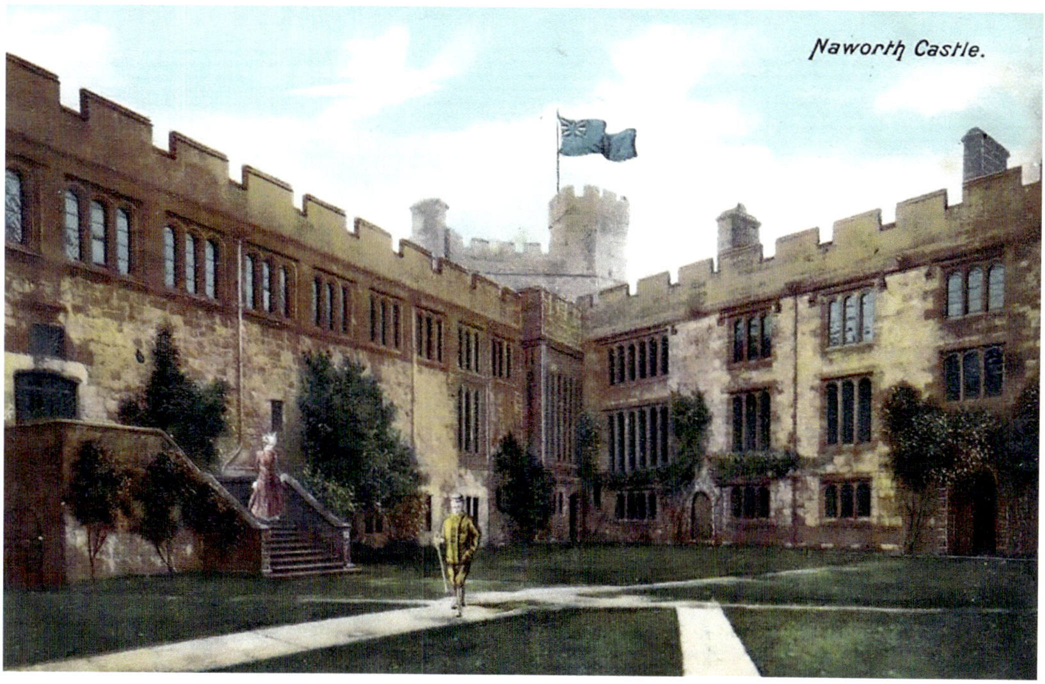

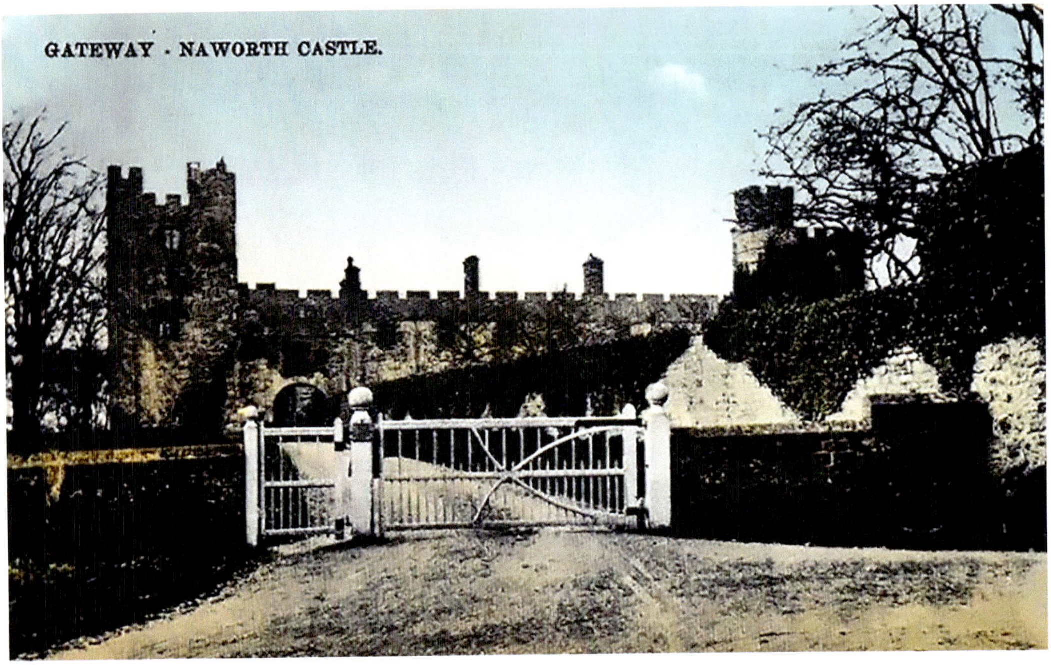

Naworth Castle, Brampton – Gateway

Thomas Dacre (1467–1525), who commanded the reserve of the English army at the Battle of Flodden, was known as the 'Builder Dacre'. He built the castle's gateway and placed over it his coat of arms with the Dacre family motto below: 'Fort en Loialte', translated to 'Strong in Loyalty'. The images show the gateway at the end of the drive accessed by the white gates in the forefront.

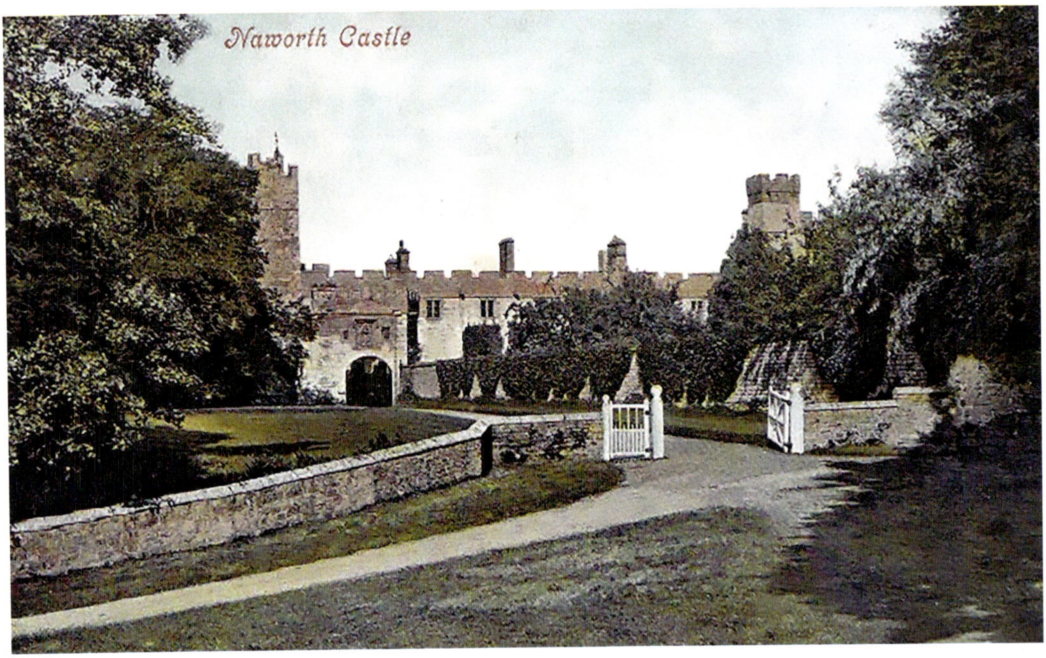

St Martin's Church, Brampton

St Martin's is located in Front Street and was built on the site of a former late seventeenth-century hospital that had been converted into a chapel in 1789. It was built for George Howard, who later became the 9th Earl of Carlisle, together with other contributors, and was constructed between 1874 and 1878. The tower was added in 1906. The architect was Philip Webb, who was closely connected with the Pre-Raphaelite Brotherhood.

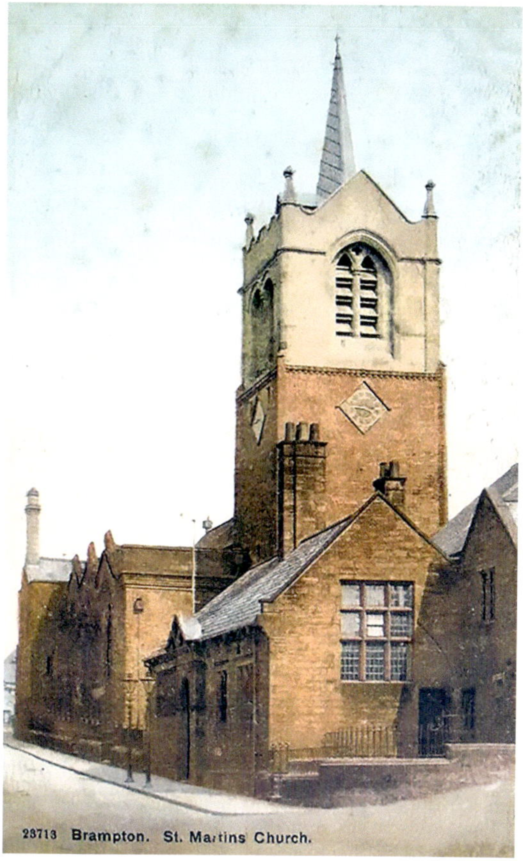

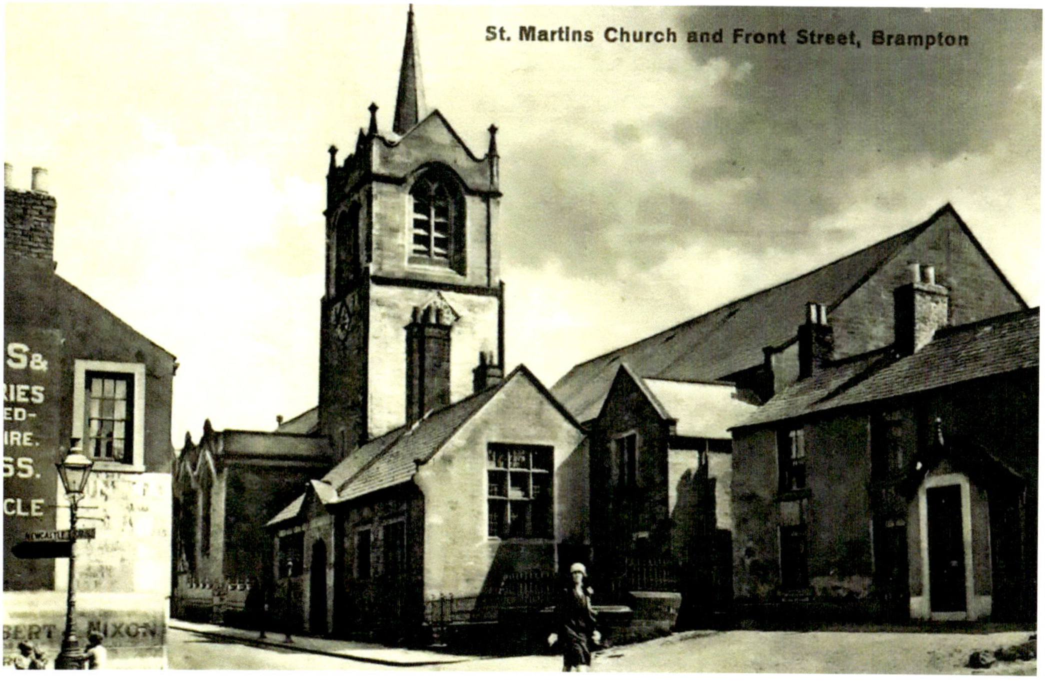

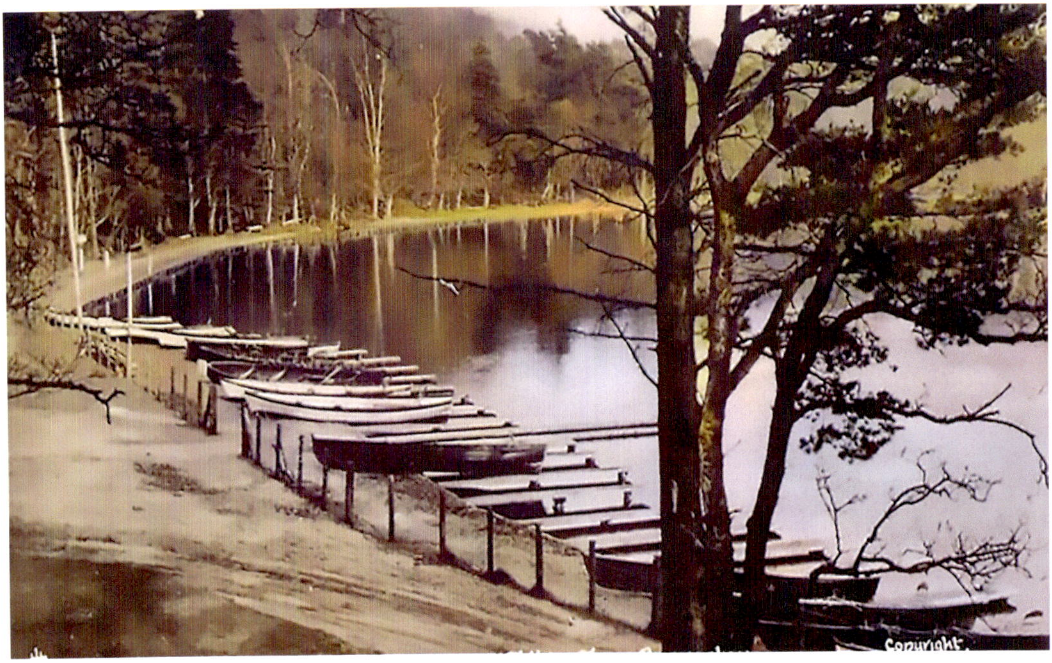

Talkin Tarn, Brampton – Views

Talkin Tarn is a kettle-hole lake formed by the immense force of glaciers 10,000 years ago. Moving ice scoured and carved the landscape, leaving glacial sand hills and a natural bowl. Talkin may be a hill name meaning 'white brow'. 'Tarn' is derived from Old Norse 'tjǫrn' and then Middle English 'terne', meaning 'small mountain pool' or 'small lake'. Rowing is the main activity on the lake.

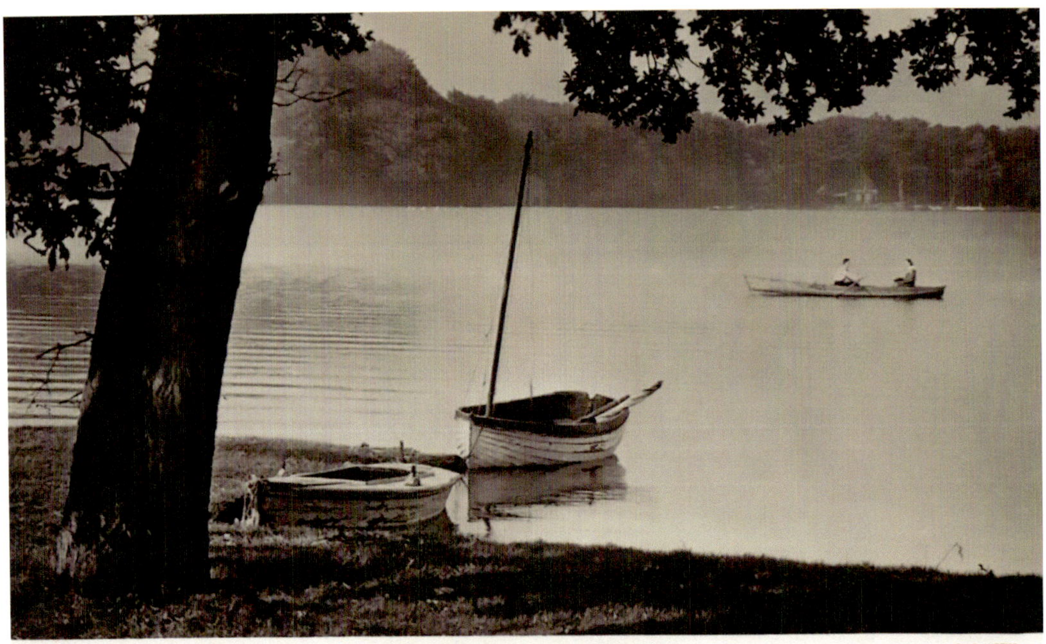

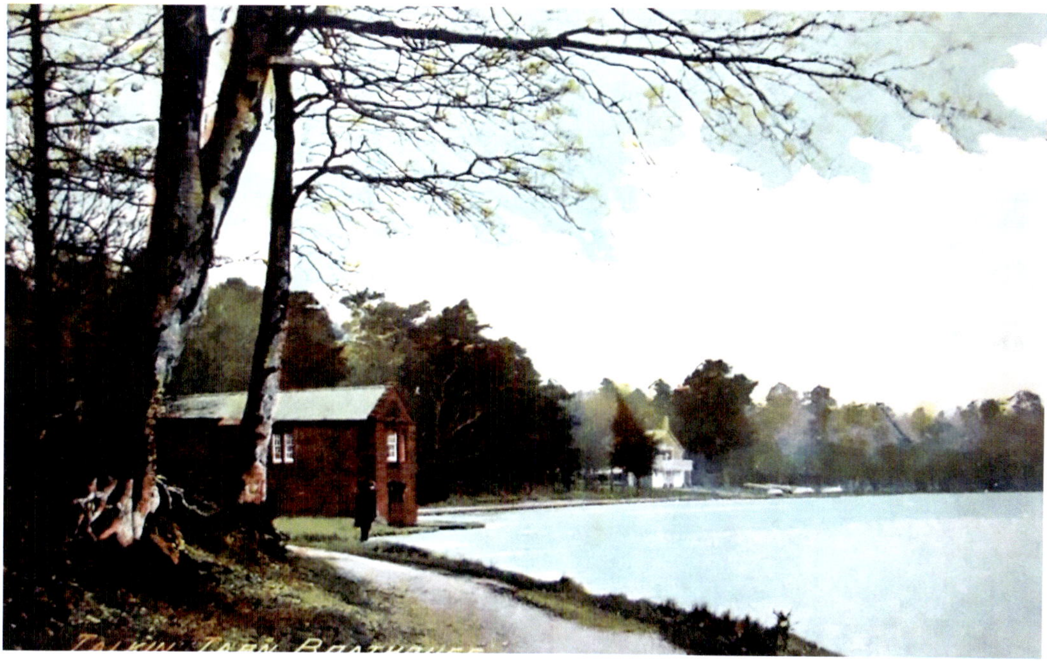

Talkin Tarn, Brampton – Boathouse

The boathouse shown on the left of the above image and on the right of the one below was built by Joseph Bell of Farlam in 1843 and ownership passed through his son John to his grandson Joseph Bell, who was the chief engineer of RMS *Titanic*.

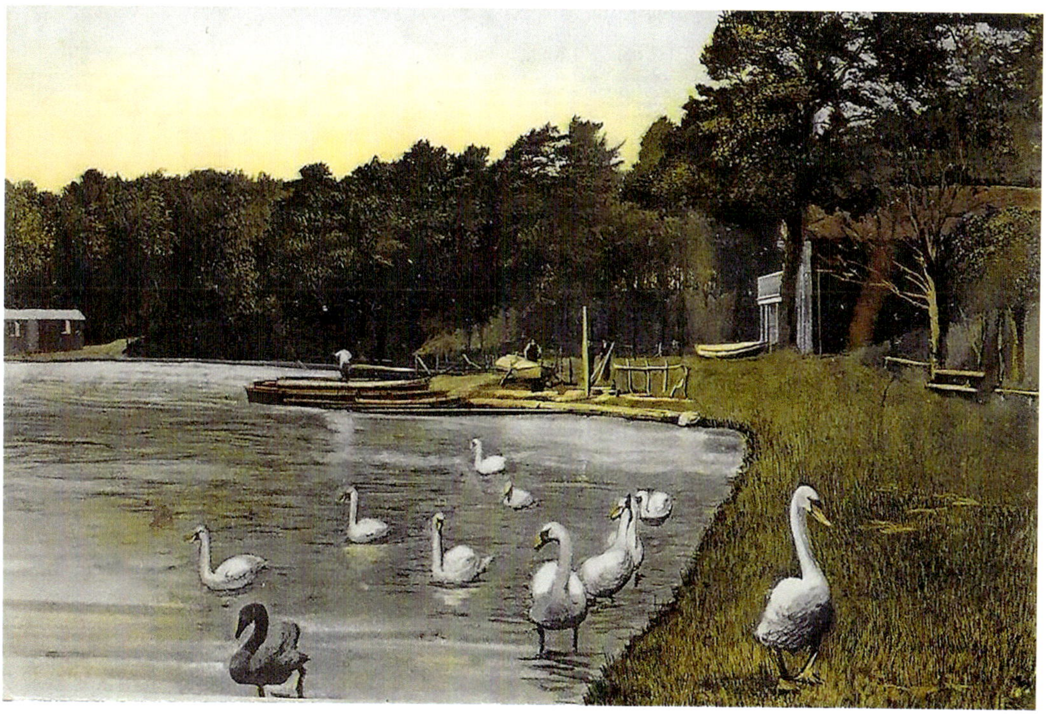

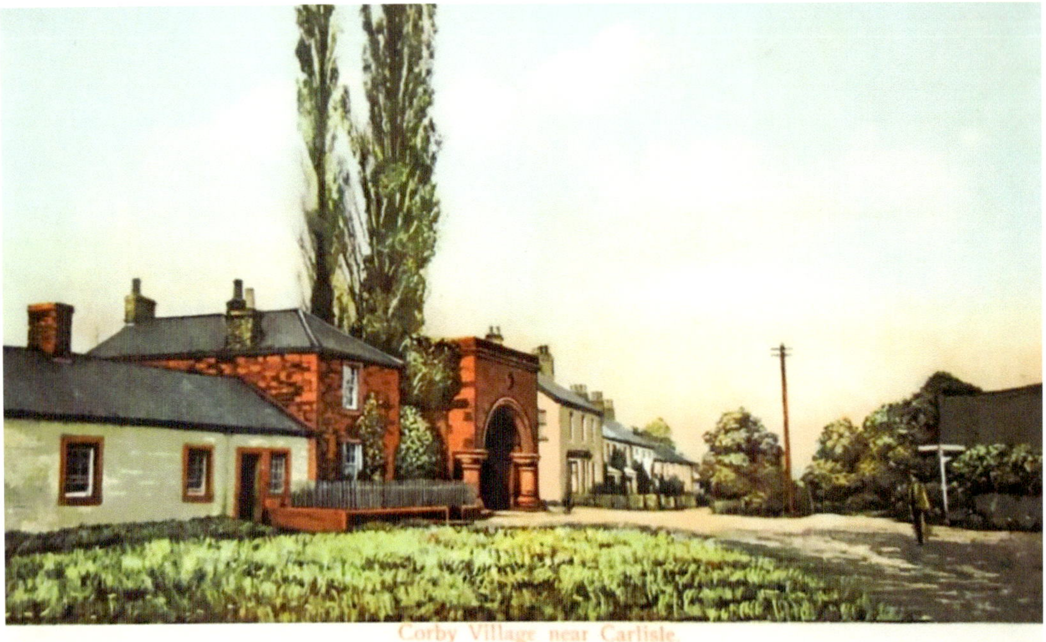

Corby

These images are looking north-easterly across the village green with Ferry Walk to the left of the image. The blacksmith's forge is the building with the arched entrance. The image below appears to be an earlier one based on the dress of the people and that there is no telegraph pole as in the upper image.

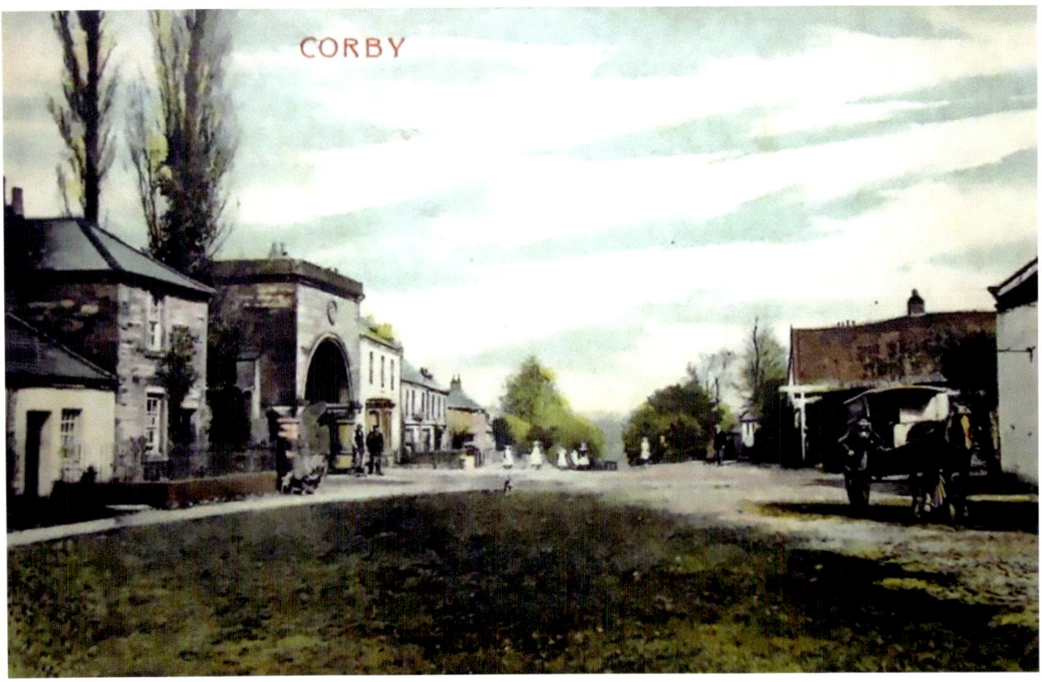

Corby – Blacksmith's Forge

This unusual building was built as a blacksmith's shop in 1833 for the Howard family of Corby Castle. It was built to represent Vulcan's forge. The covered porch was used for shoeing horses.

Apollo in the Forge of Vulcan, sometimes referred to as *Vulcan's Forge,* is an oil painting by Diego de Velázquez completed after his first visit to Italy in 1629.

1833 in Roman numerals is inscribed on one pillar and initials C.M.H. on the other.

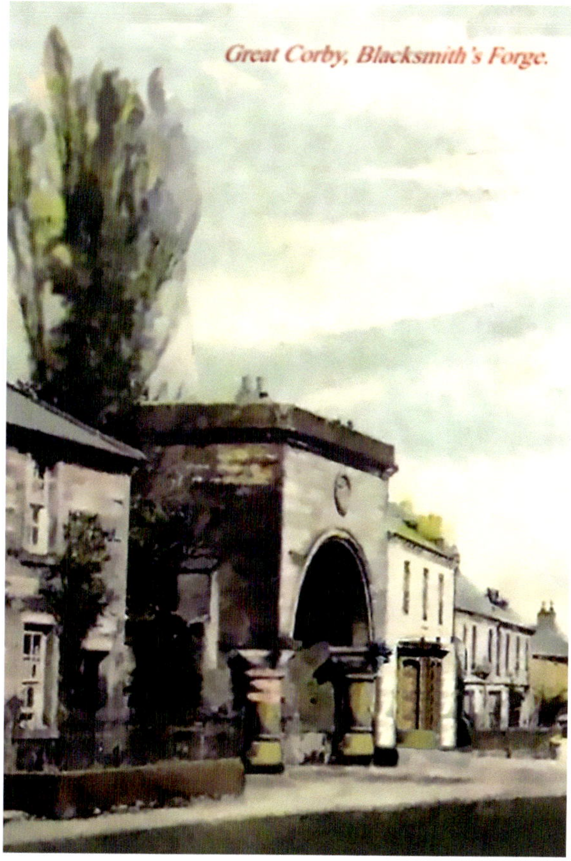

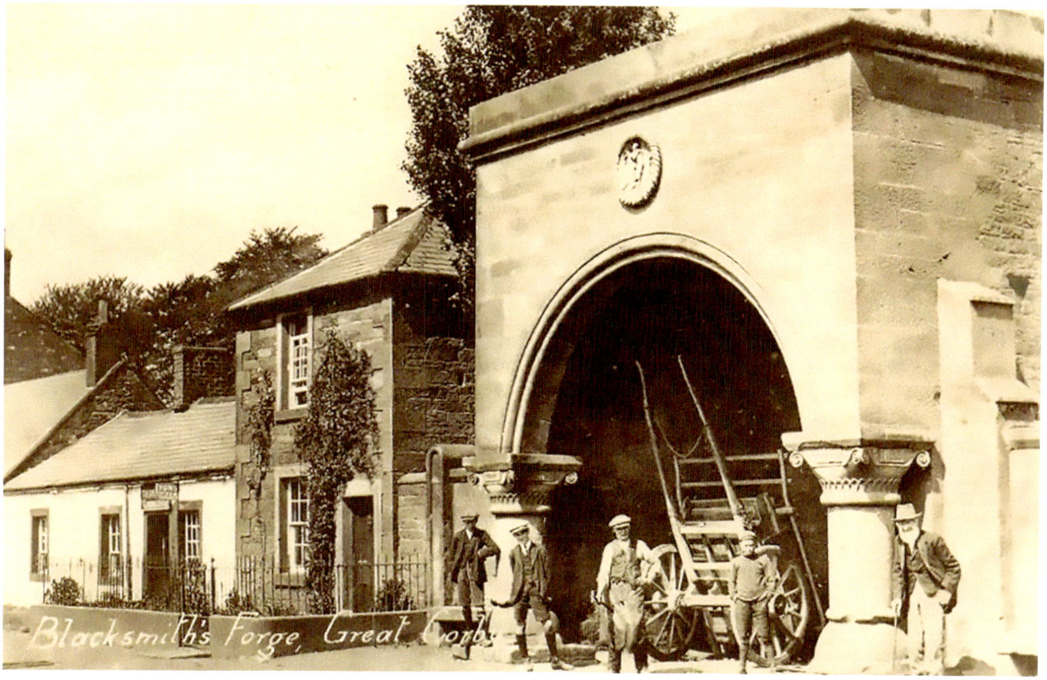

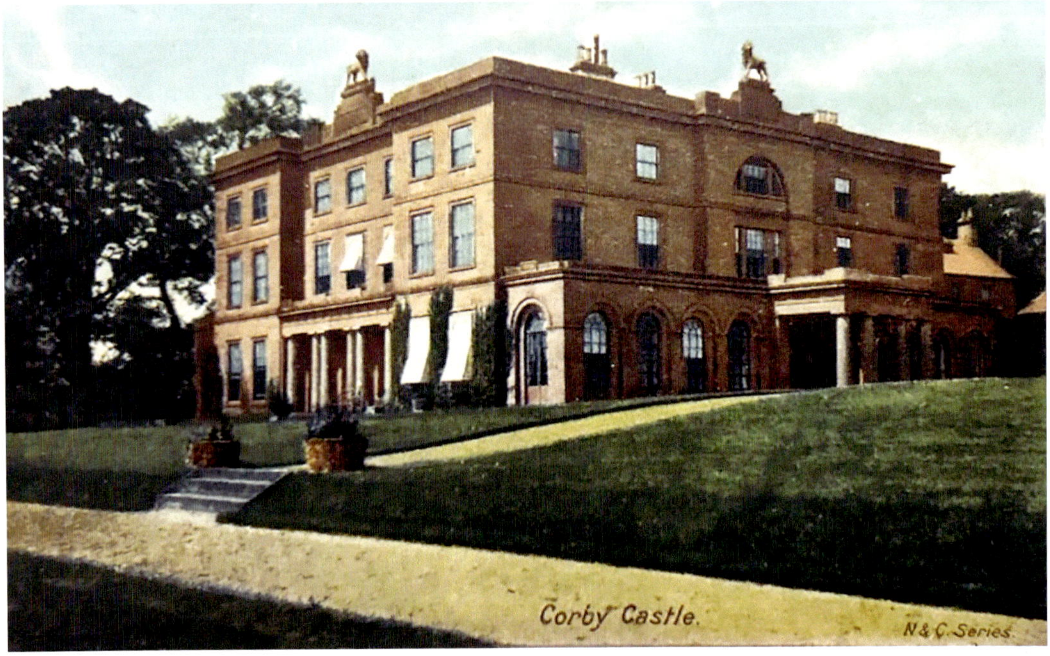

Corby Castle

Situated on the southern edge of the village of Great Corby, the castle was originally built in the thirteenth century as a red-sandstone tower house by the Salkeld family. It was sold in 1611 to Lord William Howard who added a two-storey, L-shaped house onto the peel tower. Henry Howard inherited the estate from Sir Francis Howard. The present facade was built for Henry by Peter Nicholson between April 1812 and September 1817.

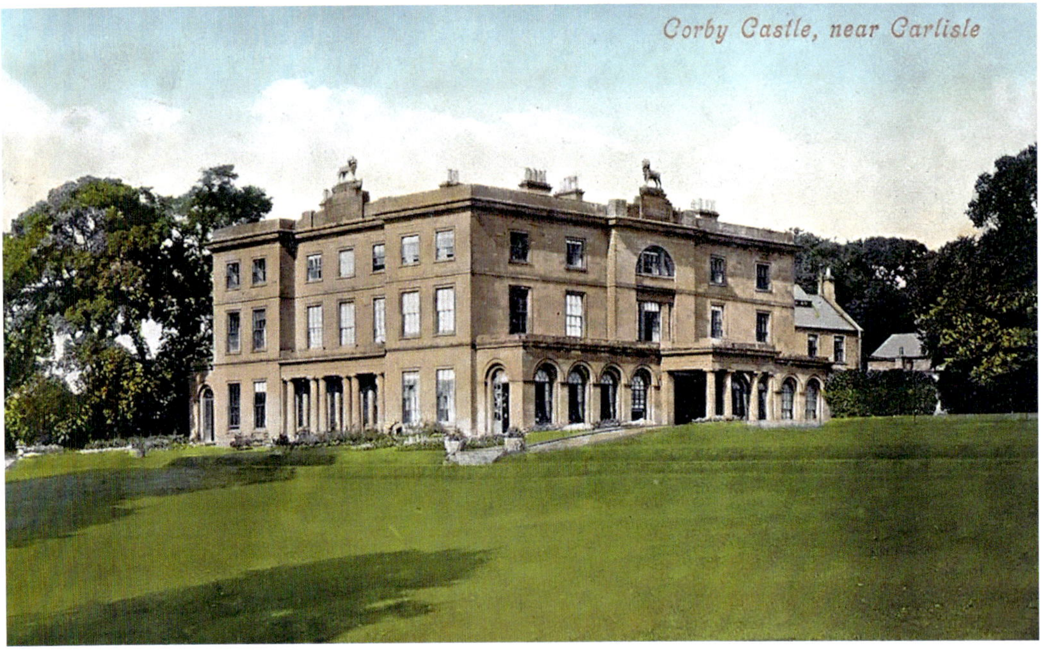

Corby Castle

Between 1708 and 1729 a Venetian summer house with cascade of four steps leading to oval pond, with a terrace and river wall was constructed. The arched steps, one of which has a grotto behind, form the cascade, falling around 12 yards to the pond, which formerly had a fountain in the centre but now has a statue of Nelson.

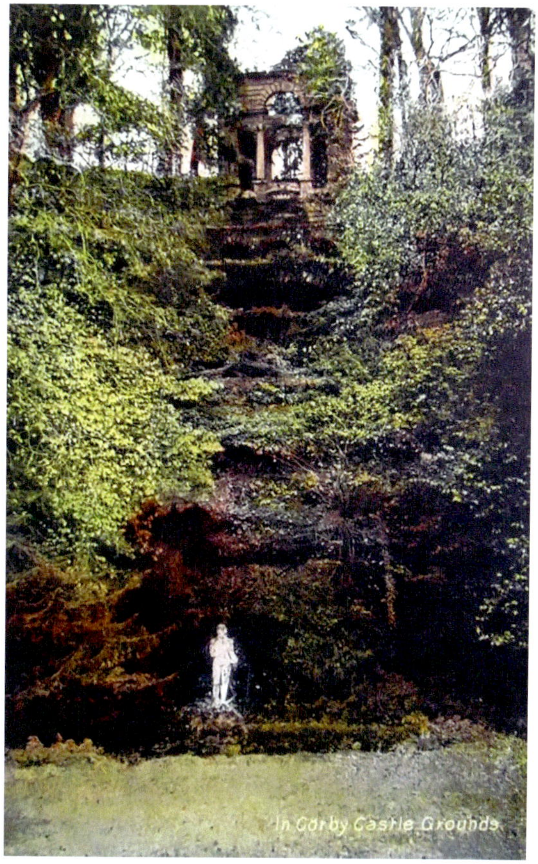

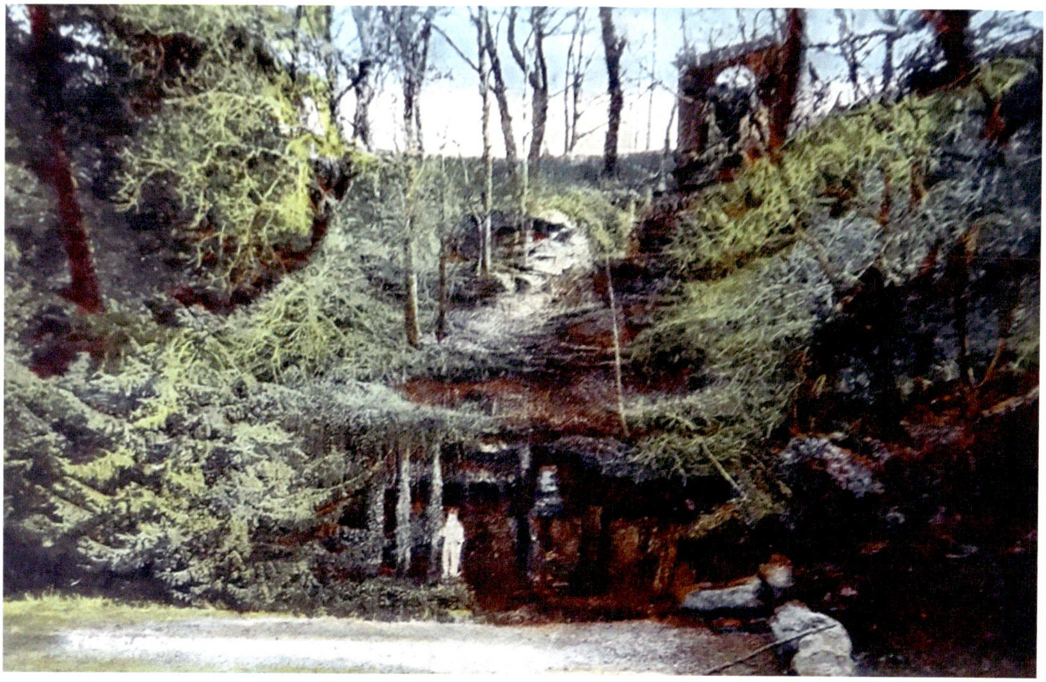

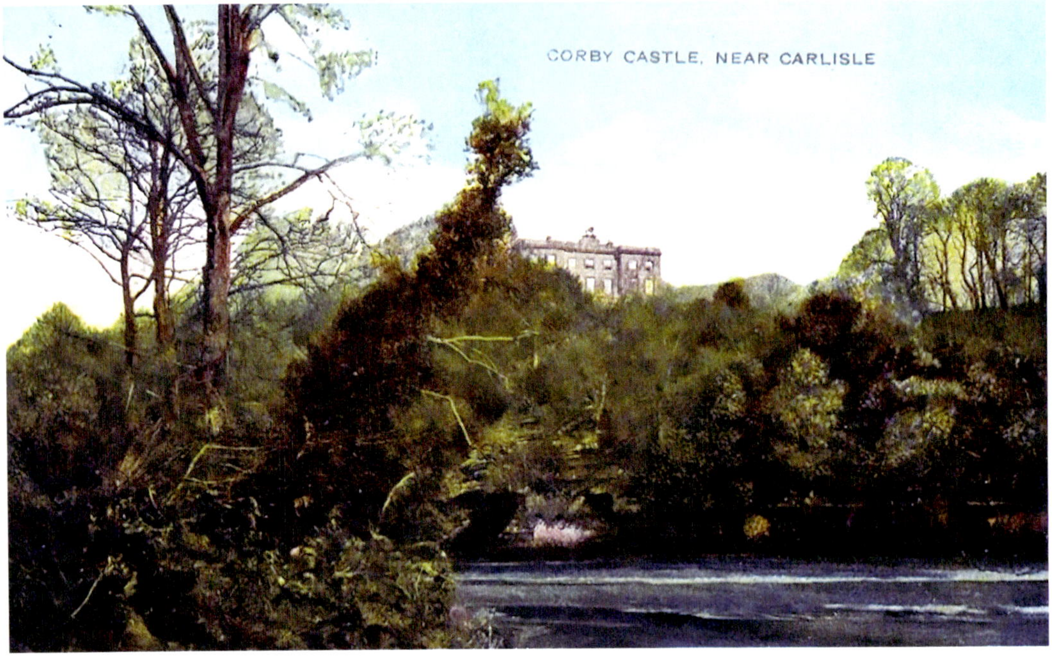

Corby Castle

The images are looking across the River Eden from the grounds of Wetheral Abbey. In the centre foreground are caves known as the St Constantine's Cells which are believed to have been excavated in medieval times by the monks of Wetheral Priory.

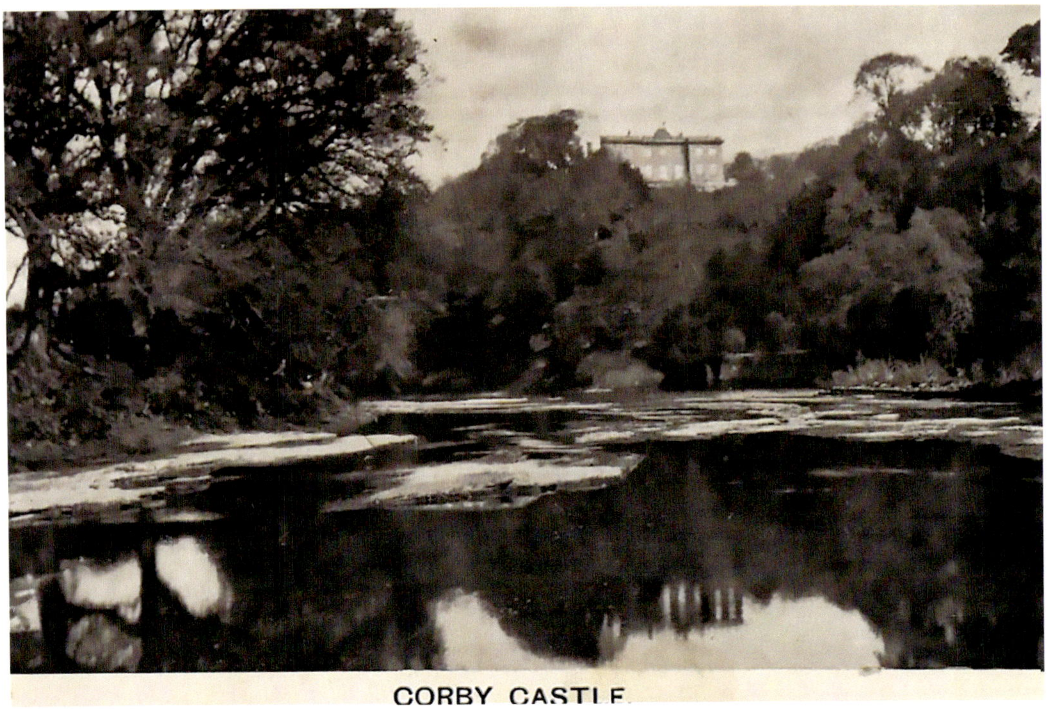

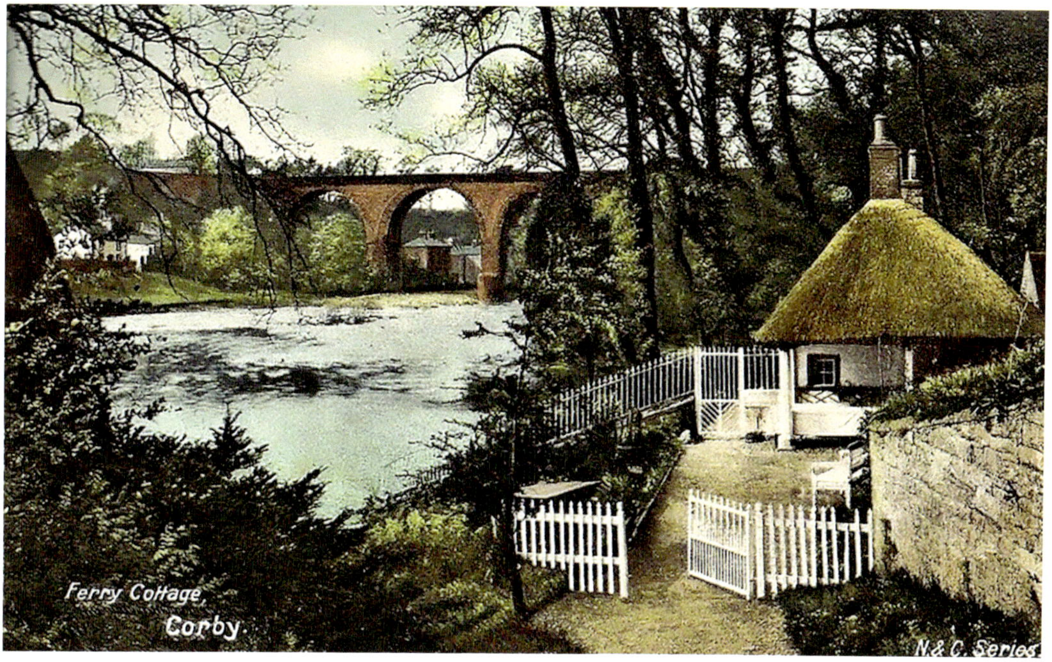

Corby – Ferry Cottage

The Ferry Cottage was a thatched building on the Great Corby banks of the River Eden. The building was situated approximately 60 yards north of where the ferry landed. The images are looking north with the Corby Bridge Railway Viaduct in the background.

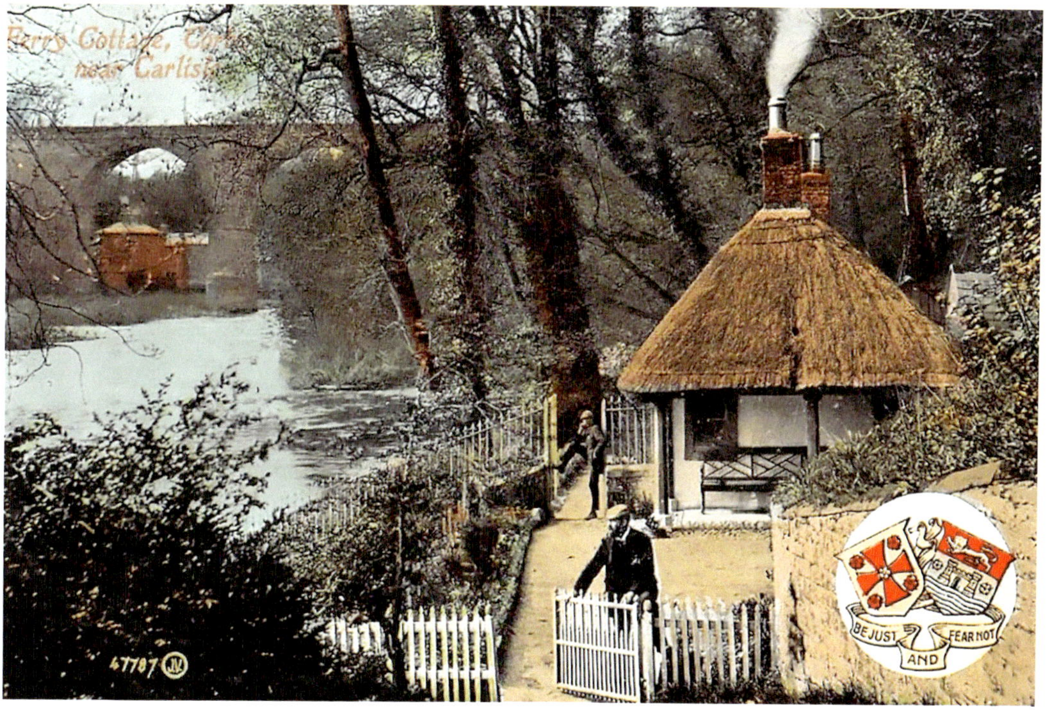

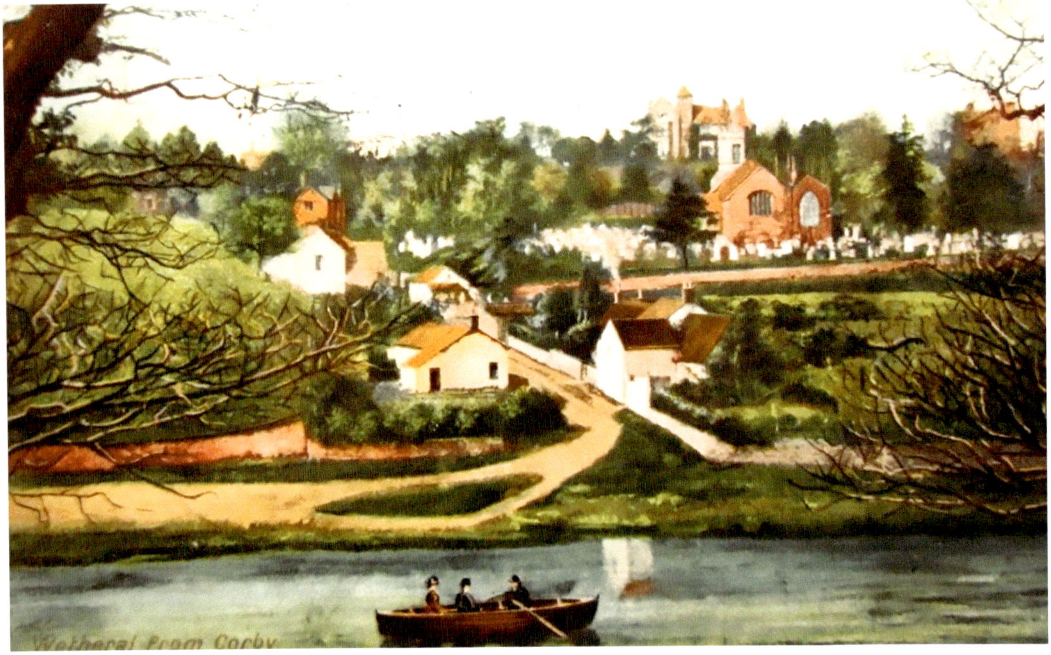

Wetheral – View from Corby

Ferry across the River Eden at Corby – first known record is in 1688. Looking west across the River Eden to the ferry landing at the end of Ferry Hill in Wetheral,

Holy Trinity church and graveyard can be seen on the right. Fish Inn is the second building on the left going up Ferry Hill.

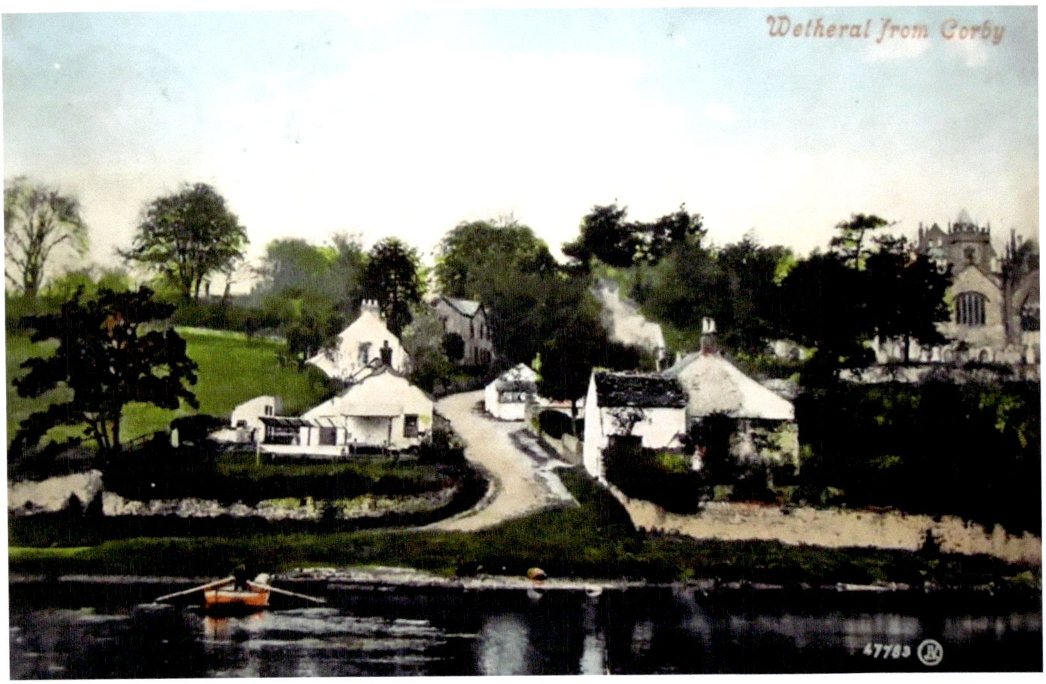

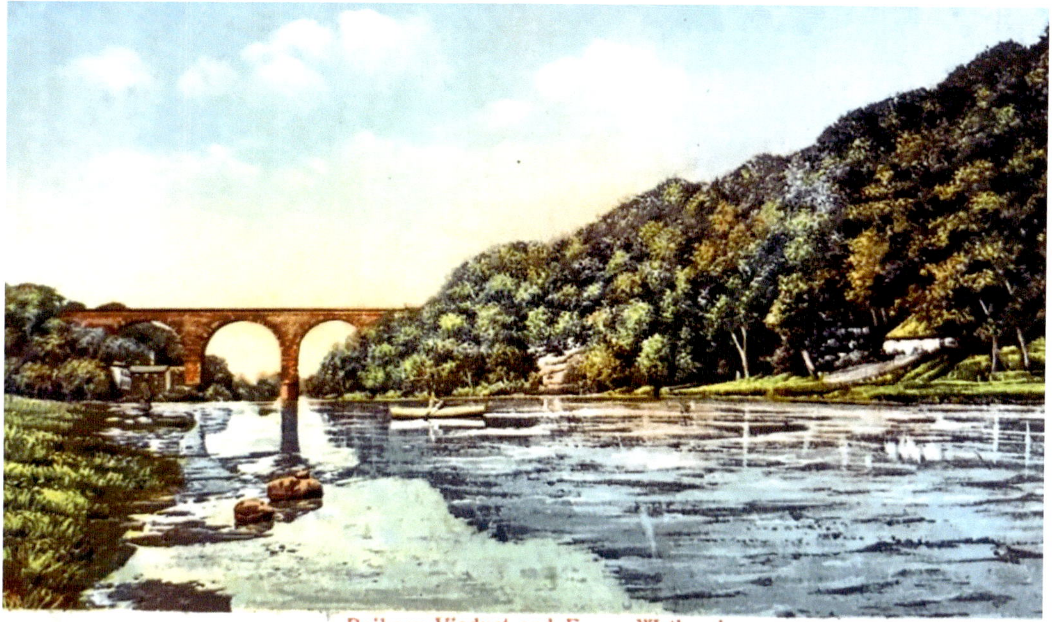

Wetheral – Viaduct and Ferry

Looking north from the west bank of the River Eden and south of the ferry crossing with the landing at Wetheral on the left and that at Great Corby to the right just below the Ferry Cottage. The crossing distance at a slight diagonal across the river was approximately 72 yards.

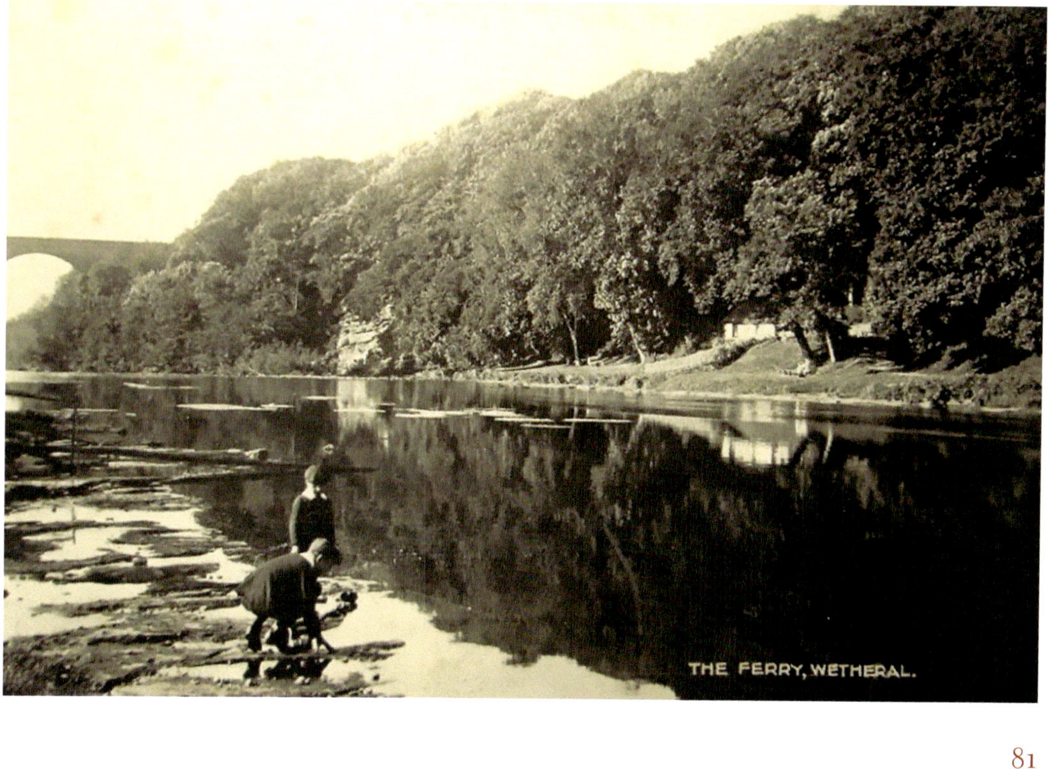

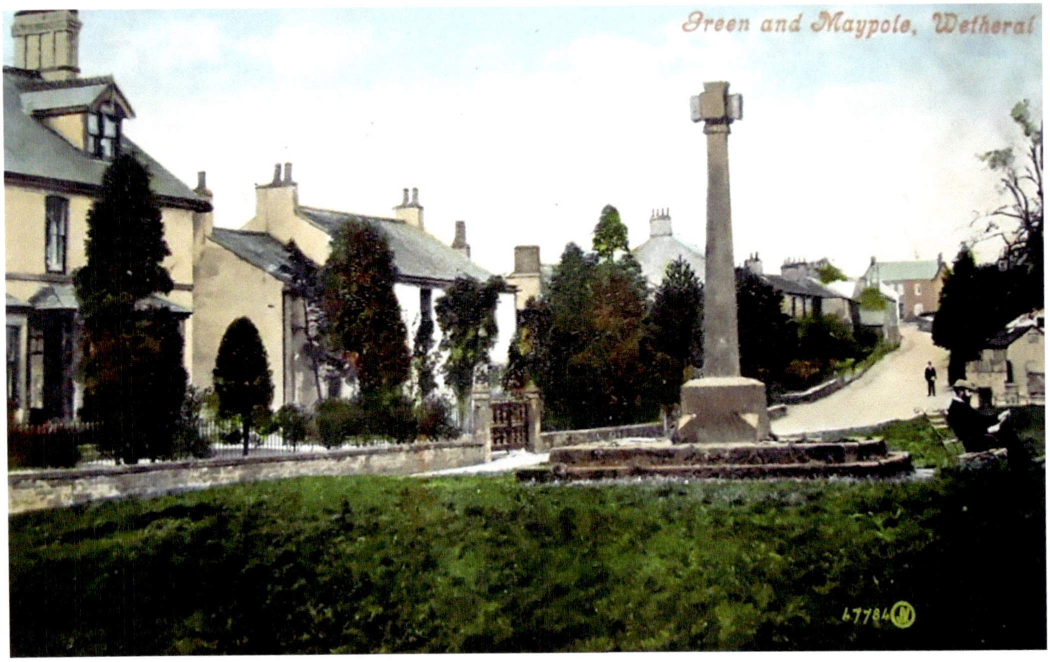

Wetheral – The Cross

Red sandstone 3½ metres high. Formerly the steps were in the centre of The Green and formed the base for a wooden maypole, which was erected at the expense of Henry Howard, of nearby Corby Castle, in 1814. Later replaced by a stone cross, when moved to its present location.

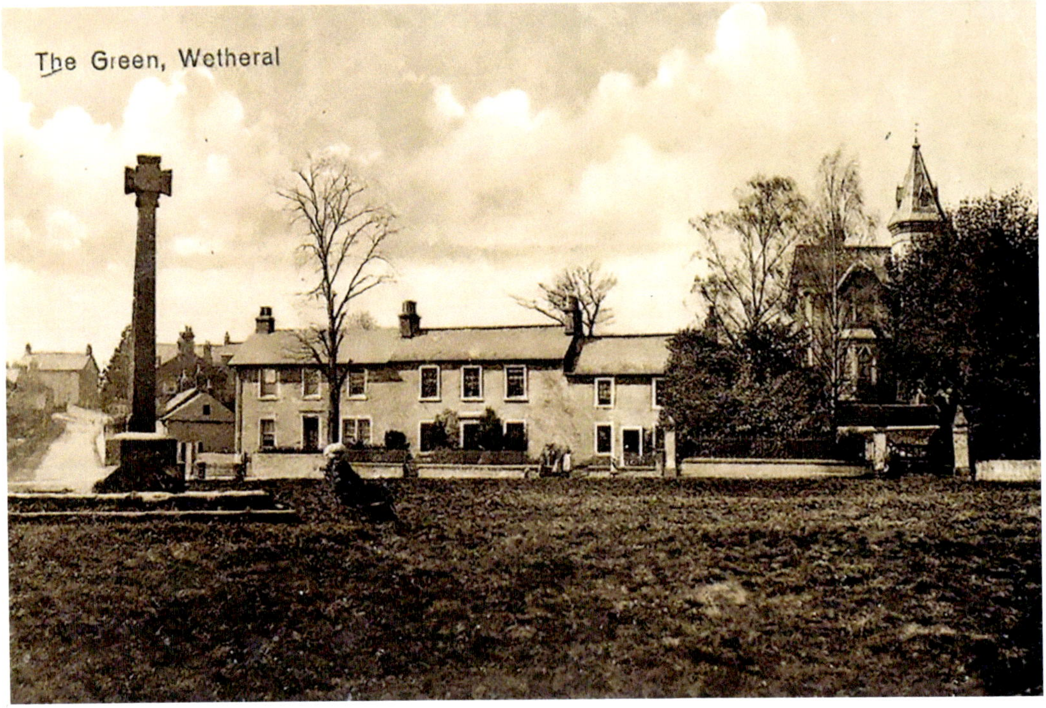

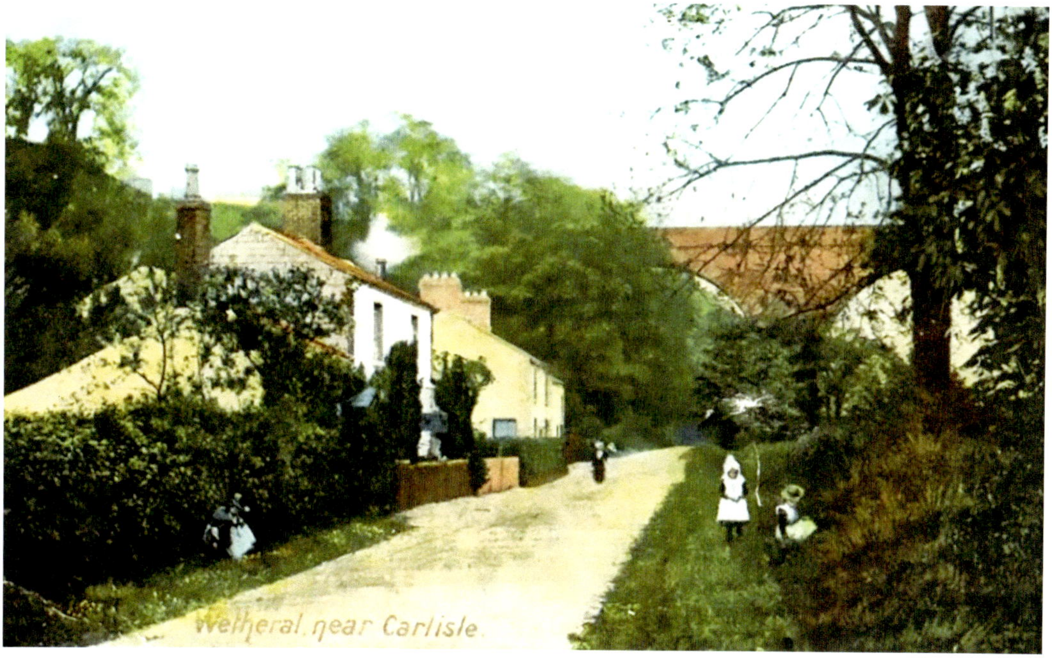

Wetheral – Bridge and Cottages

This view is looking north on the west side of the River Eden and is from approximately 160 yards south of the bridge. The bridge is immediately east of Wetheral railway station and was constructed between 1830 and 1834. It is 920 feet long and 100 feet high. The cottage shown nearest to the bridge was built in the early nineteenth century and is known as Riverhouse. The next building south is a pair of cottages which are late eighteenth century with later additions and are known as Edenside.

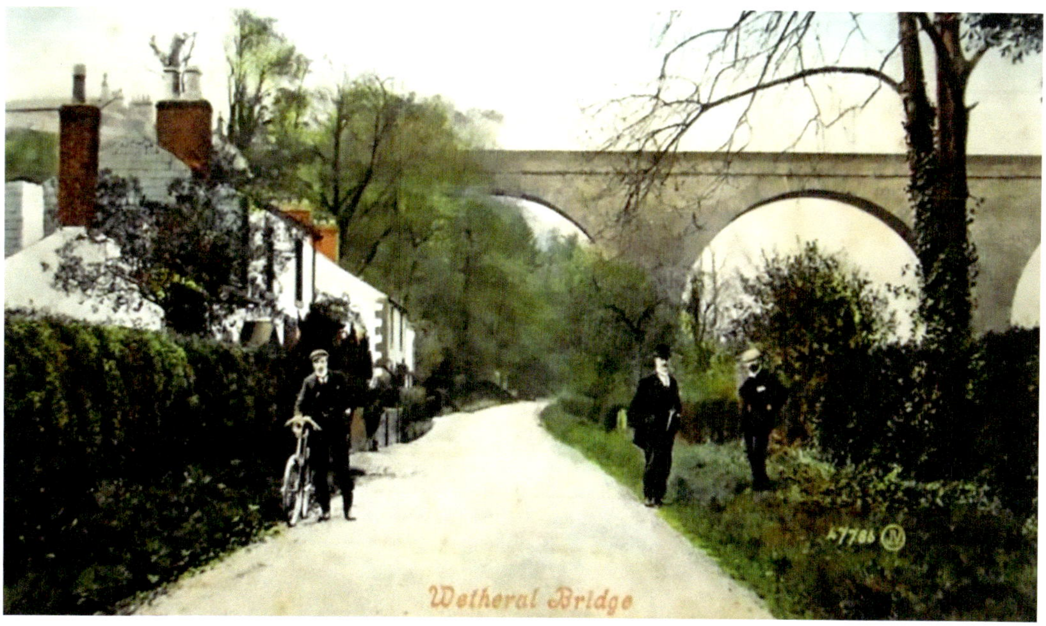

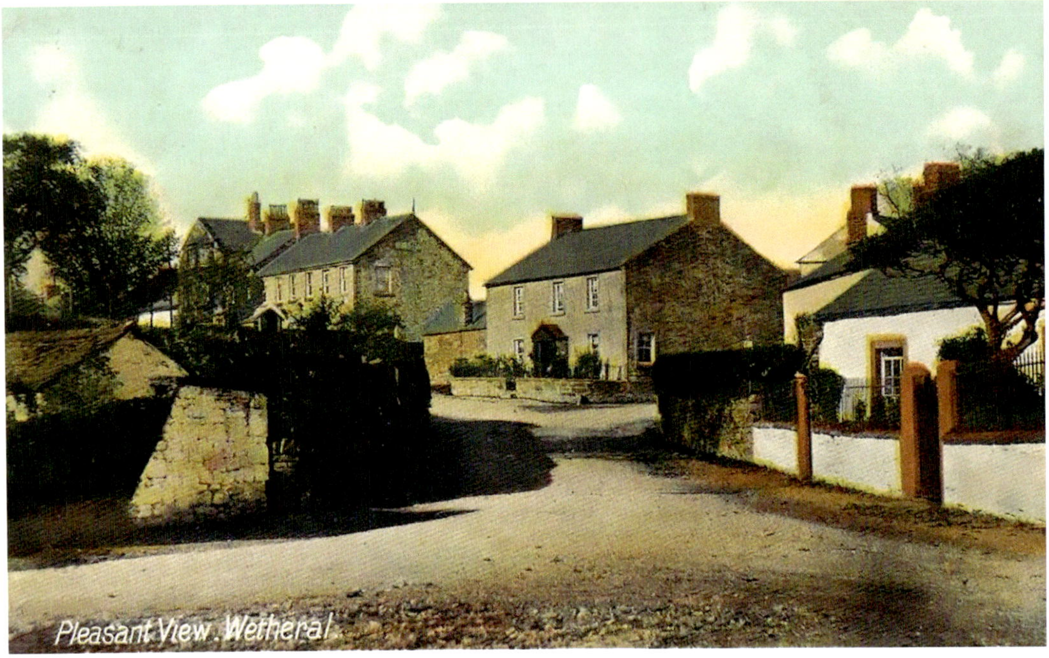

Wetheral – Views of the Village

Looking north from just below Yew Tree Cottage on the right at the junction of the road to the west of the Green and Station Street. The lane to Colby is off to the left and the road to the right road passes over the Carlisle to Newcastle railway bridge.

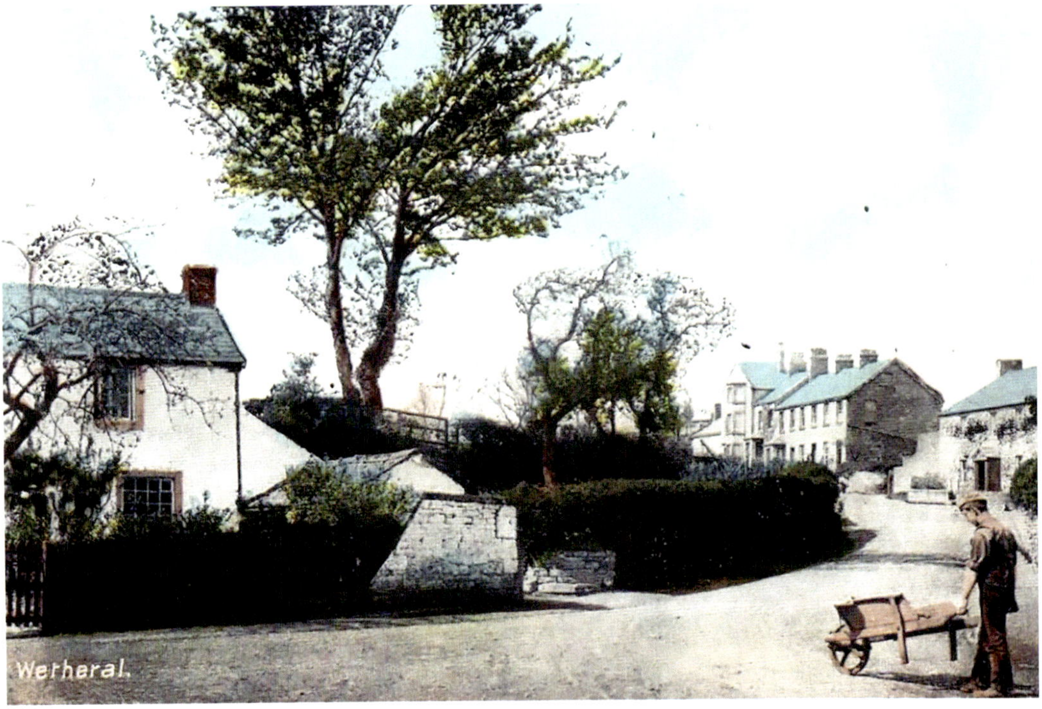

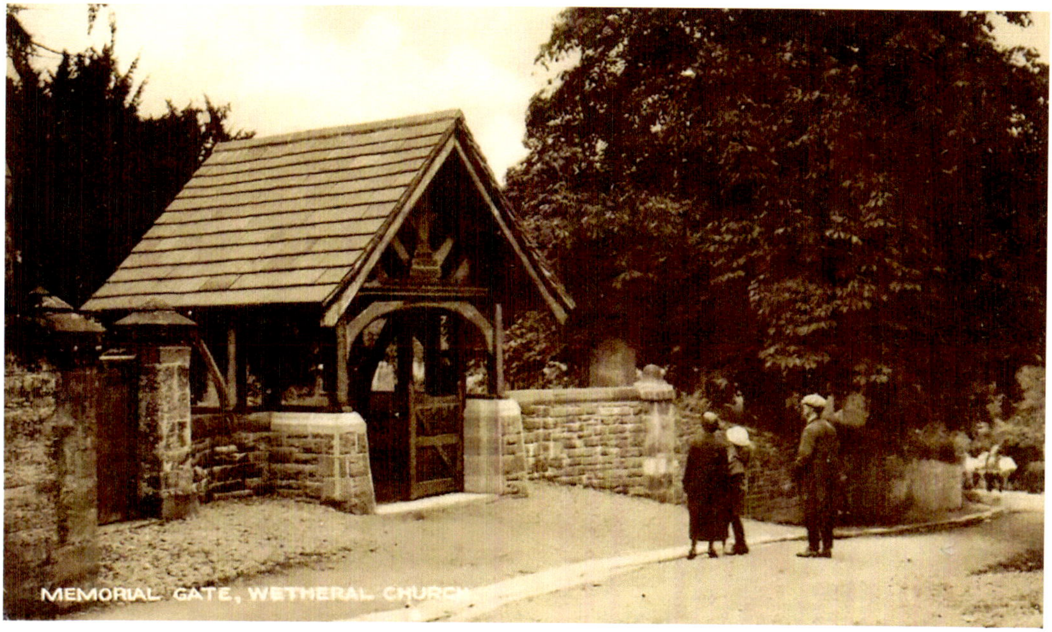

Wetheral – Lychgate

The lychgate is at the entrance to the Church of the Holy Trinity and St Constantine situated on Ferry Road. It is the parish war memorial and was originally dedicated on 10 July 1921 following the First World War and was built according to a design by Mr J. H. Martindale. The names of the fourteen parishioners who died in the First World War are listed on wooden panels inside the lychgate. After the Second World War, the date 1939–1945 was added to the gate and wooden panels along with the names of another fourteen parishioners who had lost their lives in that conflict.

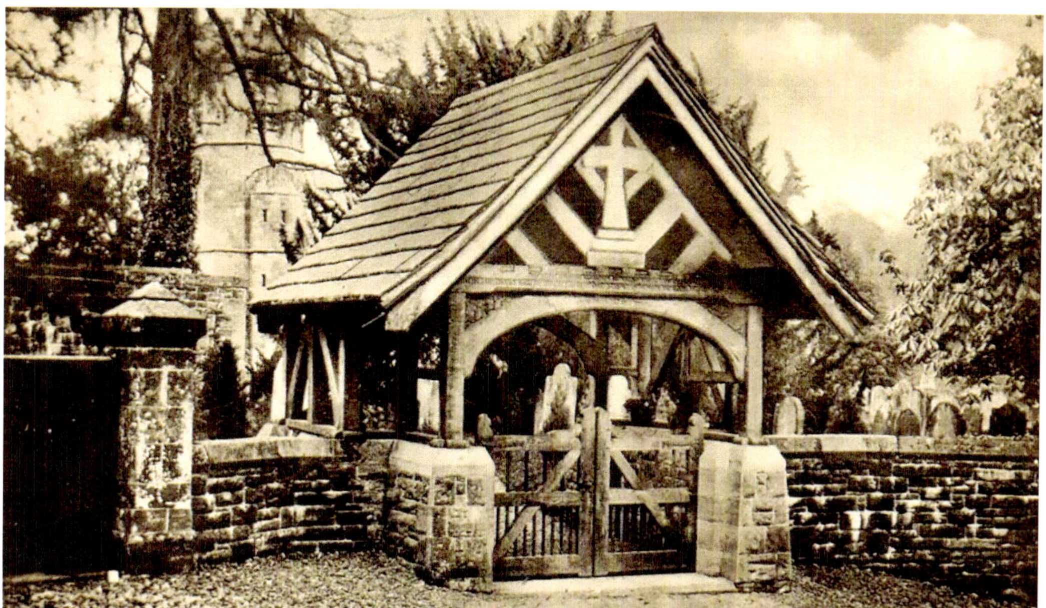

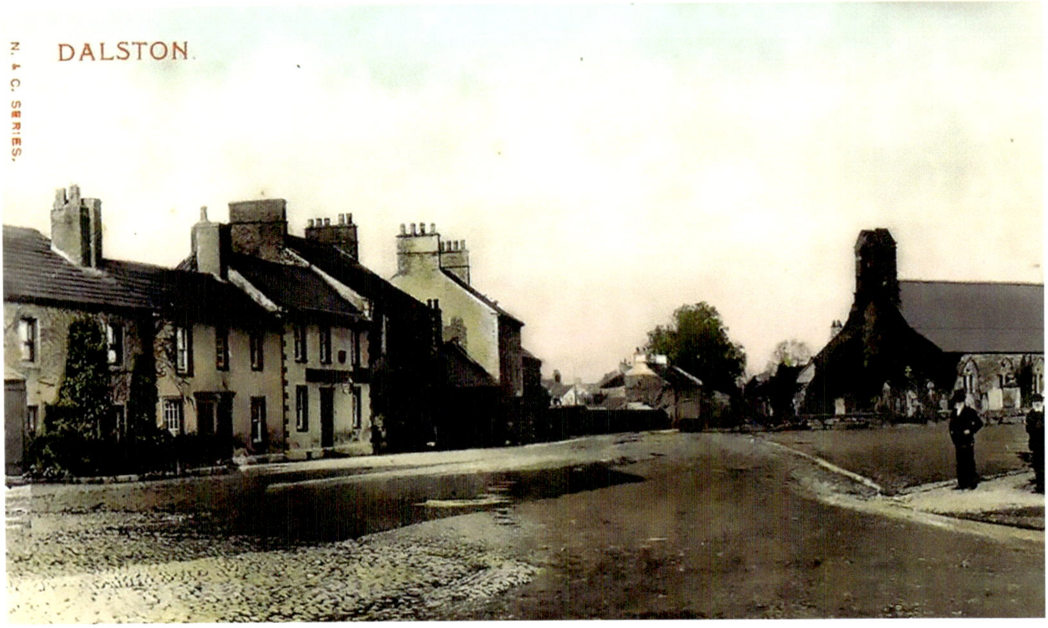

Dalston – The Square and Church

The Church of St Michael and all Angels is located at the north end of The Square and consists of a nave, chancel and small transept on the south side. The red-sandstone church was originally built in the twelfth century. It was partly rebuilt in 1749 but retains some medieval elements. The entrance porch, vestry and organ chamber date from 1890, when the church was extensively restored by C. J. Ferguson. The church is also notable for its nineteenth-century double open bell-cote.

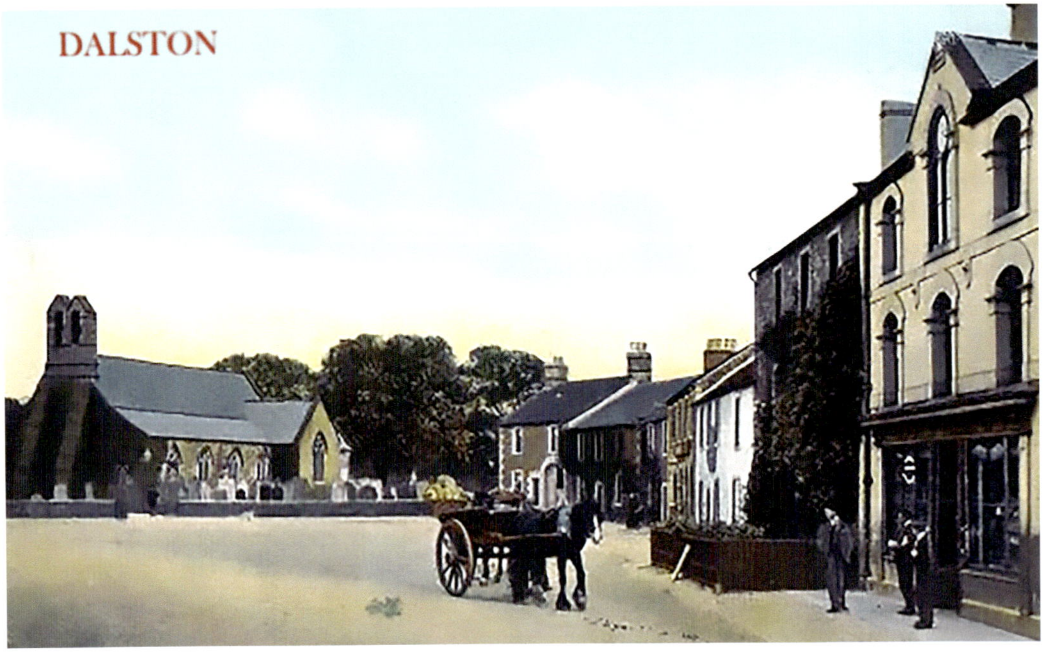

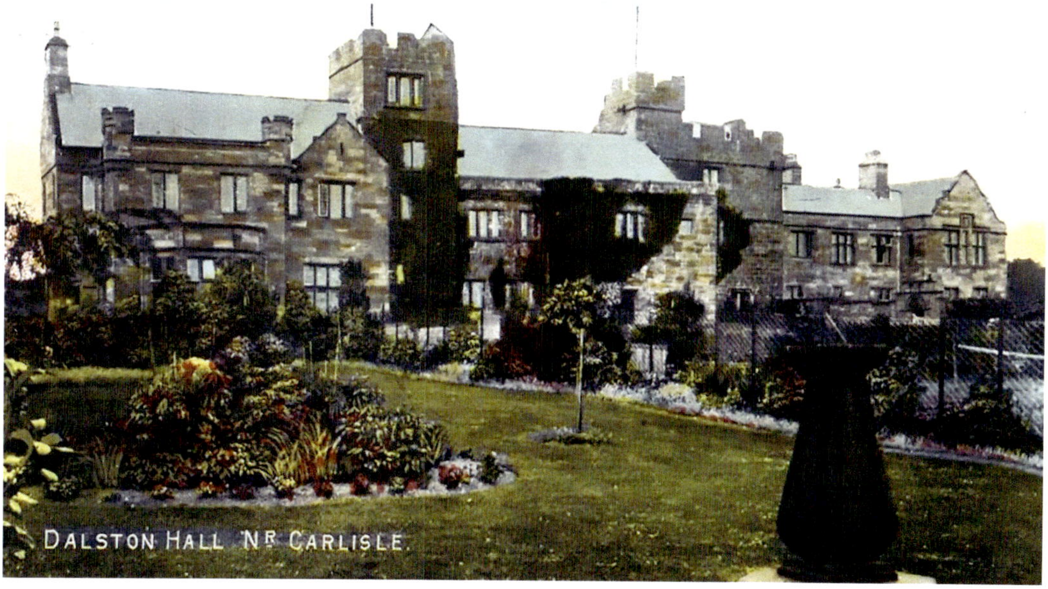

Dalston Hall

Dalston Hall was built around 1500 by John Dalston and incorporated a Peel tower and a baronial hall. A west wing was added in 1556. The house remained in the possession of the Dalston family for many generations. In 1761, Monkhouse Davison, a London grocer, bought the house and owned it for thirty-two years until his death. In 1897, the hall was acquired by Edmund Wright Stead, owner and director of Stead McAlpin, calico printers, who commissioned architect C. J. Ferguson to remodel the frontage in red sandstone in 1899.

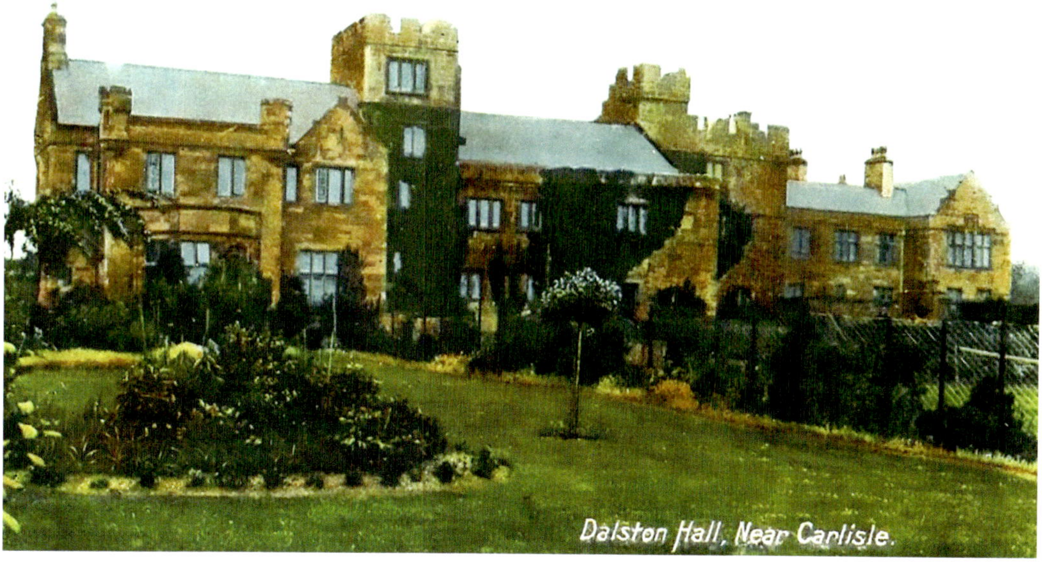

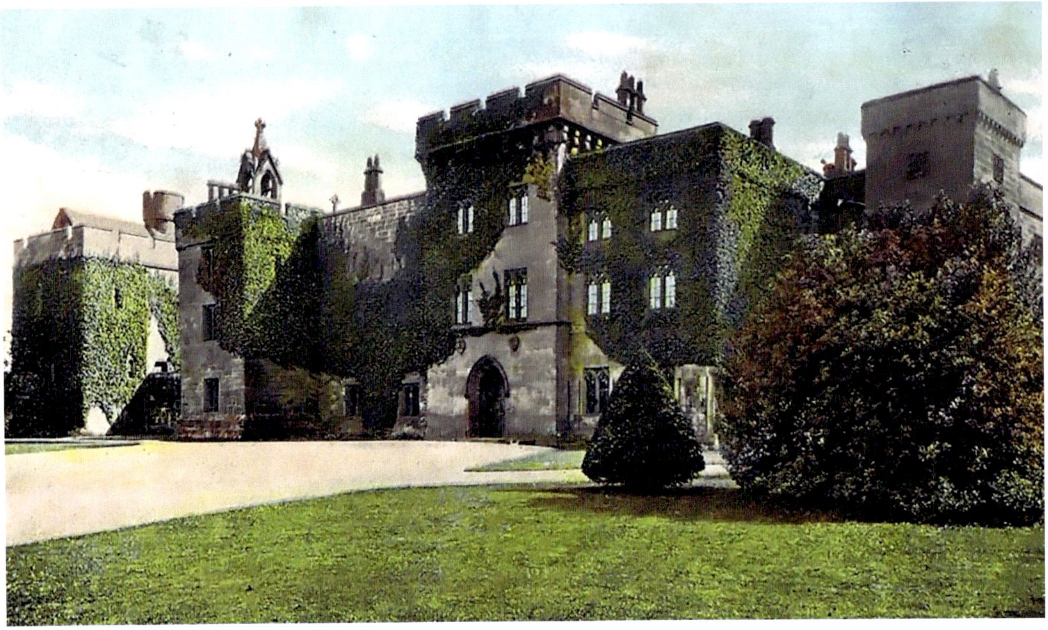

Dalston Rose Castle

Rose Castle is a fortified house and was the residence of the bishops of Carlisle from 1230. The licences that were needed to crenellate it were granted by the King in 1336 and 1355. Strickland Tower on the right of the images was built in 1400–19. Towers were added by Bishop Bell in 1488 and Bishop Kite in 1522–4. It was partly destroyed during the Civil War and repaired by William Heveningham as a private house in 1653. Alterations of 1673–5 for Bishop Rainbow were by William Thackery. More alterations were carried out for Bishop Lyttelton in 1762–9. Extensive alterations and additions for Bishop Percy by Thomas Rickman were made in 1828–31.

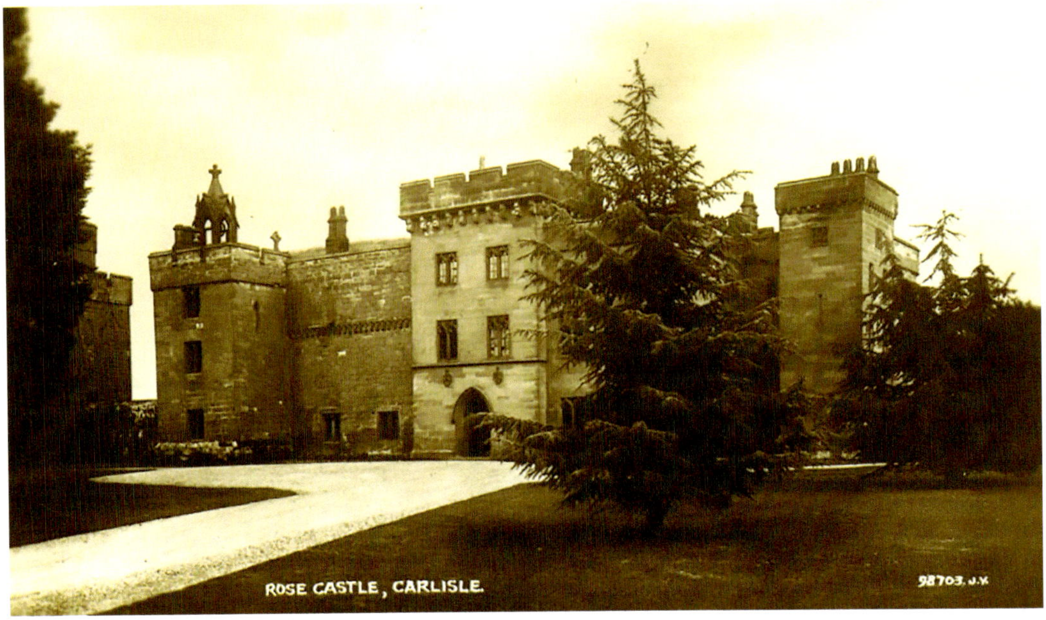

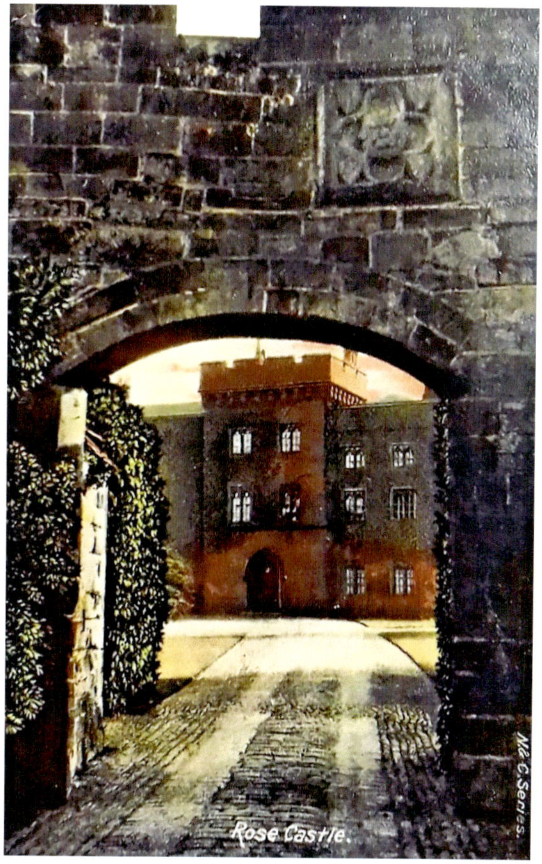

Dalston Rose Castle Gateway

Looking south from the Rose Causeway showing the gateway and flanking buildings which were constructed for Bishop Kite in the early sixteenth century. Alterations were made in the eighteenth century. The gateway is through a curtain wall with a small tower to left and lodge to the right. It is a large segmental arch with, above it, a sixteenth-century carved stone panel of a rose in quatrefoil and corner shields. There is pedestrian access to the right with a pointed arch. The twin-gabled building on the left to the rear of the gateway is an eighteenth-century gardener's storehouse. The lodge to the right is mostly demolished but its outer walls form part of the curtain wall. The gateway gave access and egress over a previous moat.

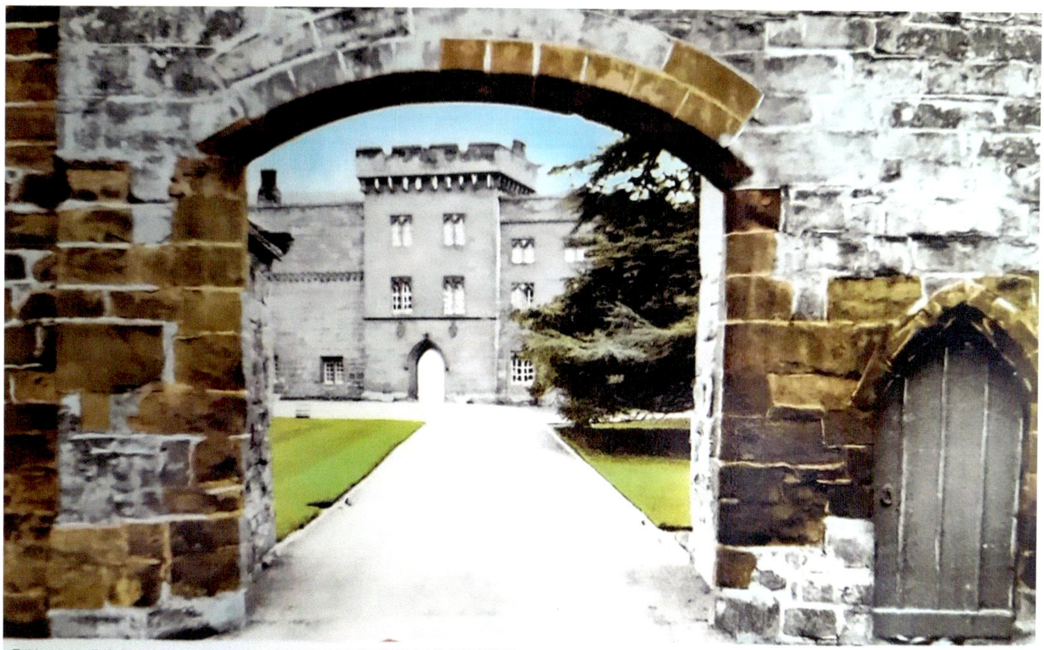

P/No 14 ROSE CASTLE, DALSTON, FROM THE OLD GATEWAY

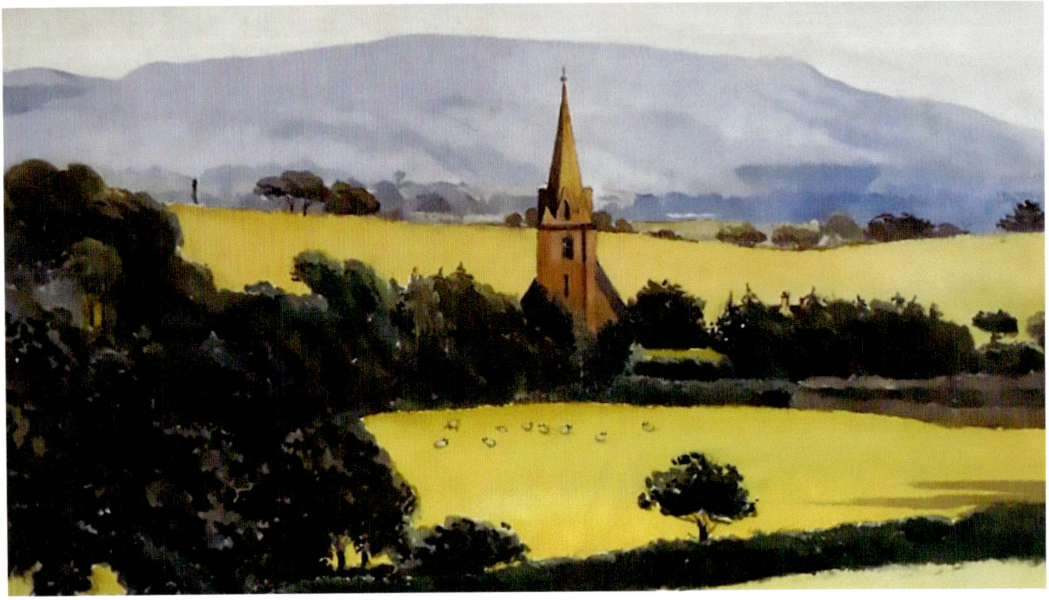

Holme Eden – St Paul's Church

St Paul's Church at Cumbria's Warwick Bridge was built and funded by Peter Dixon. The church and the surrounding churchyard were consecrated by Hugh Percy, Bishop of Carlisle, on Tuesday 2 September 1845. Its architect, John Dobson of Newcastle upon Tyne, ensured that there were no pillars or columns interfering with one's view of the front. It is a very simple design in red sandstone with a slate roof, and consists of a nave, a small chancel with an apse at the east and, a spire 110 feet tall at the west end over the entrance porch, and a small vestry at the south-east corner. There are stained-glass windows at the east and west ends by John Scott.

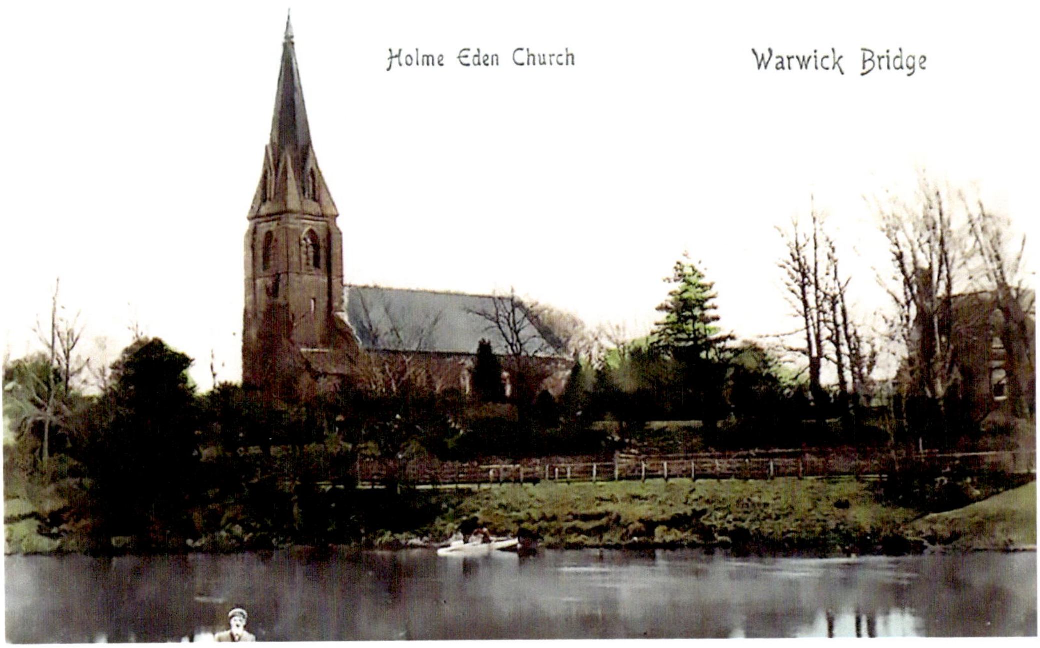

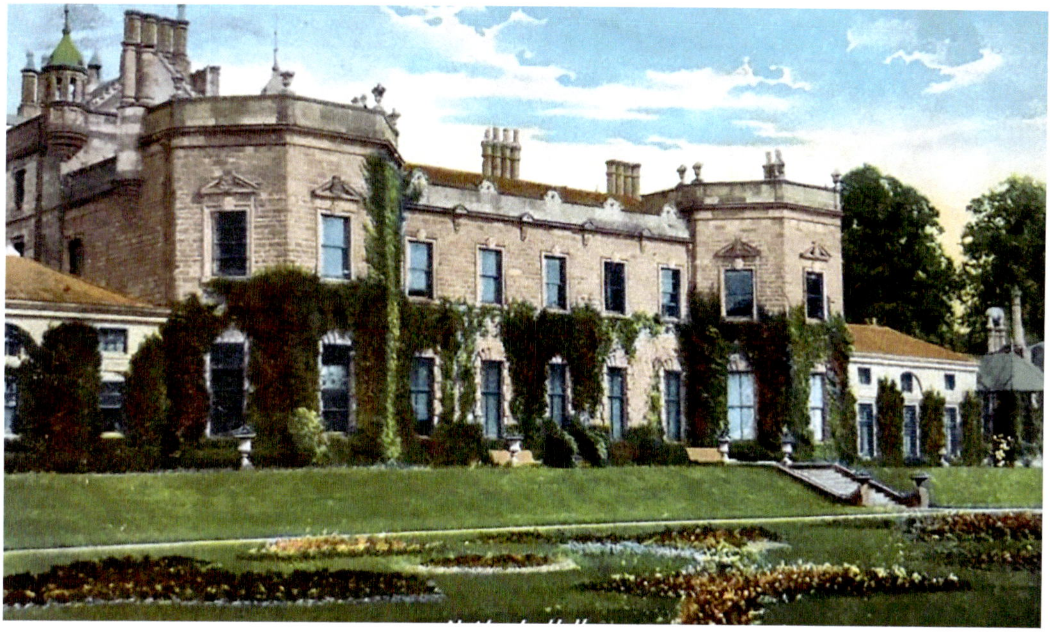

Netherby – The Hall

Located near Longtown in Dury Lane, the Georgian home was created by Robert Graham, a doctor of divinity who was responsible for enlarging the house in the 1760s and 1770s. The remains of an older house were incorporated in the construction which was executed in two phases. The main block with the principal rooms was the first phase in the 1760s, by an unknown architect. The second phase then flanked the main block by an unusual arrangement of lower, three-bay pavilions with canted, full-height projecting windows. These pavilions probably date to around 1776 and were almost certainly designed by John Carr of York. The frontage was remodelled by the architect William Burn between 1833 and 1836 for Sir James Graham, 2nd Baronet.

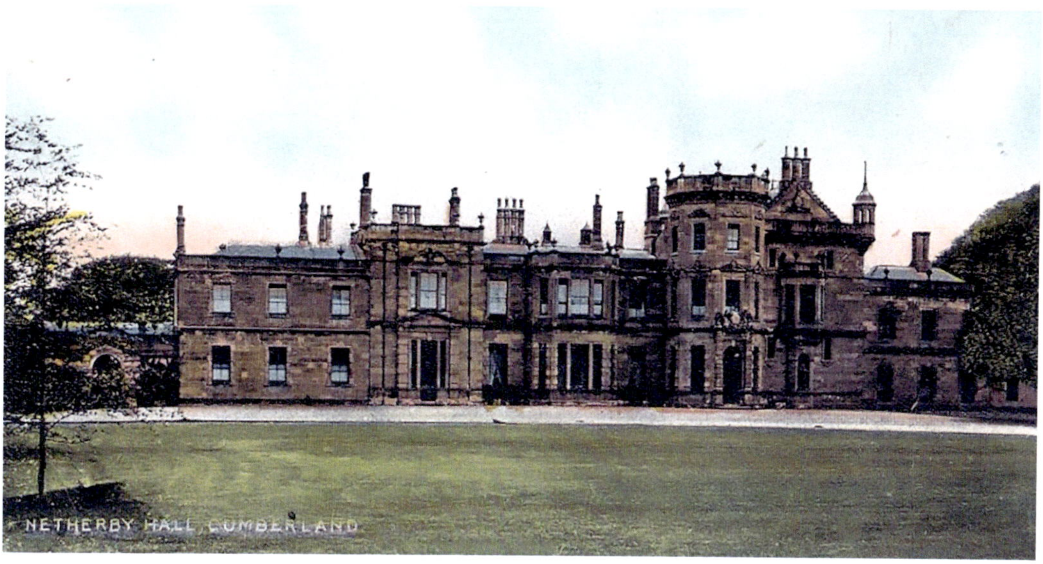

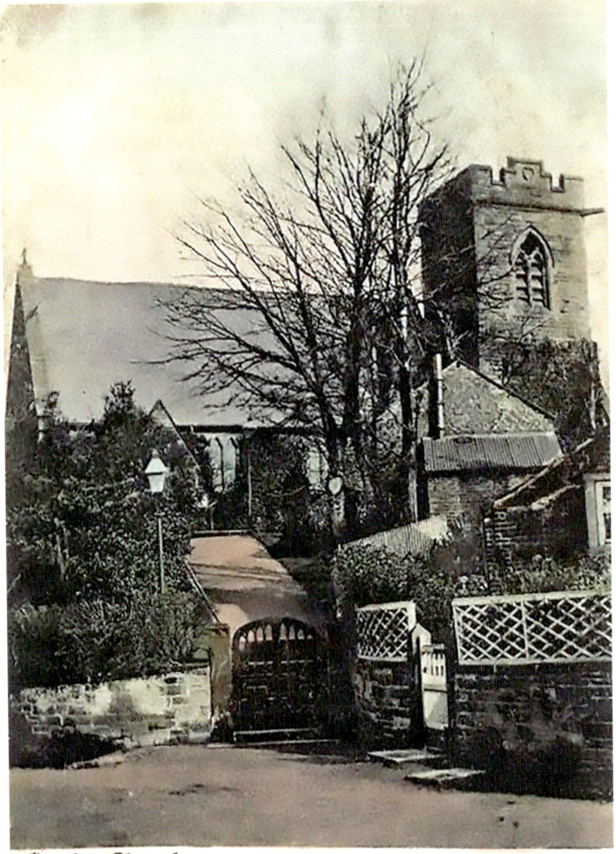

Scotby Church.

Scotby – All Saints Church

All Saints Church was designed by Anthony Salvin for George Head Head and consecrated in 1854. It has a two-storey, south-east, square tower which projects from the south wall between nave and chancel, with a single-storey nave of five bays and a two-bay chancel. The East Window, of Christ with little children, is by William Morris & Co.

Image on the left is looking north-westerly showing the gateway.

Image below is looking north from Village Road.

Church Of All Saints, Scotby, Carlisle.

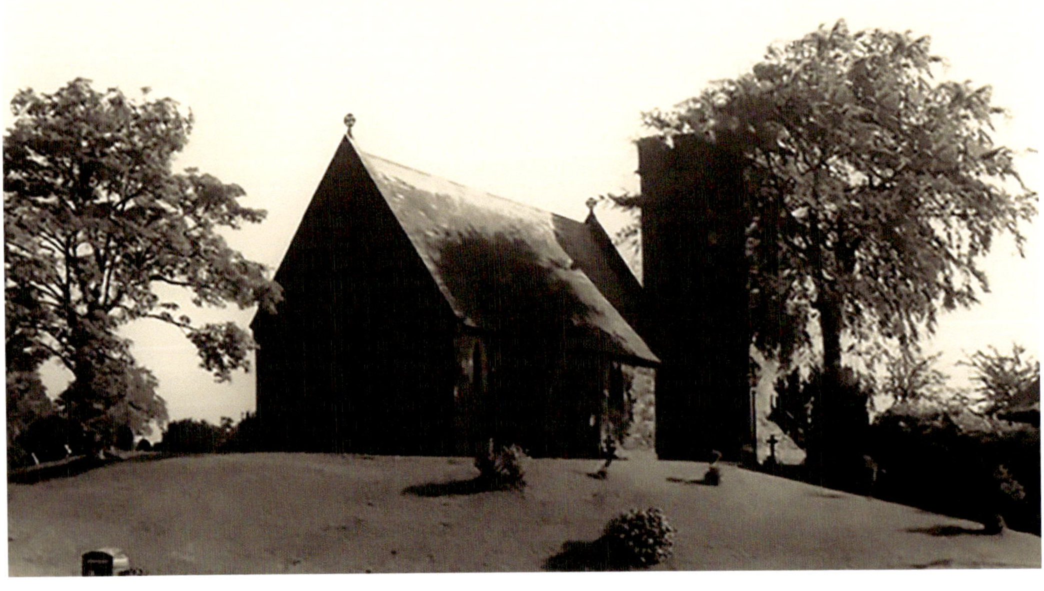

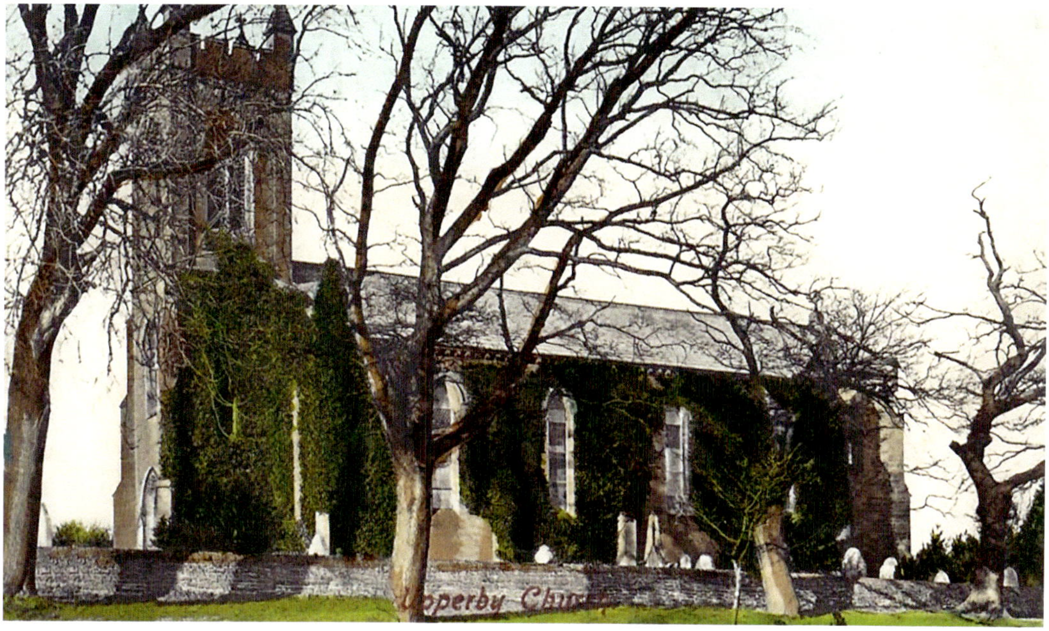

Upperby – St Jude the Baptist Church

The church of St John the Baptist, understood to have been built in 1840 in early Gothic Revival style, has a church tower and exposed roof structure practically identical to those of the church of St John the Evangelist, Houghton. The principal characteristic of both church towers is the bold short conical pinnacles with fleur-de-lis finials and corbelled castellated parapet. Also, as at Houghton, the corner buttresses to the nave have similar pinnacles and a simple stone cross terminates the gable over the chancel arch. The similarities are so marked that it must be assumed that both churches are the work of the same architect.

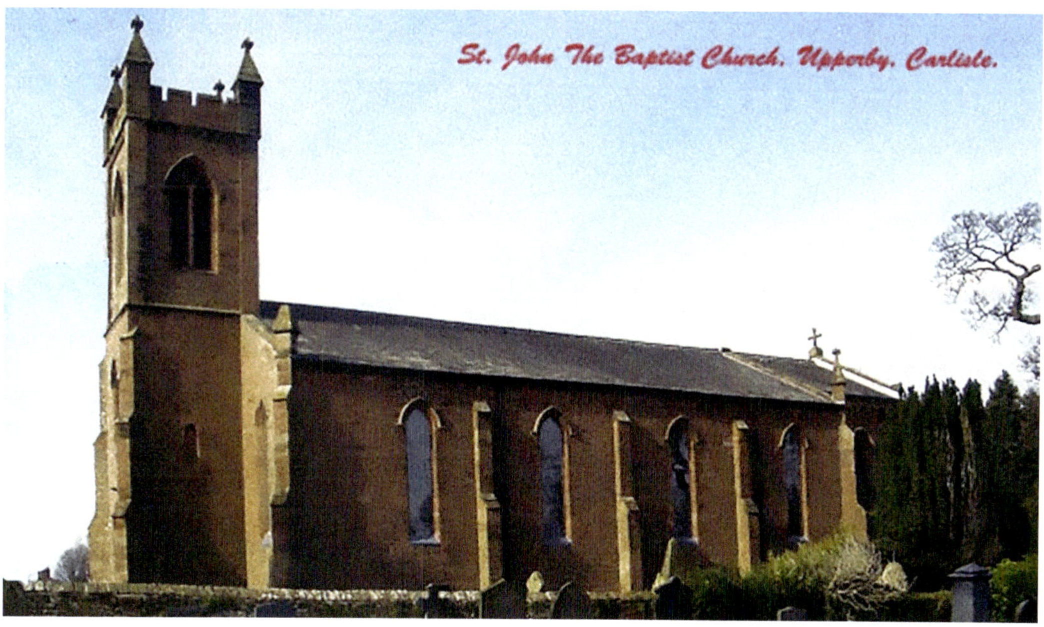

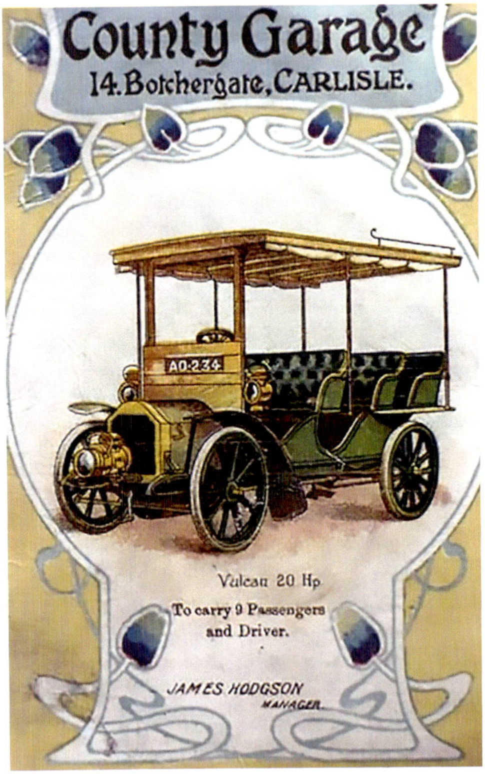

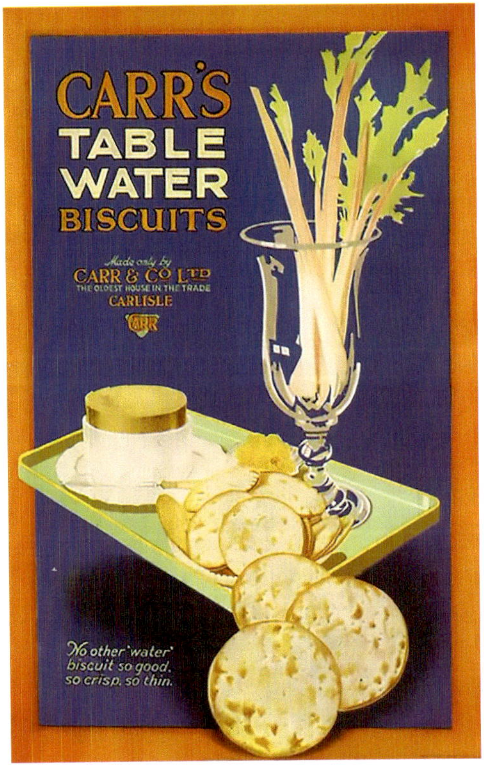

Advertising Postcards

An advertising postcard is a postcard used for advertising purposes, as opposed to a tourism or greeting postcard, and was used in advertising as an alternative to or to complement other print advertising.

The image top left shows a postcard advertising the County Garage located at 14 Botchergate. In the 1930s they were dealers for Alvis, Standard, Rover and Sunbeam vehicles.

The image bottom left shows a postcard advertising Carrs Table Water Biscuits. In 1831, Carr formed a small bakery and biscuit factory in Carlisle and he received a royal warrant in 1841. Within fifteen years of being founded, it had become Britain's largest baking business.

Carr's business was both a mill and a bakery, being an early example of vertical integration. It produced bread by night and biscuits by day. The biscuits were loosely based on dry biscuits used on long voyages by sailors. They could be kept crisp and fresh in tins, and despite their fragility, could easily be transported to other parts of the country by canal and railway.

Novelty Postcards

In the early 1930s cartoon-style saucy postcards became widespread. After the Second World War production of postcards continued although they tended to be in different style than they were before. Demand for postcards decreased, especially as telephone usage grew. As tastes changed, publishers began focusing on scenic views, humour, fashion and promotion of places. Many of the postcards were standard postcards with the name of the place added.

The card on the left opens up to show images of Carlisle.

The card below is decorated with glitter.

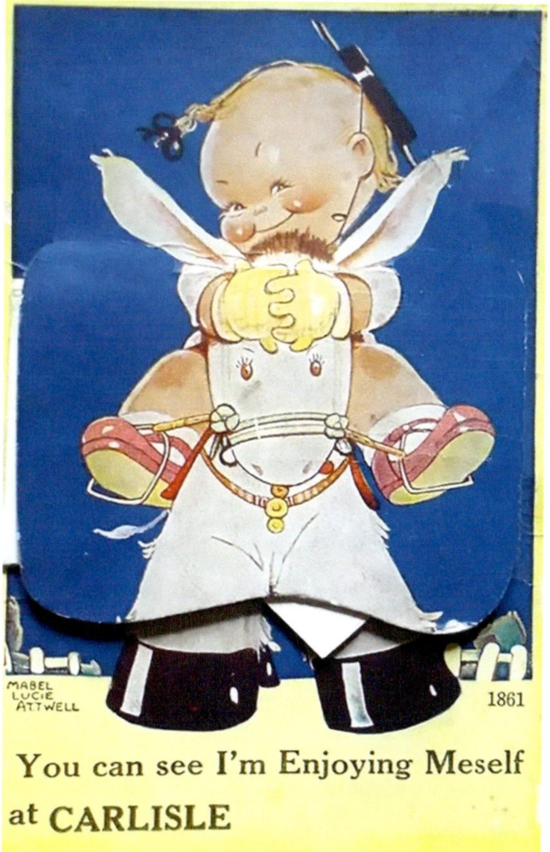

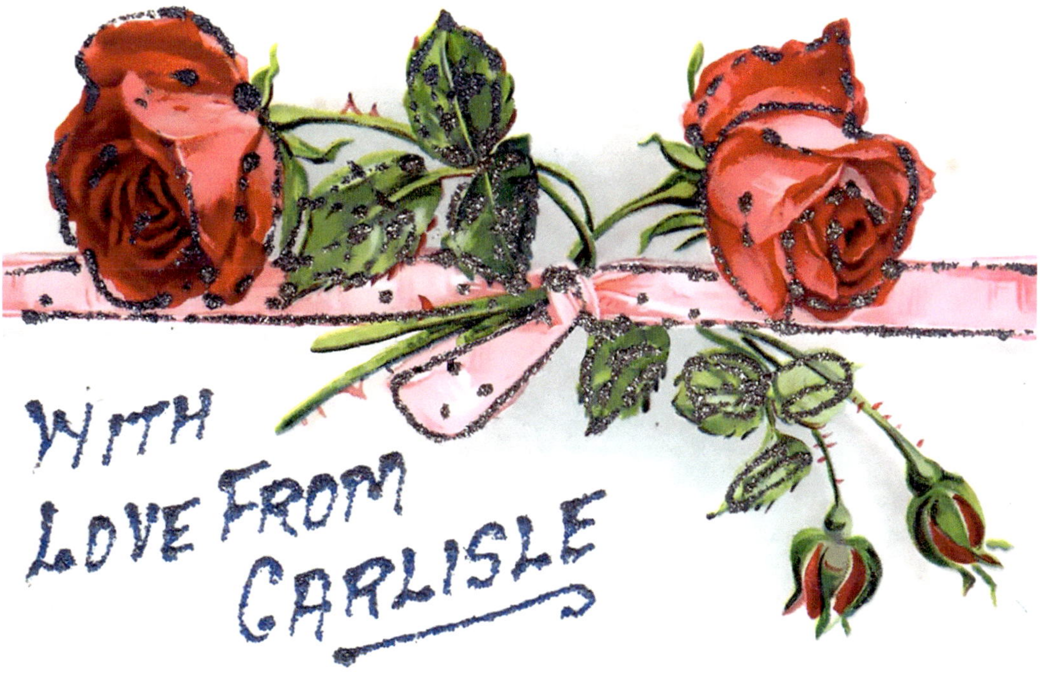

SOURCES

The following have been particularly useful in the writing of this book:

Wikipedia, Google Earth, National Library of Scotland Side by Side Referenced Maps

ABOUT THE AUTHOR

Alan Spree BSc CEng MICE MCIHT was born in Nottingham in 1944 and was educated at Glaisdale Bilateral School in Bilborough. He moved to Portsmouth with his family in 1959 and completed his secondary education at Eastney Modern School. He took an apprenticeship as a bricklayer in Portsmouth Dockyard and as part of that he received further education at Highbury Technical College. He then gained a degree in Civil Engineering at Portsmouth University before becoming a professionally qualified civil engineer. Alan worked with the Department of Environment at Portsmouth, Reading, London and Germany until voluntary retirement in 1998. He then worked for Berkshire County Council and Preston City Council before retirement to Spain in 2006.

His other *Postcard Collection* books published by Amberley are as follows:

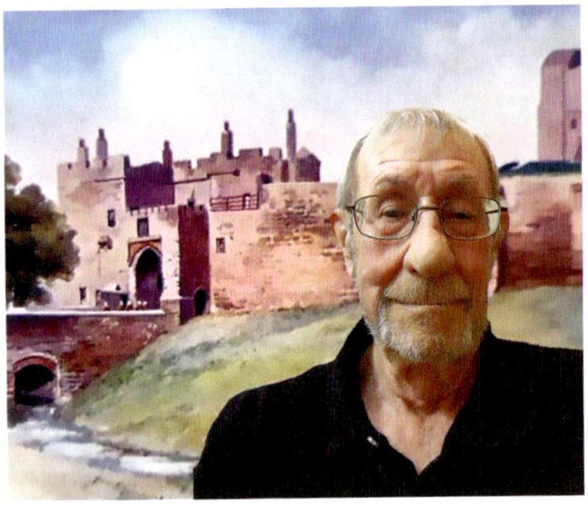

John Henry Spree's Nottinghamshire
Nottingham: The Postcard Collection
Hastings & St Leonards: The Postcard Collection
Portsmouth: The Postcard Collection
Liverpool: The Postcard Collection
Lincoln: The Postcard Collection
Newcastle Upon Tyne: The Postcard Collection
Leicester: The Postcard Collection
Bath: The Postcard Collection
Exeter: The Postcard Collection
Birmingham: The Postcard Collection